New Inside Out CD

Ceri Jones, Tania Bastow & Amanda Jeffries

Advanced

Student's Book

MACMILLAN

WB = **Workbook**. Each unit of the Workbook contains a one-page section which develops practical writing skills.

Conversation

Grammar Position of adverbials. Aspect
Vocabulary Describing conversation styles. Conversation collocations. Word building
Useful phrases Opening conversations

Speaking & Vocabulary

1 **Work with a partner. Look at the photos (a–c) and discuss these questions.**

a) Who do you think the people in the photos are? Where do you think they are? How do you think they know each other?

b) What do you think they're talking about?

2 **In the box there are some adjectives which are commonly used to describe conversations. Categorise the adjectives under the headings in the table. Use a dictionary if necessary.**

> animated   bizarre   ~~boring~~   frustrating   hilarious   in-depth   intense   intimate
> lengthy   meaningful   one-sided   pointless   predictable   stimulating

Positive	Negative	Neutral
	boring	

Add one or two more adjectives under each heading. Compare with your partner.

Look at the photos in Exercise 1 again. Which adjectives would you use to describe each conversation?

3 **Work with your partner. Answer these questions.**

a) Which of the conversations below have you had recently in your own language?

- a quick word in passing with a friend or colleague
- a brief exchange with a complete stranger
- a long heart-to-heart with a close friend or family member
- a hurried exchange of text messages
- an online chat

b) What did you talk about? Choose an adjective from Exercise 2 to describe the conversations.

Listening & Vocabulary

1 **Work in small groups. Discuss these questions.**

a) What makes a conversation enjoyable?
b) What makes a conversation frustrating?
c) What's your definition of a good conversationalist?

Compare your answers with the rest of the class.

2 🌐 **1.01–1.06 Listen to six people, Joanna, Mike, Phil, Jessica, Bryony and Rafe, answering one of the questions in Exercise 1. As you listen, decide which question (*a*, *b* or *c*) each person is answering.**

Did the people interviewed have similar opinions to those expressed by your class?

3 **Complete these extracts from the speakers' answers in Exercise 2. Use the words and collocations in the box.**

> butt in   drones on and on   flows   hog   hunt around   on the same wavelength
> put across   something to say

a) … it helps if there aren't some people who _____ the conversation all the time …
b) … you need a conversation that _____ …
c) … it's someone who's got a point that they want to _____ during the conversation. Someone with _____ as opposed to someone who just talks endlessly about various subjects …
d) … some people don't care about whose turn it is to talk, so they just, you know, _____ when you're in the middle of a thought …
e) I really hate it when I'm with someone who just _____ in a conversation, and who doesn't give you a chance to speak at all.
f) … you're _____ and you can share the same tastes or experiences …
g) … that's really bad, when you're having to _____ for things to say …

Listen again and check.

4 **Match the definitions (*1–8*) to the words and collocations in Exercise 3.**

1 work hard to find
2 join a conversation without being asked
3 dominate
4 an interesting point to make
5 able to understand the way the other person thinks
6 explain or communicate
7 continues in an easy, natural way
8 talks for a long time in a very boring way

5 **Work with your partner. Which words and collocations from Exercise 3 do you associate with …**

1 an uncomfortable silence?
2 a conversation where one person is dominating?
3 a successful conversation?

Speaking

1 **Think about the last time you had a conversation in English outside the context of your English course. Work with your partner and discuss these questions.**

a) Who were you talking to? Did you know them well?
b) What did you talk about? How long did the conversation last?
c) Were you happy with your English? Why? / Why not?
d) Who did most of the talking, you or the other person/people? Why?

2 **Compare your answers with the rest of the class. Decide whose conversation was …**
a) the most challenging.   b) the most satisfying.

Conversation **5**

1 **Work in small groups. Look at these statements. To what extent do you agree or disagree with them? Explain why.**

a) Women talk more than men.
b) Women communicate better than men.
c) Men are more factual and honest than women.
d) A conversation between two men is different from one between two women.

2 **You are going to read about a book that explores the differences between men and women. Work with a partner. Look at the book cover and answer these questions.**

a) The book is based on the premise that men and women are very different, especially in the way they communicate with each other. Do you agree with this premise?
b) What differences do you think the book describes?
c) Which of the words in the box do you think the book associates with men and which with women? Why?

> autonomy conversation cooperation gadgets and gizmos power romance shopping spirituality sports success technology

3 **Work with your partner. You are going to read two extracts from the book. Student A read about life on Mars below, Student B read about life on Venus on page 7. As you read make notes about …**

a) what the people there value most.
b) how they experience fulfilment.
c) what they are most interested in.

4 **Use your notes to tell your partner about your extract and then discuss these questions.**

a) Do you identify with the description given of your sex? Why? / Why not?
b) The book was written in the US in the 1990s but it is still very popular today. What do you think most people in your country would think of these ideas?

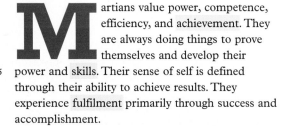

Life on Mars

Martians value power, competence, efficiency, and achievement. They are always doing things to prove themselves and develop their
5 power and skills. Their sense of self is defined through their ability to achieve results. They experience fulfilment primarily through success and accomplishment.

They are more interested in 'objects' and 'things'
10 rather than people and feelings. Even today on Earth, while women fantasise about romance, men fantasise about powerful cars, faster computers, gadgets, gizmos, and new powerful technology. Men are preoccupied with the 'things' that can help them
15 express power by creating results and achieving their goals.

Achieving goals is very important to a Martian because it is a way for him to prove his competence and thus feel good about himself. Martians pride

20 themselves on doing things all by themselves. Autonomy is a symbol of efficiency, power, and competence.

Understanding this Martian characteristic can help women understand why men resist so much
25 being corrected or being told what to do. To offer a man unsolicited advice is to presume that he doesn't know what to do or that he can't do it on his own. Men are very touchy about this, because the issue of competence is so very important to them.

30 Because he is handling his problems on his own, a Martian rarely talks about his problems unless he needs expert advice. He reasons: 'Why involve someone else when I can do it by myself?' He keeps his problems to himself unless he requires help from
35 another to find a solution. Asking for help when you can do it yourself is perceived as a sign of weakness.

Vocabulary

1 **Complete the glossary with the highlighted words in the extracts.**

> **Glossary**
>
> **a)** *skills* **noun [C]:** the knowledge and abilities that enable you to do something well, which can often be learnt
> **b)** _____ **noun [C]:** something which someone has succeeded in doing, especially after a lot of effort
> **c)** _____ **noun [C]:** the general ability to do something well or efficiently
> **d)** _____ **noun [U]:** the quality of being able to do a task successfully without wasting time or effort
> **e)** _____ **noun [U]:** the pleasure you feel when you have done something well
> **f)** _____ **noun [U]:** the feeling you have when a hope, dream or ambition has been realised
> **g)** _____ **adj:** thoughtful towards other people
> **h)** _____ **verb [T]:** to think that something is important and to appreciate it

Which words in the extracts were associated with a) men b) women c) both?

2 **Complete the table with the noun, verb, adjective and adverb forms for your answers in Exercise 1.**

Noun	Verb	Adjective	Adverb
skills	–	*skilful/skilled*	*skilfully*

3 **Complete these sentences with words from the table in Exercise 2.**

a) I always try to take other people's points of view into _____ before *making a decision*.
b) I find *helping others* very _____ .
c) *Honesty* is the thing I _____ most in a friend.
d) I always feel really _____ when I *manage to reach a deadline*.
e) *Getting a degree* has been my greatest _____ so far.
f) I really admire people who are *super-* _____ *and always manage to do everything on time*.
g) *My job* is the one thing that gives me real _____ .
h) *Using a computer* is probably one of the most important _____ I've learnt *in my present job*.

4 **Look at sentences (*a–h*) in Exercise 3. Replace the words in italics so that the sentences are true for you. Compare your sentences with a partner.**

Life on Venus

Venusians have different values. They value love, communication, beauty, and relationships. They spend a lot of time supporting, helping, and nurturing one another. Their sense of self is
5 defined through their feelings and the quality of their relationships. They experience fulfilment through sharing and relating. Rather than building highways and tall buildings, the Venusians are more concerned with living in harmony, community, and loving cooperation. Relationships
10 are more important than work and technology. In most ways their world is the opposite of Mars.

Communication is of primary importance. To share their personal feelings is much more important than achieving goals and success. Talking and relating to one another is a
15 source of tremendous fulfilment.

This is hard for a man to comprehend. He can come close to understanding a woman's experience of sharing and relating by comparing it to the satisfaction he feels when he wins a race, achieves a goal, or solves a problem.

20 Instead of being goal-oriented, women are relationship-oriented; they are more concerned with expressing their goodness, love and caring. Two Martians go to lunch to discuss a project or business goal; they have a problem to solve. In addition, Martians view going to a restaurant
25 as an efficient way to approach food: no shopping, no cooking and no washing dishes. For Venusians, going to lunch is an opportunity to nurture a relationship, for both giving support to and receiving support from a friend. Women's restaurant talk can be very open and intimate,
30 almost like the dialogue that occurs between therapist and patient.

Venusians are very intuitive. They pride themselves in being considerate of the needs and feelings of others. A sign of great love is to offer help and assistance to another
35 Venusian without being asked.

Speaking & Listening

1 Work in small groups. Brainstorm a list of common complaints girlfriends and boyfriends make about each other, for example:

- *He/She talks about himself/herself too much.*
- *He/She spends too much time with his/her friends.*

Which do you think are made about men, which are made about women?

2 Work in two groups, Group A and Group B. You are going to act out a telephone conversation between a girlfriend (Suzi) and a boyfriend (Brian). Look at page 128. Read the information about your character and discuss what you are going to say.

3 Work with a partner. One student should be from Group A and one student from Group B. Act out the telephone conversation between the couple.

4 🌐 1.07 Listen to a similar conversation. Was it very different from yours?

5 Work with your partner. Here are some extracts from the telephone conversation in Exercise 4. Who said each line, the boyfriend (Brian) or the girlfriend (Suzi)?

a) … a bit stressed out, had a hard day at work, you know, the usual.
b) What's going on?
c) I just don't fancy it tonight …
d) Have I done something wrong?
e) But not tonight, eh? The football's more interesting …
f) … shall I come and pick you up?
g) Let's just drop it.
h) Whatever. Just please yourself.

Listen again and check your answers.

6 What do you think Brian should do now?

Pronunciation

1 Work with your partner. Look at these two extracts from the telephone conversation in Speaking & Listening, Exercise 4 and discuss the questions.

a) But not tonight, eh? The football's more interesting I suppose.
b) No, forget it! I wouldn't want you to go out of your way or anything!

Does the girl mean what she says? How does she convey her anger?

2 🌐 1.08 Listen to the two extracts being repeated, first in a normal tone and then angrily. What's the difference?

Look at the Recordings on page 146. Find other phrases where the girl uses an angry tone of voice. Work with your partner and read the conversation aloud.

Grammar

Position of adverbials

We stayed **at home**.

I'm coming **tomorrow**.

He spoke **quickly**.

He came **to see us**.

We meet **every week**.

Frankly, I never believe a word he says **about Jane**.

Jeff has been working **late at the office every night this week**.

Jeff handed in the project **on time with a huge sigh of relief**.

1 Work with a partner. Suzi is talking to her sister about Brian. Look at the adverbials in bold and answer the questions.

a) He **never** used to want to spend so much time **on his own**.

b) He said he wanted to do something **tomorrow**, but I don't believe him.

c) He just sits and watches TV **on the sofa**.

d) I end up shouting **dramatically** and slamming the phone down **like an overgrown teenager**.

e) **Frankly**, I've had enough.

Which adverbial(s) ...

1 describe(s) how something is done? 4 describe(s) where something is done?

2 describe(s) how often something is done? 5 add(s) emphasis?

3 describe(s) when something will happen?

2 Look at this sentence and answer the questions below.

(1) *Suzi* (2) *used to discuss her problems* (3) *with her twin sister* (4).

In which position *(1–4)* would you normally add these adverbials to the sentence?

a) when she was younger c) in secret e) from time to time

b) always d) only f) probably

What do you notice about the position of the one-word adverbials?

Make the sentence negative. How does this affect the position of the adverbials?

3 Modify the sentence in Exercise 2 so that it is true for you. Add at least three adverbials.

I (1) *never used to discuss my problems* (2) *in depth with my parents* (3) *when I was a teenager*.

Compare your sentence with your partner.

4 Look at the pairs of sentences below. The underlined adverbials are in different positions. How does this change the meaning of the sentences?

For example:

1 *Actually, he's performing in the play tomorrow.* (and not doing something else)

2 *He's actually performing in the play tomorrow.* (and not just sitting in the audience)

a) 1 Honestly, I can't speak to her any more.

2 I can't speak to her honestly any more.

b) 1 Earlier, I had wanted Rich to come to the meeting.

2 I had wanted Rich to come to the meeting earlier.

c) 1 I get into arguments when I'm particularly angry.

2 I get into arguments, particularly when I'm angry.

5 Write answers to these questions. Use at least five adverbials in your answers. Compare your answers with your partner.

a) Who do you speak to most on a day-to-day basis?

b) What do you talk about?

I **usually** work **from home** so I speak to colleagues **on the phone,** and I **always** try to get in touch with my sister **in the evening / for a long chat / on the phone or online.**

6 Grammar *Extra* 1, Part 1 page 134. Read the explanations and do Exercise 1.

Speaking

1 Underline the correct alternative to complete the definitions.

a) Secretly listening to other people's conversations is called **eavesdropping / overhearing**.

b) Accidentally hearing a conversation between other people is called **eavesdropping / overhearing**.

2 Work in small groups. Discuss these questions.

a) In what kind of situation is it difficult not to overhear another person's private conversation? How do you feel when this happens?

b) Describe the last time you overheard a conversation in a public place. Who was talking? Did they notice (or mind) that you were listening to them?

c) Who would you like to eavesdrop on? What do you imagine them saying?

Listening

1 🌐 1.09–1.10 You are going to listen to two conversations. Listen and match the conversations (*1* and *2*) to the photos (*a* and *b*). For each conversation, answer these questions.

a) What is the relationship between the two people involved in the conversation?

b) What are they talking about?

2 Work with a partner. Look at these sentences. Which conversation from Exercise 1 do you think they refer to, *1*, *2* or both?

a) They often speak to each other.

b) There's some tension between them.

c) One of them may not be being completely truthful.

d) They're enjoying their conversation.

Listen again and check your answers.

3 Work with your partner. Look at the Recordings for the second conversation on page 146. What do you think the other person was saying? Act out the complete conversation.

Grammar

Aspect

Perfect forms
have + past participle:
You'll **have received** it by then.

Continuous forms
be + *ing*:
He **was driving**.

Perfect continuous forms
have + *been* + *ing*:
He must **have been doing** something important.

1 **Work with a partner. Complete the extracts from the conversations in Listening, Exercise 1 using the past participle or *ing* form of the verbs in the box.**

> be   begin   come (×2)   complete   finish   get   realise   take   talk   wait (×2)   work

a) I'd been _____ and _____ … and … I was _____ to think … he wasn't _____ …
b) … I thought he might have _____ caught up at work or something …
c) … there are two Italian restaurants called Casa Mia, and neither of us had _____ …
d) I'm just on the train actually. It's just _____ into the station now.
e) We've been _____ on it all week.
f) … we've already _____ the initial plans …
g) … I'm sure we'll have _____ by then …
h) You must have been _____ to the wrong person …
i) … there must have _____ some kind of misunderstanding.
j) I'll be _____ care of it personally. You can be sure of that.

2 **Work with your partner. Look at the sentences in Exercise 1. Find three examples of each of the verb forms (1–3).**

1 a perfect verb form   2 a continuous verb form   3 a perfect continuous verb form

3 **Work with your partner. Underline the correct form of the verb.**

a) We **'d waited / were waiting / 'd been waiting** for over half an hour by the time *it* finally turned up.
b) We'll **have finished / be finishing / have been finishing** *it* by the end of the day.
c) He must **have put / be putting / have been putting** some extra time in at work. *He*'s usually here by now.
d) I **'ve already posted / 'm already posting / 've already been posting** *them* on my website.
e) We **'ve seen / 're seeing / 've been seeing** *each other* for about six months.
f) Sorry, I can't find *it*. I think I may **have left / be leaving / have been leaving** *it* at home! Can you pay this time? Thanks!

Look at the words in italics. What do you think they refer to?

4 **Work with your partner. Look at the pictures. Complete the thought bubbles with an appropriate form of the verb, as in the example.**

5 **Work in small groups. Discuss these questions.**

a) When was the last time you had to make an excuse because you were late or had forgotten to do something?
b) What exactly did you say?
c) Did the other person believe you?

6 **Grammar *Extra* 1, Part 2** page 134. Read the explanations and do Exercise 2.

Useful phrases

1   Work with a partner. Read the tips on the right and answer the questions.

Do you think it's good advice? Is there anything you'd like to change or add?

What would you say in these situations, if you wanted to …

a) start a conversation with a person you don't know at a party?

b) introduce yourself to a new member of staff or a new student in your class?

c) start a conversation with a friend you haven't seen for a long time?

d) speak to the person standing next to you at the bus stop or in a check-out queue?

2   🌐 1.11 Listen to conversations (1–4). Match them to the situations (a–d) in Exercise 1.

How to start a conversation:

Always approach the person you want to talk to with a smile.

Use a question to start the conversation, but don't make it too direct.

Better still, comment on something in your surroundings.

Or pay the person you're talking to a genuine compliment (for example, 'Where did you get your T-shirt? It's great!').

To keep the conversation going, use follow-up questions or introduce a new topic.

3   Look at the four conversation openers. Do they follow the advice in the tip sheet in Exercise 1?

a) Fancy *meeting you here*! How are *things*?

b) Sorry, have you got *the time*?

c) You must be *Ruben*. I've *heard a lot about you*.

d) Great *party*, isn't it?

Are the conversation openers similar to the ones you came up with in Exercise 1?

4   Match the responses (1–4) to the conversation openers (a–d) in Exercise 3.

1   Hi, you must be Steve. I've heard a lot about you too!

2   Hi! How are you? You're looking great!

3   Yes, it really is. I hadn't been to their house before. It's really nice, isn't it?

4   No, I haven't, sorry. But there's a clock over there, look.

Listen to the conversations again. Which responses do you prefer, the ones above or the ones in the Recordings?

5   Look at the Recordings on page 146–147. Underline all the questions the speakers used to continue their conversations. Which conversation do you think is the most successful? Why?

6   Work with your partner. Look at the conversation openers in Exercise 3. Think of as many ways as possible to replace the words in italics.

7   You are going to talk to some of the other students in your class. Look at the list and prepare a conversation opener for each context.

- something that's been in the news or on TV recently
- an item of clothing or accessory your partner is wearing
- something that really annoys you

Stand up and start a conversation with one of the students in your class. Use one of your conversation openers. Keep the conversation going until your teacher gives you a signal to stop. Close your conversation and change partners. Start a new conversation using a new conversation opener.

Vocabulary *Extra*

Multiple meanings and uses of *talk*

1 Work with a partner. Look at the proverbs and answer the questions.

> *One must talk little and listen much.*
> (African proverb)

> *Those who know do not talk, those who talk do not know.*
> (Turkish proverb)

> *It's not the same to talk of bulls as to be in the bullring.*
> (Spanish proverb)

a) What do they mean?
b) Which do you like best?
c) Do you know of any other proverbs about talking?

2 Work with your partner. Look at the list below. It shows some of the most common uses and forms of the word *talk*. Which part of speech is used in each sentence: noun (countable or uncountable), verb or adjective?

A small man was **talking** intently to the woman on his left.

My mother has **talked** of little else since meeting you.

The next stage will be **talks** between the American and Russian ministers.

I was already hearing **talk** about the merger of the two companies.

He's quite a smooth **talker**, don't you think?

Morris gave a riveting **talk** on his visit to East Africa.

He's not very **talkative** but you certainly feel his presence.

She has become the **talk** of the town since her very public affair.

In this brief **talk** I will ask three key questions.

We listened to Fred's hilarious **talk** about how to avoid becoming a millionaire.

After the meeting the main **talking** point was the threat of redundancy.

You can't **talk**! You never do any exercise!

All that **talk** of food made me feel extremely hungry.

There's fresh **talk** of a strike at the car factory.

3 Work with your partner. Look at the sentences in Exercise 2 again and answer these questions.

a) What does *the talk of the town* mean? And *smooth talker*?
b) In what situation would you say *You can't talk!* ?

Check your own dictionary. Look for other words formed using *talk*.

4 Complete these sentences using one of the forms of *talk*.

a) Are there any international peace _____ going on at the moment?
b) Who's the most _____ person you know?
c) What's the main _____ point amongst your friends these days?

5 Work with your partner. Discuss the questions in Exercise 4.

---

talk¹ /tɔːk/ verb ★★★

1 communicate	6 send information
2 discuss	7 have power to persuade
3 give lecture	+ PHRASES
4 give secret information	+ PHRASAL VERBS
5 achieve sth by talking	

talk² /tɔːk/ noun ★★★
1 [C] a conversation with someone: **have a talk (with sb)** *We had a nice talk yesterday.* **1a. talks** [plural] discussions between important people from opposing sides designed to help them agree about an issue: **+with** *He visited Egypt in March for talks with the president.* ♦ **+between** *the outcome of talks between the government and the rebels* ♦ **+on** *preliminary talks on the future of the steel industry* ♦ **have/hold talks** *The management will be holding informal talks with union officials.* ♦ **a round/session of talks** *the need for a fresh round of peace talks* ♦ **talks break down/collapse** *Talks broke down last week over the issue of overtime pay.* ♦ **talks resume/reopen** *The trade talks will resume next month.*
2 [C] an informal lecture about a subject: **give/deliver a talk (on sth)** *Williams gave a talk on his travels in Nepal.*
3 [U] ordinary conversations between people: *I sat there listening to the sailors' talk.* ♦ **+of** *Talk of housework bored her.* ♦ **the talk turns to sth** (=the conversation begins to be about something) *Then the talk turned to the upcoming exam.* **3a.** conversations and discussions about what may happen: **+of** *There was no talk of any cuts in wages.* ♦ **+about** *There is a lot of talk about welfare reform.* ♦ **hear talk** *We hear talk nowadays about being good Europeans.* **3b.** the activity of talking, especially when you think it does not achieve anything: *Most radio stations need less talk and more music.* ♦ **be all/just talk** *She appears to be an expert on men, but it's all talk!* ♦ **despite/for all sb's talk** *For all the government's talk, it does nothing to improve housing conditions.* **3c.** discussion of other people's private lives: *At first there was a lot of talk, but people soon lost interest.* **3d.** a style of talking used by a particular group of people: *girl/boy talk* ♦ *youngsters using up-to-the-minute street talk* (=a fashionable way of talking)
PHRASES **talk is cheap** *informal* used for saying that you do not believe that someone will in fact do what they are saying they will do
the talk of sth if something is the talk of a place, people there talk a lot about it: *a fashion display that was the talk of London society* ♦ **the talk of the town** *The couple had suddenly become the talk of the town.*

talkative /ˈtɔːkətɪv/ adj a talkative person talks a lot

talker /ˈtɔːkə(r)/ noun [C] *informal* someone who talks a lot or who talks in a particular way: *She's quite a talker.* ♦ **a smooth talker** (=someone who is good at persuading people by saying nice things) *Your brother certainly is a smooth talker, isn't he?*

talking point /ˈtɔːkɪŋ ˌpɔɪnt/ noun [C] something interesting that people are likely to want to discuss

2 Taste

Grammar Noun phrases. Describing nouns and order of adjectives. Fronting
Vocabulary Describing places to eat. Word building. Idioms with *taste*
Useful phrases Agreeing and disagreeing

Speaking

▲ Julia, art teacher

1 The people in the photos *(1–4)* were asked 'If you were a food, what food would you be?' Which of the four do you think gave each of the answers *(a–d)*? Why?

a) 'Baked beans, because they're full of protein and good for you.'
b) 'A cauliflower, because it's flowery and intricate.'
c) 'A bar of dark chocolate, because it's smooth and velvety like me!'
d) 'Nuts, because they're hard, but worth opening for what's inside!'

Check your answers on page 128.

2 If you were a food, what would you be? Why? Discuss your answer with a partner.

Listening

1 Work in small groups. What kind of food or drink would you associate with the following situations? Why?

a) being in love
b) waiting at a bus station
c) rainy days
d) summer
e) the end of a hard day
f) your grandmother's house

2 🌐 1.12 Listen to six people giving their answers to Exercise 1. Answer these questions for each person *(1–6)*.

a) Which situation *(a–f)* are they talking about?
b) What food do they associate with that situation?

3 Complete the descriptions of the foods you heard in Exercise 2.

a) b_____ coffee i_____ a p_____ c_____
b) big bowls of f_____ salad w_____ h_____-m_____ d_____
c) huge plates of r_____ lamb s_____ w_____ m_____ p_____
d) the b_____ gravy y_____ h_____ e_____ t_____
e) c_____ m_____ c_____ biscuits d_____ i_____ c_____
f) s_____ s_____ strawberries w_____ f_____ c_____
g) some kind of m_____ convenience food t_____ d_____ n_____ a_____ c_____

Listen again and check your answers.

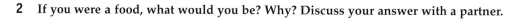

▲ Colin, army officer

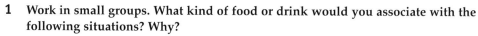

▲ Max, sailor

▲ Janet, pensioner

Noun phrases

some coffee
a cup of coffee

Describing noun phrases
a milky coffee served in an
enormous mug

Order of adjectives
delicious, spicy, home-made,
French onion soup

Grammar

1 **Read the descriptions (*a–d*) and decide which best fits the photo.**

a) bitter vending machine coffee in a plastic cup
b) the espresso coffee that you can get in the bar round the corner
c) a mug of strong, black coffee with two or three sugars
d) hot, milky coffee steaming in a mug

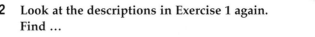

Which of the descriptions above is most similar to the coffee served in your country?

2 **Look at the descriptions in Exercise 1 again. Find …**

1 the head: the main noun (it is the same for all the descriptions).
2 an adjective.
3 a noun used as an adjective.
4 a prepositional phrase (preposition + noun phrase).
5 a relative clause.
6 a participle clause.

Answer these questions.

- Which parts of speech (2–6) are used **before** the head?
- Which are used **after** the head?

3 **Work with a partner. Put the words and phrases in the correct order.**

a) tea / with a / green / slice of lemon / a cup of
b) Greek / served / yoghurt /creamy / with nuts and dried fruit
c) freshly-made / dripping with maple syrup / a pile of / pancakes
d) two / of bacon / cooked to a crisp / rashers

Do you ever have any of these things for breakfast? Write a complex noun phrase describing your favourite breakfast food.

4 **Look at these descriptions. Which (if any) appeals most to you right now? Why?**

a) a slice of delicious home-made apple pie
b) a glass of refreshing, ice-cold lemon tea
c) a strong wake-me-up Italian espresso

5 **Look at the adjectives in Exercise 4 and answer these questions.**

a) Which adjectives describe …
1 the basic ingredients or qualities (for example, the country it comes from)?
2 the ways it can be prepared or served (for example, *fresh, frozen, home-made*)?
3 the speaker's personal opinion?
b) What order are they used in?

6 **Complete these menu descriptions with the words and phrases given. Which dish would you most like to try?**

a) a selection of _____ cheeses (French / local / delicious)
b) a bowl of _____ chowder (piping hot / clam / tasty)
c) half a dozen _____ crayfish (freshwater / exquisite / grilled)
d) a _____ pancake (savoury / mouth-watering / vegetable)

7 **Work in small groups. Expand the sentence below as much as possible. You have three minutes. The group with the longest and most coherent sentence wins.**

The restaurant served food.

8 Grammar *Extra* 2, Part 1 page 134. Read the explanations and do Exercise 1.

Reading

1 **Read the introduction to a restaurant review and answer these questions.**

a) When did the writer first visit the restaurant?

b) How is it different from other restaurants? List as many unusual things about it as you can.

c) Why do you think the writer liked it so much?

I first reviewed Le Palmier ten years ago. At the time I wrote that it was one of the most unusual and enjoyable seafood restaurants I had ever visited – not least because of its location on Croix
5 St Michel, a tiny island just off the coast near St Laurent. Back then it was run by a married couple, Marianne and Didier. He was the cook and fisherman, while she tended the vegetable gardens and ran the restaurant. There was only
10 one waiter, their son Alex.

Access to the island was by a small launch with room for no more than five passengers. There were no advance bookings. You simply turned up at the jetty in St Laurent and waited. Eventually
15 Marianne would come along in the launch and pick you up. Sometimes you had to wait for an hour or more. To make the wait more agreeable, their daughter, Dominique, had set up a tiny bar on the jetty. It was really just a kiosk with a couple
20 of tables where you could take a glass of white wine (from vines grown on the island) and enjoy the scenery.

The trip to the island took ten minutes. As the coastline receded, Marianne would tell you what
25 was on the day's menu and what was going on in the village. She always seemed very well-informed. Or, perhaps, very imaginative.

Le Palmier was in the only building on the island; a three-storey house looking over the
30 water to the mainland. On the upper floors lived the family. Their rooms had balconies filled with glorious geraniums and bougainvillea. The restaurant occupied the ground floor, opening out onto a sea-side terrace. A striped canopy provided
35 shelter from the sun. There were only four

tables, each one covered with a crisp, white linen tablecloth and provided with a basket of wonderful home-made bread.

The menu was, frankly, limited, but while
40 choice was restricted, there were rarely any complaints about price, which was absurdly low, or about quality. Basically, you ate whatever Didier had caught in the waters of the bay that morning. On my first visit, I had squid for the first time in
45 my life. It was barbecued with red peppers and served with fresh salad from the restaurant gardens to the sound of *La Traviata*: Didier was singing in the kitchen. For dessert I chose pears in red wine.

This summer, my wife and I went to St Laurent
50 as an anniversary celebration, my first visit in several years.

2 **Work with a partner. Answer these questions.**

a) Is this the type of restaurant you would enjoy eating at?

b) What three changes would you make to the restaurant to make it more profitable?

3 **You are going to read the rest of the review. Divide into two groups. Group A: read text A on page 17 and make notes about the changes that had been made ...**

a) in the area surrounding the bar.

b) in the bar on the jetty.

c) to the boat and the journey to the island.

Group B: look at page 128 and read the instructions.

Compare your answers with a member of your group.

4 **Work with a partner from the other group. Close your book and use your notes to tell your partner about the changes that had been made.**

5 **Work with a partner. Discuss these questions.**

a) Were any of the changes the owner made similar to the ones you thought of?
b) What was the writer's attitude towards the changes? Do you think the review was fair?
c) Do you know of anywhere, not necessarily a restaurant, that has undergone modernisation? Were the changes for the better or the worse?

TEXT A

My wife had heard all about Le Palmier and was looking forward to our visit as much as I was. Driving to the jetty, we were surprised to find that what had once been a tiny village was now a
5 thriving tourist town. As I parked the car I looked across the water to the island, where I saw a brand new sign with the restaurant's name in lights. We set off for Dominique's bar in the hope of finding her still serving exquisite wine from a barrel.
10 It was not to be. At the edge of the water stood a large bar with tables inside and out. As I pushed open the door, pop music blared out at me. I made my way to the bar to find out about the possibility of getting a table that evening. The woman I spoke
15 to looked familiar and I realised I was speaking to Dominique. As she looked at her list of bookings, I noticed that a number of coach parties were booked in. It all looked terribly efficient.
We were in luck – there had been a late
20 cancellation. We ordered a drink and settled down to wait for our turn on the launch. But while the wait was the same – about an hour – the surroundings were not. As we sat sipping our pricey beers people came and went all around
25 us. The bar clearly catered for more than the restaurant clientele, but the number of people who were looking expectantly out across the water worried me slightly. Eventually our names were called along with around twenty others. I
30 wondered how we were all going to fit into the five-seater launch that I remembered from my earlier visit.
But there was no small launch any more. Instead, bobbing up and down at the end of

35 the walkway, I saw a sleek boat with plenty of seating and an enormous motor at the back. We were helped aboard by a smartly-dressed crew member. As the boat sped off towards the island I glanced back towards our rented car, and
40 saw a crowd of teenagers gathered around it. I wondered whether the satnav would still be there when we returned.
The journey across the water was speedy and efficient. Gone was the opportunity to chat with
45 Marianne and find out what Didier had caught that day. Instead we listened to more music.

Vocabulary

1 **Work with a partner who read the same text as you and follow the instructions. Students from Group A: prepare to teach four of the words in the box from your part of the review to a student from Group B.**

| blared out   bobbing   clientele   exquisite   launch   pricey   sped off   thriving |

a) Read the text again and find the words.
b) Discuss their meanings with your partner. Think about the best way to explain them.

Students from Group B: look at page 129.

2 **Work with a partner from the other group and follow the instructions.**
• Teach your partner the words.
• Ask your partner to write sentences using the new words.
• Check that the words have been used correctly in the sentences.

Grammar

Fronting

Use for changing emphasis and adding dramatic effect.

Gone were the days when we could sit and enjoy a quiet meal.

Over the sea came a boat.

Why it had changed, we couldn't say.

1 Look at these sentences (a–e), which have been taken from the restaurant review. Write the words in the correct order without looking back.

a) floors / family / the / lived / upper / on / the (page 16)
b) at / large / water / the / stood / bar / a / edge / the / of (page 17)
c) chat / to / gone / Marianne / was / with / opportunity / the (page 17)
d) ran / between / tables / waiters / the (page 128)
e) there / a / on / tablecloth / basket / paper / was / the (page 128)

2 Work with a partner. Check your completed sentences in Exercise 1 with the review and answer these questions.

a) Are the sentences in the review different from yours?
b) In what way is the word order different from usual?
c) In which sentence has a word been dropped? Which word?
d) What information has been brought to the front of each sentence? What effect does this have?

3 Rewrite these sentences to change the emphasis.

a) The peaceful little restaurant we once knew was gone.
b) There was a modern monstrosity in its place.
c) We didn't know when exactly the change took place.
d) The chef lived above the restaurant.
e) The path, lit by small twinkling candles, went down to the beach.
f) We went home, tired and hungry.

4 Complete these sentences about a place you remember from your past which has changed a lot since you first went there.

a) Many a time did we …
b) Gone is the …
c) Why … I don't really know.

Compare your answers with your partner and ask for more information about the place and the changes that have taken place.

5 Grammar *Extra* 2, Part 2 page 134. Read the explanations and do Exercise 2.

Speaking: anecdote

You are going to tell your partner about the last time you ate out at a restaurant.

- Ask yourself the questions below.
- Think about *what* to say and *how* to say it.
- Tell your partner about your experience.

a) When did you last eat out?
b) Where did you go?
c) Who did you go with?
d) Why did you decide to go there?
e) What was the place like?
f) Did you like the atmosphere? Why? / Why not?
g) Do you go there often or was it the first time?
h) What did you order?
i) Did you enjoy it? Why? / Why not?
j) Was the service good? Did you leave a tip?
k) Would you recommend it to someone else? Why? / Why not?

Writing

1 Write a review for the restaurant you described in Speaking: anecdote. Before you start, look at the points below and think about what you are going to write and the language you will need.

   a) Think about the kind of person who goes to that kind of restaurant and the kind of information they would be interested in.

   b) Decide what information you are going to include. Look at this list.
- the address and phone number
- the opening times
- some information about the people who run the place
- anything they said of interest that you could report
- the menu
- some typical dishes
- a description of a particular dish
- a description of the decor
- a description of the atmosphere
- a personal recommendation (A dish? A good time of day to go?)
- some information about the history of the place (How long it's been open? The history of the building?)
- any particular incident that gives an insight into the restaurant
- anything else you'd like to add

   c) Decide what order to present the information in.

2 Write a short review of no more than 200 words.

3 Work in small groups. Read each other's reviews. Can you guess what kind of person the review is written for? Which restaurant would you like to eat at?

Listening

1   Work in small groups. Think of one typical dish for as many countries as you can. You have three minutes.

2   Compare your answers with the rest of the class and discuss these questions.
   a) Have you tried any of the dishes you mentioned in Exercise 1? Do you know what the ingredients are?
   b) Have you got a favourite foreign dish?
   c) When you travel, do you make a point of trying the local specialities?

3   🔊 1.13–1.16 Listen to Anne, Kim, Bill and Steve talking about their eating experiences abroad. Did they like the food in the countries they visited?

   Listen again and list the food vocabulary you hear each person use.

4   Work with a partner. Compare your lists and discuss these questions.
   a) Which countries do you think they are talking about? Check your answers on page 128.
   b) Which diet appeals to you the most/least? Why?
   c) How do these foods differ from the food you're used to eating?

Pronunciation

1   Look at these extracts from the conversation in Listening, Exercise 3. Underline the words and sounds the speakers stress to express their enthusiasm or reservation.
   a) Mmm, it's superb, really hot and spicy …
   b) Well, it took a bit of getting used to actually.
   c) Well, to tell you the truth, I didn't really like it that much.
   d) … and hmm, I don't really like cabbage that much …
   e) … no, it isn't really my favourite.
   f) It isn't particularly elaborate, but it's good.

   🔊 1.17 Listen and check your answers.

2   Listen to the extracts in Exercise 1 again. Pay particular attention to the intonation of the words and sounds that were stressed by the speakers. In which sentences does the speaker use intonation to …
   a) show enthusiasm?
   b) show that he/she has some reservations?
   c) soften criticism?
   d) emphasise good qualities?

3   Work with your partner. Discuss these questions.
   a) How do the sounds of *mmm* and *really* change according to their meaning?
   b) Do you use *mmm* in your own language to do the same thing?
   c) We often use intonation to communicate what we are thinking or feeling. What other techniques can we use to show enthusiasm or reservation?

4   Work with your partner. Look at the two short exchanges below. Use the words and intonation in Exercise 1 above and add your own ideas to make the conversations sound a) more enthusiastic b) less enthusiastic.
   a) A: How was the trip then?   b) A: So, how was the food last night?
        B: Interesting.   B: Unusual.

Vocabulary & Speaking

1 **Work in small groups. Answer these questions.**

a) How many words can you form from the root word *taste*?
b) What verbs or adjectives can you think of that are often used with *taste*?
c) The word *taste* has several meanings. How many can you think of?
d) Do you know of any sayings or idioms with *taste*?

2 **Complete these sentences with words and expressions in the box.**

> accounting   acquired   bad taste   of her own medicine   poor taste   share   tastefully
> tasteless   tasty   victory

a) The new bar is very lively, with very _____ food and a good selection of drinks.
b) When they asked him if he had enjoyed the liqueur he was very diplomatic and said that it was an _____ taste.
c) We found a charming little hotel with _____ furnished bedrooms and lots of facilities.
d) 'They get along well.'
   'Yes, they _____ the same taste in music.'
e) She forgot to put salt in, so the bread was absolutely _____ .
f) She's always keeping him waiting, so when he left her waiting in the pub for half an hour so she got a taste _____ .
g) The new boss left without offering a round, which left a _____ in everyone's mouths.
h) The joke was in very _____ and quite a few people were offended.
i) An orange fur coat! There's no _____ for taste.
j) They finally tasted _____ when their team won 3–0.

Look at the idiomatic sayings with *taste*. Do you use the same sayings in your own language?

3 **Work with a partner. Write a short definition of *good taste*. Use no more than twenty words. Share your definition with the rest of the class. Which one do you like best?**

4 **Look at the list of actions and decide which of the following you consider …**

a) completely unacceptable.
b) acceptable in certain circumstances.
c) totally acceptable at all times.

- chewing gum
- using your mobile telephone on public transport
- kissing in public
- spitting in the street
- swearing
- losing your temper in public

5 **Compare your views with your partner. Would your parents have given the same answers? How many of these are you actually guilty of? What other things do you consider 'not in good taste'?**

Useful phrases

1 🌐 **1.18–1.20 Listen to three short conversations. As you listen, answer these questions.**

a) Match each conversation (*1–3*) to one of these topics:
   a) shopping   b) giving presents   c) eating out.

b) Decide who is speaking in each conversation (*1–3*):
   a) a married couple   b) colleagues on the phone   c) a parent and a child.

2 **Work with a partner. In each conversation the people are disagreeing about something. What exactly is the nature of the disagreement?**

Listen again and check your answers.

3 **Complete the extracts from the conversations in Exercise 1 with the useful phrases in the boxes. There is one useful phrase too many in each case.**

a) | That can't be | I think you'll find | That may be but |
   |---|---|---|

   A: Because you could have used the company's dining facilities.
   B: Yes, but it was a breakfast meeting with a client.
   A: (1) _____ it's company policy.
   B: (2) _____ that it's only company policy if we're entertaining in-house guests.

b) | I suppose you're right | No way! | That's a load of rubbish |
   |---|---|---|

   A: Well, apart from the fact that it doesn't help the environment, imported fruit doesn't taste as good.
   B: (1) _____ . These strawberries are absolutely delicious!
      ...
   A: What about the environment?
   B: Okay, okay, (2) _____ , it's not brilliant for the environment, but I couldn't resist them.

c) | I rest my case | I know it's awful, isn't it? | Oh, I don't know |
   |---|---|---|

   A: I can't believe he got her a Hoover® for her birthday.
   B: (1) _____ . It's the thought that counts.
   A: No! Come on! He couldn't have given it much thought, if that's all he came up with.
   B: You gave me a drill on my last birthday.
   A: So?
   B: (2) _____ .

Listen again and check your answers.

4 **Work with your partner. Look at the useful phrases in Exercise 3 again. Use them to complete the table below.**

Agreement	Disagreement	Closing an argument
strong:	total:	
reluctant:	polite:	

5 🌐 **1.21 Listen to four people saying *yes* and *no*. Decide whether the speaker is …**
a) uncertain   b) in total agreement   c) in total disagreement.

6 🌐 **1.22 Work with your partner. Listen to six statements (*a–f*) and respond with *yes* or *no* so that your partner can tell if you agree, disagree or are uncertain.**

7 **Work in small groups and discuss two or three of the statements from Exercise 6. Use the useful phrases above to agree or disagree with each other.**

Writing *Extra*

Letter to a newspaper

1 Work in small groups. Look at the photos and discuss the questions.

    a) Do you like wearing jeans? Why? / Why not?

    b) Have you got any jeans that look like the ones in the photos?

    c) Would you wear these jeans, or any other jeans …

- to work?
- to a job interview?
- to class?
- to a party?

2 Look at this headline from a local newspaper. What do you think is the story behind the headline?

Schools ban baggy, ripped and super-skinny jeans

3 Read one woman's reaction to the story. Would you class her reaction as …
a) moderate? b) reasoned? c) exaggerated? d) extreme?

Can you think of any other adjectives to describe her tone?

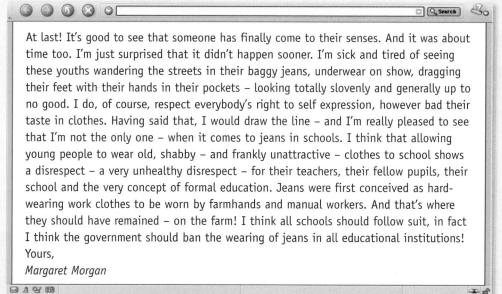

At last! It's good to see that someone has finally come to their senses. And it was about time too. I'm just surprised that it didn't happen sooner. I'm sick and tired of seeing these youths wandering the streets in their baggy jeans, underwear on show, dragging their feet with their hands in their pockets – looking totally slovenly and generally up to no good. I do, of course, respect everybody's right to self expression, however bad their taste in clothes. Having said that, I would draw the line – and I'm really pleased to see that I'm not the only one – when it comes to jeans in schools. I think that allowing young people to wear old, shabby – and frankly unattractive – clothes to school shows a disrespect – a very unhealthy disrespect – for their teachers, their fellow pupils, their school and the very concept of formal education. Jeans were first conceived as hard-wearing work clothes to be worn by farmhands and manual workers. And that's where they should have remained – on the farm! I think all schools should follow suit, in fact I think the government should ban the wearing of jeans in all educational institutions!
Yours,
Margaret Morgan

Do you agree with anything the woman says? Why? / Why not? How would you feel if the same ban was suggested in your town?

4 Look again at the woman's reaction to the story in Exercise 3 and find expressions to complete the table.

Expressing agreement or approval	Accepting someone's arguments without necessarily agreeing with them	Expressing disagreement or disapproval
It's good to see that …		

5 Add these expressions to the table in Exercise 4.

I can sympathise with the view that …   *I find it hard to believe that …*
I take exception to …   *There is no doubt some truth in …*
Whilst not in total agreement with …   *However, …*
I couldn't agree more.

6 Write a reply to the woman's comment. Use the expressions in Exercises 4 and 5 to help you.

3 City

Grammar Hedging. Inversion after negative and limiting adverbials
Vocabulary Describing cities. Describing tourist spots
Useful phrases Adding emphasis

Listening

1 How much do you know about cities around the world? Do this quiz and find out.

Cities of the world

1 **What proportion of the world's population lives in cities?**
a) Over 80%.
b) About two-thirds.
c) About a third.
d) About half.

2 **Which is the world's largest capital city?**
a) Mexico City.
b) Seoul.
c) Tokyo.
d) New Delhi.

3 **Which is Europe's noisiest capital city?**
a) Athens.
b) Madrid.
c) Rome.
d) Paris.

4 **Which is the world's oldest capital city?**
a) Baghdad.
b) Damascus.
c) Cairo.
d) Amman.

5 **Which is the world's highest capital city?**
a) La Paz (Bolivia).
b) Lima (Peru).
c) Quito (Ecuador).
d) Kathmandu (Nepal).

6 **Which was the first city to reach a population of one million?**
a) Mexico City.
b) New York.
c) London.
d) Rome.

🔊 1.23 Listen and check your answers. Were there any surprises?

2 Listen to the radio programme again. Replace the words in italics with the words used by the speaker.

a) It *seems* that there is a steady movement towards urban areas …
b) … there is still some *debate* as to which is the world's largest capital.
c) … it is *commonly accepted* that Athens is the European capital which suffers from the worst noise pollution levels.
d) It's *unclear as to* whether this information is based on popular opinion or on statistical data from the Greek authorities …
e) Sources *would appear* to suggest that the Syrians are right …
f) There is *absolutely no question* about which of the world's capital cities is the highest.

Grammar

Hedging

Use hedging expressions to distance yourself from facts or opinions that you cannot prove are true.

Hedging with verbs

it **seems** that ...
it **appears** that ...
sources **seem to suggest** ...
the results **would appear** to show ...

Hedging with *would*

it **would** seem that ...
it **would** appear that ...

Hedging with the passive voice

it **is** widely **recognised** that ...
there **are** not **believed** to be ...
it **is** not **known** ...

Hedging with noun phrases

there is **no / little / some doubt** ...
there is **no / little / some evidence** ...
there is **some discussion** ...

1 Work with a partner. Look at the expressions you added to the extracts in Listening, Exercise 2 and find expressions that show the writer believes there is ...

a) very strong evidence.   c) weak evidence.
b) fairly strong evidence.   d) unreliable evidence.

2 Read the sentences (*a–e*) and look at the information below. Decide if the sentences are true or false. Correct the ones that are false.

a) It seems that most people enjoy life in the country.
b) It appears that very few people who live in a city would prefer to live in the country.
c) The results from the first survey seem to suggest that most people are happy to stay in the country.
d) On the other hand, the second survey would seem to show that most people who live in the country would prefer to move to the city.
e) Older people are not believed to be as happy with city life as younger people. But there is little evidence in the surveys to back this up.

The results of two new surveys have just been published in which people living in rural and urban areas were asked about how happy they are with where they live. Below are some of the results.

	Survey 1	Survey 2
People who enjoy living in cities	79%	72%
People who live in a city, but would prefer to live in a rural area	35%	43%
People who live in a city, but spend as much time as possible outside the city	47%	29%
People who live in rural areas, but would prefer to live in a city	62%	36%
Percentage of these who are under 30	84%	–
Percentage of these who are over 50	13%	–

Do you think the results would be the same in your country?

3 Look at the sentences (*a–e*) in Exercise 2 again and underline all the hedging expressions.

4 Work with your partner. Rewrite these statements using the words in brackets.

a) Most young people prefer to live in large cities because of the job opportunities. (seem)
b) Older people living on their own get very lonely in big cities. (little doubt)
c) People who live in the country are generally more healthy than city dwellers. (some discussion)
d) Life in the country is much less stimulating than life in a big city. (would not appear)
e) There is far less violent crime in the country. (generally accepted)
f) People suffer from sleep deprivation in big cities. (little evidence)

Do you agree with the sentences you've written?

5 ● 1.24 Listen to Sharon and Derek discussing a newspaper story about the survey. Make notes about the reasons young people prefer to live in a city.

6 Work with your partner. Write the story as it would have appeared in the newspaper. Use no more than 120 words. Then compare your story with the version on page 129.

7 Grammar *Extra* 3, Part 1 page 136. Read the explanations and do Exercise 1.

▲ Sharon and Derek

Speaking

Work with a partner. Discuss these questions.

a) What is the capital of your country famous for? Does it attract a lot of visitors?
b) Which capital city would you most like to spend a weekend in?
c) Do you live in a city, a town, a village or out in the country? Have you always lived there? Do you like it? Why? / Why not?

1 There is little point in portraying it as something it is not. Its beauty is not as awe-inspiring as other cities. It is not even particularly old, and much of what may have constituted its historical legacy has over the centuries
5 been all too quickly sacrificed to make way for the new. It is a largely modern city, a product of the 19th and 20th centuries, and the expanses of its outer dormitory suburbs and peripheral high-rise apartment jungles are an oppressive introduction for anyone driving into the city for
10 the first time.

It may lack the historical richness and sophistication of other European capitals, but it oozes a life and character that, given the opportunity to work its magic (it doesn't take long), cannot leave you indifferent. Leaving aside the
15 great art museums, the splendour of the main square and the Royal Palace, and the elegance of the city park, the essence of this city is in the life pulsing through its streets. In no other European capital will you find the city centre so thronged so late into the night as here, especially if you
20 go out at weekends. Everyone seems to stay out late, as though some unwritten law forbade sleeping before dawn. In this sense it is a city more to be lived than seen.

2 The city is like a history lesson come to life. As you walk among the long stone palaces or across the Charles Bridge, with the Vltava flowing below and pointed towers all around, you'll feel as if history had stopped back in the
5 18th century. Goethe called it the prettiest gem in the stone crown of the world. A millennium earlier, in 965, the Arab-Jewish merchant Ibrahim Ibn Jacob described it as a town of 'stone and lime'. For these reasons the city is on the UNESCO World Heritage list.
10 Today it is a city of over a million inhabitants, the seat of government and leading centre of much of the country's intellectual and cultural life. Unlike other capitals in this region, which were major battlefields during WW2, it escaped almost unscathed and after the war, lack of
15 modernisation prevented haphazard modern development. Since 1989, however, the city centre has been swamped by capitalism as street vendors, cafés and restaurants take over pavements, streets and parks, as they did prior to 1948.
How you feel about the city's current tourist glut may
20 depend on where you're coming from. If you're arriving from Western Europe it may all seem quite normal, but if you've been elsewhere in Eastern Europe for a while, you'll be in for a bit of a shock. As you're being jostled by the hawkers and hordes of tourists, you may begin to feel that it has become a
25 tacky tourist trap, but try to overcome that feeling and enjoy this great European art centre for all it's worth.

3 The sheer level of energy is the most striking aspect of this capital city. It's true the larger picture can be somewhat depressing – shoebox housing estates and office blocks traversed by overhead expressways crowded with traffic.
5 But this is the country's success story in action. The average suburb hasn't fallen prey to supermarket culture though: streets are lined with tiny specialist shops and bustling restaurants, most of which stay open late into the night. Close to the soaring office blocks exist pockets of another
10 time – an old wooden house, a kimono shop, a small inn, an old lady in a traditional dress sweeping the pavement outside her home with a straw broom. More than anything else, this is a place where the urgent rhythms of consumer culture collide with the quieter moments that linger from
15 older traditions. It's a living city and you'll never run out of things to explore.

4 They don't come any bigger than this – king of the hill, top of the heap. No other city is arrogant enough to dub itself 'Capital of the World' and no other city could carry it off. It is a densely-packed mass of humanity – seven million
5 people in 309sq miles (800sq km) – and all this living on top of one another makes the inhabitants a special kind of person. Although it's hard to put a finger on what makes it buzz, it's the city's hyperactive rush that really draws people here.
10 In a city that is so much a part of the global subconscious, it's pretty hard to pick a few highlights – wherever you go you'll feel like you've been there before. Bookshops, food, theatre, shopping, people: it doesn't really matter what you do or where you go because the city itself
15 is an in-your-face, exhilarating experience.

Reading

1 Work in small groups. Look at the guidebook extracts on page 26. They describe four of the world's most famous cities. Read the descriptions and decide which city is being described.

Turn to page 129 if you need help.

2 Read through the guidebook extracts again and underline the information that helped you decide which cities were being described.

3 Work with a partner. Discuss these questions about the guidebook extracts.

a) Which description appeals to you most? Why? Choose two or three phrases which you find evocative.
b) Have you been to any of these cities? Do the extracts reflect your experiences?
c) Do the extracts make you want to visit any of these cities?

Vocabulary

1 Match the adjectives (a–f) to the definitions (1–6). Then decide which of the adjectives you would use to describe the noun phrases in the box below.

a) awe-inspiring   1   giving a feeling of respect and amazement
b) haphazard   2   full of people who are very busy or lively (especially a place)
c) tacky   3   not organised, not arranged according to a plan
d) bustling   4   very tall or high in the sky (especially buildings or trees)
e) soaring   5   so loud, big or noticeable that you just can't ignore it
f) in-your-face   6   cheap and badly-made or vulgar

> advertising campaigns   coastal resorts   collection of people   market
> plastic souvenirs   scenery   seaside postcards   tower blocks   tree tops

2 Find the adjectives (a–f) in Exercise 1 in the guidebook extracts on page 26. What are they describing?

3 Work with your partner. Look at the verbs (1–5). Without looking back at the guidebook extracts, match each verb to an appropriate phrase.

1   to make   a finger on
2   to work   prey to
3   to fall   on top of one another
4   to live   its magic
5   to put   way for the new

Now check your answers.

4 Complete these sentences with the phrases in Exercise 3. Make any changes to the phrases that are necessary.

a) It's very easy _____ the charm of the market stallholders and people often end up spending much more than they'd expected to.
b) The old town was built on the edge of a cliff overlooking the gorge, using up every bit of spare space. Some houses were even built into the cliff face and people _____ in a warren of narrow cobbled streets.
c) It is difficult _____ exactly what makes this grey, industrial town such a popular tourist destination.
d) No matter how stressed you feel, once you let the beauty of the beach and the warmth of the sun _____ on you, you will begin to wind down and relax.
e) Far too often historic town centres are carved up and charming old buildings torn down _____ .

5 Work with your partner. Look at the sentences in Exercise 4 again. Have you ever visited a town or city that matches one of the descriptions? Tell your partner about it.

Grammar

Inversion after negative and limiting adverbials

Not only was it the most expensive city I'd ever stayed in, it was also the most dangerous.

Seldom have I seen anything more beautiful.

1 Work with a partner. Look at the adverbials in the box and decide which of them have negative or limiting meanings.

at once   even in the summer   frequently   never   not a word
not until he'd finished   on no account   only after a long night
only after a long wait   only then   quite often   rarely   seldom
under no circumstances   usually

2 Look at these pairs of sentences and answer the questions.

1A *In no other European capital* **will you find** the city centre so thronged so late into the night.

1B **You won't find** the city centre so thronged so late into the night *in any other European capital.*

2A *Not until I actually lived there* **did I understand** just how great the lifestyle is.

2B **I didn't understand** just how great the lifestyle is *until I actually lived there.*

a) Which sentences, the As or Bs, would be more likely to be spoken?
b) What happens to the word order when the adverbial phrase is placed at the beginning of the sentence?
c) What effect does this have on the sentence?

3 Rewrite these sentences, starting with the word or words in brackets.

a) You will rarely see such a superb example of modern architecture.
    Rarely will you see such a superb example of modern architecture.

b) I rarely visit a city more than once, but this place is really special. (Rarely)
c) I had never seen anything so breathtakingly beautiful before. (Never before)
d) You will only be able to experience the heart of this beautiful old town by wandering down its narrow side streets. (Only by)
e) You will only begin to understand the special charm of this place after you have spent an evening there. (Only after you)
f) You can't really understand exactly how beautiful the view is until you climb to the top. (Not until)
g) You shouldn't leave the town without first tasting its famous local delicacies. (On no account)

4 Work with your partner. Think of a town, city or village to fit each sentence in Exercise 3.

5 Grammar *Extra* 3, Part 2 page 136. Read the explanations and do Exercise 2.

Writing

1 You are going to write a short description of a famous town or city in your country.

- Choose the town or city you are going to write about.
- Decide what kind of tourist or visitor you are writing for. (Young backpackers? Families? Culture vultures?)
- Decide on three or four main points to include in your description.
- Write a short description (about 200 words) in the style of a guidebook. Include **at least one** inversion after a limiting or negative adverbial and **at least three** of the words and expressions from the Vocabulary exercises on page 27. Do NOT include the name of the town or city.

2 When you have finished writing, work in groups of three or four. Read your description to the group. Listen to the descriptions and try to guess which town or city they are describing. What information helped you get the answer?

VANCOUVER
heaven and earth

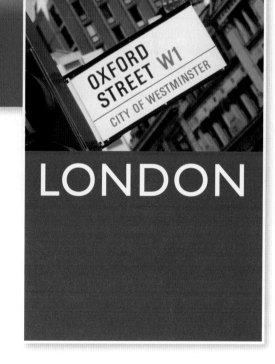

LONDON

1 Work in small groups. Look at the tourist posters, compare them and discuss these questions.

a) What aspects of the city are they promoting?
b) What kinds of tourists are they appealing to?
c) Which poster appeals to you most? Why?

2 Work in your groups. Make a list of the things a city can offer a visitor that the beach, the mountains or the countryside can't.

Which aspects would attract you most? Choose the top three. Compare your answers with the class.

3 Work in new groups. Discuss these questions.

a) Which city in your country attracts most visitors? Why?
b) What is there for them to see and do there?
c) What time of year would you recommend a visitor go there? Why?
d) Do you know of any advertising campaigns for that city? What aspects of the city are they trying to sell?
e) Choose three adjectives to sum up the atmosphere of that city.

4 Work with a student from another group. Tell each other about the city or cities you discussed in Exercise 3. If you discussed the same city, did you come to the same conclusions? If you discussed different cities, which one do you think is the most successful as a tourist attraction. Why?

Reading & Vocabulary

1   What do you know about Leicester Square? Match the questions (a–d) to the answers (1–4).

a)   Where is it?

b)   What is it?

c)   On a bad day?

d)   What's with the funny spelling?

1   Okay, it's spelt funny, but it's pronounced *Lester*.

2   A loud, brash, sweaty mass of seething humanity.

3   On a good day, it's a huge meeting place for the world.

4   Between Piccadilly and Covent Garden, just north of Trafalgar Square.

2   Read the article and answer these questions.

a)   What type of entertainment does Leicester Square offer?

b)   What type of people go to Leicester Square?

c)   What money-saving tips does the writer mention?

LEICESTER SQUARE

(1) ____ Leicester Square is one of the busiest spots in London. Buskers entertain the crowds with anything from an impromptu song to a political rant, tourists pay good money to have their faces ridiculed by cruel cartoonists
5   and suburban kids queue to dance the night away at the Hippodrome, Equinox or Maximus. (2) _____ , the whole pedestrianised area can seem like one big, youthful party. The Square is a popular meeting place for friends (3) _____ and for tourists who seem to enjoy congregating outside
10   the tube station. The cinemas claim to be the biggest and best but (4) _____ tickets are the most expensive in town. It will cost you almost double the price of a normal seat to see a blockbuster at the Empire, for example. For good value movie magic check out the Prince Charles cinema
15   on Leicester Place, (5) _____ ! People-watching is one of Leicester Square's great attractions as representatives from virtually every country on little old planet Earth walk

past (6) _____ . Ordinary people are interesting enough bu if you're really lucky you get the chance to eyeball visiting
20   stars who attend the regular movie premières. Despite its movie-made image of constant fog, London does get hot from time to time. Luckily for Leicester Square visitors, there's a handily-placed ice-cream emporium where you can gorge yourself on Triple Choc Brownie until one in
25   the morning. For main-meal feed-ups, (7) _____ avoid the overpriced chain-store eateries that front the Square and head instead for nearby Chinatown. The choice can be overwhelming with little to differentiate one prim Cantonese restaurant from another. Watching out for
30   where the Chinese themselves eat is probably the best indicator of quality. Eternally popular choices include a number of small, family-run places with menus listing up to 40 dim sum dishes and other traditional offerings. (8) _____ , Leicester Square is something of a 'must' for
35   tourists and Londoners alike. All you need to enjoy it full is plenty of time and a bit of patience!

3   Match the sentences (a–h) to the appropriate places (1–8) in the article.

a)   Especially on Friday and Saturday nights

b)   and simply gawp at each other

c)   looking for a drink and chat after a hard day's slog

d)   where tickets for a good selection of cult films start at the same price as a cup of coffee in the Square

e)   All in all

f)   your best bet is to

g)   By night

h)   consequently

4   Work with a partner. You are going to teach your partner some words from the article. Student A: turn to page 129, Student B: turn to page 130.

5   Work in small groups. Discuss these questions.

a)   Where is the busiest place in the evening where you live? What do people do there? Are there buskers or eateries? Which places would you recommend?

b)   Do you like to go out in the evenings? Where do you go? What do you do? When was the last time you went out for the evening? Tell your group where you went and what you did.

Listening & Speaking

▲ Helen

▲ Robert

1 Work with a partner. Do you agree with this statement?

Life in the city is more dangerous than life in the country.

Draw up a list of the main dangers of city life.

2 🌐 1.25 **Listen to Helen and Robert talking about the city they live in. Do they mention any of the dangers on your list?**

3 Compare your answers with your partner and discuss these questions.

a) Do Helen and Robert think they live in a particularly dangerous city?

b) What precautions do they suggest you should take when walking home at night?

c) In what places do they suggest you should take special care with your bag or wallet? Why?

d) There seems to have been an increase in crime recently. What sort of crime?

e) What exactly happened to the group of tourists?

f) What do they think the police could do to improve the situation?

Listen again and check your answers.

4 Work in groups. What advice would you give …

a) someone visiting your home town for the first time?

b) someone going abroad for the first time?

Pronunciation

1 Look at these extracts from the conversation in Listening & Speaking, Exercise 2. Complete them with *just*, *really* or *actually*.

a) … there are certain areas that you _____ know you wouldn't go into …

b) … _____ there have been a couple of stories in the papers recently about this spate of muggings that's been going on.

c) … and her wallet was snatched from her bag _____ as the train was coming into the station …

d) You've got to be _____ careful there because there is a big crowd and a lot of pickpockets …

e) I think she thought they were going to stab her husband _____ .

f) … but the sad thing was that they had only _____ arrived …

g) She didn't lose anything _____ valuable …

h) I think they need to know if a crime's happened _____ .

🌐 1.26 **Listen and check your answers. Notice the stress on *just*, *really* and *actually*.**

2 Add *just*, *really* and *actually* to the exchanges. Practise reading them with your partner.

a) A: So, what happened?

B: Well, I was coming round the corner when a boy rode past on a scooter. It all happened quickly. Next thing I knew my bag had gone.

b) A: I wouldn't walk home that way if I were you. It's dangerous.

B: I walked home that way last night. It took five minutes. It didn't look dangerous to me.

City

Useful phrases

1 **Look at the photos of a London building and discuss these questions with a partner.**

a) What do you think it's used for?

b) What does the shape remind you of?

c) Do you like it? Why? / Why not?

2 **At the time the building was opened, readers of a blog were invited to comment on the design. Read their comments. Do you agree with any? If so, which ones?**

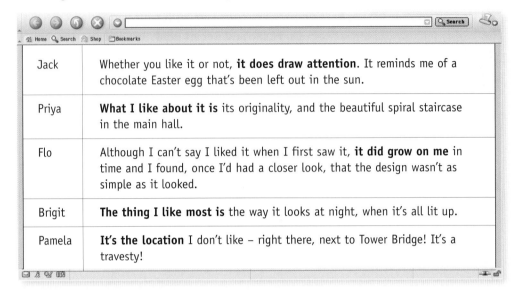

Jack	Whether you like it or not, **it does draw attention**. It reminds me of a chocolate Easter egg that's been left out in the sun.
Priya	**What I like about it is** its originality, and the beautiful spiral staircase in the main hall.
Flo	Although I can't say I liked it when I first saw it, **it did grow on me** in time and I found, once I'd had a closer look, that the design wasn't as simple as it looked.
Brigit	**The thing I like most is** the way it looks at night, when it's all lit up.
Pamela	**It's the location** I don't like – right there, next to Tower Bridge! It's a travesty!

Adding emphasis

When we want to add emphasis to a statement we can use:

1 the auxiliary **do**, **does** or **did** between the subject and the main verb.

He really *does* like it.
They really *did* come up with a great design.

Notice that the main verb is in the infinitive:

does like NOT ~~does likes it~~
did come up with NOT ~~did came up with~~.

2 cleft sentences. Cleft sentences emphasise the object of a sentence using expressions with **what**, **the thing** and **it**.

what I like is ...
the thing I like best is ...
it's the ... I love/ object to

3 **Look at the comments on the blog in Exercise 2 again. Look at the phrases in bold and match them to the rules (1 or 2) on the left.**

4 **Add emphasis to these sentences using the words in brackets. You may need to change the structure of the sentence.**

a) Although I really didn't like it to start with, I got used to it with time. (did)

b) I like the design best of all. It's really original and eye-catching. (it)

c) I like the simplicity of the design best. (the thing)

d) Initially people complained about the location. (what)

e) One thing it certainly does is provoke discussion. (do)

f) It needs a more identifiable shape. (one thing)

🌐 1.27 Listen and check your answers.

5 **Listen again. Mark the main stresses in the sentences you wrote in Exercise 4. Then listen and repeat.**

6 **Work in small groups. Look at three more modern buildings in London (a–c). Which do you like best? Why?**

Write three sentences about the buildings using emphasis. Report back to the class.

7 **Work with your partner. Discuss these questions.**

a) Are there any similar buildings in your town or in your country?

b) What did people think of them when they first went up?

c) What do they think of them now?

Vocabulary *Extra*

Lexical sets and collocations with *city* and *urban*

▲ Chongqing, China – the world's fastest growing city

▲ Ny-Ålesund, Norway – one of the northernmost settlements in the world

1 Look at the photos and think of two nouns and two adjectives that would best describe each one. Compare with a partner.

2 Work with your partner. Look at the words in the box and answer the questions.

> city   conurbation   hamlet   megalopolis   metropolis
> outpost   satellite   settlement   town   village

   a) Can you order them from the largest to the smallest?
   b) Can you think of an example of each in your immediate area? Which do you live in?
   c) Which words would you be more likely to find in a geography textbook or geography magazine?

Check your answers in Section A on the right.

3 Complete the sentences with the nouns or compound nouns in Section B on the right to make collocations.

   a) The country is undergoing a steady process of _____ , as towns and cities grow at an incredible pace.
   b) More and more villages and small satellite towns are getting eaten up in the _____ surrounding the capital city.
   c) A _____ search has begun for the Birmingham-based mystery lottery winner.
   d) The _____ is one of the most impressive buildings in the capital.
   e) The current government has pledged to spend more money on _____ as more and more people move to the cities.
   f) The country is probably better known for its spectacular _____ than its natural landscapes.

4 Work with your partner. Look at the sentences in Exercise 3 again. Are the sentences true for your country?

Section A

city /ˈsɪti/ noun [C] ★★★
1 a large important town: *a thriving industrial city on the Tasmanian coast* ♦ **major city** (=a large important city) *New and better hotels are springing up in most of Russia's major cities.* **1a.** [usually singular] the political, legal, and ADMINISTRATIVE institutions of a city: *The city has agreed to pay damages to those involved.* ♦ *city employees/officials* ♦ *city hospital/court/legislature* **1b.** the people who live in a city: *a city that is very optimistic about the future* **1c.** a European town that has a CATHEDRAL

hamlet /ˈhæmlət/ noun [C] a small village

megalopolis /ˌmegəˈlɒpəlɪs/ noun [C] a large city, or an area that contains a lot of large cities

metropolis /məˈtrɒpəlɪs/ noun [C] *mainly literary* a big city, especially considered as somewhere that is very busy and exciting

outpost /ˈaʊtpəʊst/ noun [C] **1** a military camp that is far away from the army **2** a small town far away from other towns, usually where trading takes place

satellite /ˈsætəlaɪt/ noun ★★
1 [C] an object that is sent into space to travel round the Earth in order to receive and send information: *a spy/communications/weather satellite* ♦ *France was the third country to launch* (=send into space) *an artificial satellite.* ♦ **via satellite** (=by satellite) *We have pictures of the disaster live via satellite.* ♦ **by satellite** *The new equipment will link vehicles by satellite to their office.* **1a.** a natural object such as a moon that moves around a planet: *Jupiter's satellites*
2 [C] something that is controlled by a larger thing or that depends on a larger thing but is separate from it: *She works in a satellite office.* **2a.** a town or city that is close to and depends on a larger city **2b.** a country that depends on another, more powerful, country

settlement /ˈset(ə)lmənt/ noun ★★
2 [C] a place where people have come to live permanently, usually when there were very few people living there before: *They discovered the remains of an early Anglo-Saxon settlement.* **2a.** [U] the process of going to live in a place with few people and starting to make it into a community

town /taʊn/ noun ★★★
1 [C] a place where people live and work that is larger than a village but smaller than a city: *a small town* ♦ *an industrial town in China* ♦ *Mountains overlook the town on three sides.* ♦ *a town on the River Thames* ♦ **+of** *the northern Belgian town of Onkerzele*

village /ˈvɪlɪdʒ/ noun [C] ★★★
1 a very small town in the countryside: *a Scottish fishing village* **1a.** the people who live in a village: *The whole village attended the meeting.* **1b.** [only before noun] in a village, or relating to a village: *the village shop/church* ♦ *village gossip*

Section B

ˌcity ˈhall noun *American* [C/U] the building where the council members and officials who manage a city work = TOWN HALL **a.** [U] the council members and officials who manage a city
cityscape /ˈsɪtiˌskeɪp/ noun [C/U] the way that a city looks, or a particular view of a city: *architectural projects that have changed the Paris cityscape*
citywide /ˈsɪtiˌwaɪd/ adj involving the whole of a city: *Police launched a citywide hunt for the gunman.*

urbanisation /ˌɜː(r)bənaɪˈzeɪʃ(ə)n/ noun [U] the process by which towns and cities grow bigger and more and more people go to live in them: *The 18th century was a period of rapid urbanisation.*
ˌurban reˈnewal noun [U] the process of making areas of a city more attractive and rich by creating new buildings and parks, more business activity etc
ˌurban ˈsprawl noun [U] a very large area of buildings, industries etc that has spread from a city into the countryside surrounding it, especially in a way that is not attractive: *We drove through several miles of urban sprawl.*

Review A

▶ Grammar *Extra* pages 134–137

Grammar

1 Underline the correct alternative.

I had (1) **waited / been waiting** for ages. I (2) **was getting / had got** really bored. I didn't know how much longer I was going to wait. Why (3) **was he taking / had he taken** so long? (4) **Had something terrible happened / Was something terrible happening** to him? At last I saw him.

'Sorry! There's a demo in town. Thousands of people (5) **are protesting / have protested** outside the city hall. They've (6) **closed / been closing** all the streets to traffic.'

'Why didn't you phone? I've (7) **worried / been worrying** about you!'

'I tried, but my battery's (8) **gone / going** flat!'

When was the last time you had to wait a long time for somebody? Tell a partner what happened.

2 Work with your partner. Read the pairs of sentences. Explain the difference in meaning between them.

a) 1   I don't particularly want to go.
   2   I particularly don't want to go.
b) 1   John's only got his phone number.
   2   Only John's got his phone number.
c) 1   I did my work quickly and got ready to go.
   2   I did my work and quickly got ready to go.
d) 1   Personally, I don't think he'll apologise.
   2   I don't think he'll apologise personally.
e) 1   For a moment I didn't believe him.
   2   I didn't believe him for a moment.
f) 1   Just Sam and I went for a drink.
   2   Sam and I just went for a drink.

3 Write the phrases in the correct order.

a) beautiful / with a delicate / shirt / floral pattern / silk / A
b) coat / A / made of 100% / warm / lamb's wool / winter
c) A / old pair of / shoes / covered in mud / scruffy / running
d) bought / leather / Knee-high / that my mother / for me / boots / in Italy
e) a picture of / hand-printed / An / T-shirt / with / a cat / unusual

Do you ever wear anything similar to the clothes described? Write a detailed description of one of your favourite items of clothing. Show it to your partner.

4 Rewrite the sentences starting with the word given.

a) His name was Harry.
   Harry _____ .
b) Gambling was his game.
   His _____ .
c) His losses were great.
   Great _____ .
d) Those who suffered most were his family.
   His _____ .
e) His car was gone.
   Gone _____ .
f) Nobody knew where he had gone.
   Where _____ .

Write a short story about Harry's disappearance. Use fronting where appropriate.

5 Add words and phrases from the box to soften the statements and reflect your attitude to them.

appear believe discussion doubt evidence recognise seem suggest think

a) City life is dangerous.
   It is widely recognised that life in some cities can be very dangerous.
b) There are no job opportunities in small towns.
c) Capital cities are the best places to build a career.
d) Quality of life is more important than money.
e) Life in a small town is boring.
f) People who live in the country live longer, happier lives.

Work with your partner. Discuss your statements.

6 Match the sentence halves.

a) Never had she
b) Only then did I
c) Not only was she
d) Not a word did she
e) Never again would I

1   understand how strongly I felt.
2   say as I took her hand.
3   looked so beautiful.
4   my best friend, she was also the love of my life.
5   ask such an important question.

What do you think the question was? Discuss with your partner. Write three more sentences to continue the story.

Vocabulary

1 Complete the descriptions with the words and phrases in the box.

> butting in   drones on and on   flows   hog
> hunt around   puts it across   say
> the same wavelength

a) I think Fred can be really rude, don't you? He's forever _____ on conversations and it's not even as if he's got anything interesting to _____ !

b) Mel is very sweet but she does tend to _____ the conversation, you know, she gets started on a topic and then she just _____ forever.

c) He's amazing. The conversation really _____ when we're together. We're always on _____ . I've never met anyone like him before!

d) She's really good in meetings. She never has to _____ for words, she always knows exactly what she wants to say and she _____ so clearly. I wish I was like her!

Do you know anyone like the people described above? Tell a partner about them.

2 Complete the sentences with the correct form of the words in brackets.

a) That was probably the greatest _____ of my whole life. (achieve)

b) He tackled the problem with _____ and _____ . (competent / efficient)

c) I don't think she's particularly _____ of other people's feelings. (consider)

d) I get an enormous amount of _____ out of my family. (satisfy)

e) She's a very _____ worker and a _____ addition to the workforce. (skills / value)

f) Reaching the top of the mountain gave me an incredibly intense feeling of _____ . (fulfil)

3 Match each sentence (*a–f*) with a response (*1–6*).

a) Have you seen Tim's new hairstyle?

b) This coffee is really strong!

c) Ann hasn't phoned me for two days! Do you think she's angry with me?

d) He should really apologise.

e) It's great to see the boys playing so well together.

f) What's up with Jorg? He looks a bit glum.

1 No, she's just giving you a taste of your own medicine.

2 Yes! Just goes to show – there's no accounting for taste!

3 I agree – that comment was in poor taste.

4 Yes, it's definitely an acquired taste.

5 Yes, it's the bitter taste of defeat!

6 Well, it's no surprise. They share the same taste in practically everything!

4 Choose the correct words to complete the descriptions.

It was a busy, (1) _____ market town. We arrived at dawn. The bus station was an ugly (2) _____ block set in a (3) _____ back street behind the main square. People were already setting up their stalls. Music (4) _____ from the loud speakers of one of the vans. It was a lively scene, and behind it all, the (5) _____ view of the Andes (6) _____ above the town.

1	a) homely	b) bustling	c) bobbing
2	a) concrete	b) tacky	c) batter
3	a) haphazard	b) in-your-face	c) grubby
4	a) sped off	b) blared out	c) chugged
5	a) exquisite	b) awe-inspiring	c) reverie
6	a) thriving	b) thrusting	c) soaring

Pronunciation

1 Look at some words from Units 1–3. Say the words and add them to the table.

> animated   atmosphere   awe-inspiring   efficiency
> evocative   exquisite   fulfilment   frustrating
> haphazard   hilarious   historical   intricate
> meaningful   reverie   satisfying   stimulating

A: ☐□□	B: □☐□	C: ☐□□□	D: □☐□□
			animated

2 Underline the stressed syllables.

🔊 1.28 **Listen, check and repeat.**

4 Story

Grammar The future as seen from the past. Discourse markers in writing
Vocabulary Types of story. Expressions with *story* and *tale*. Deception and belief
Useful phrases Responding to a story

Speaking

1 Read the text about six-word life stories. Which is your favourite story and why?

One Life. *Six words.* What's yours?

Legend has it that the novelist Ernest Hemingway was once challenged to write a story in six words. He came back with, 'For sale: baby shoes, never worn.' Some say he called it his best work. Others dismiss the anecdote as literary folktale. Either way, the six-word story was born, and it's been around ever since. The following stories were amongst thousands submitted to *Smith* magazine in New York:

I was never the pretty one.
Followed rules, not dreams. Never again.
Barrister, barista. What's the difference, Mum?
Found true love, married someone else.
Time heals all wounds? Not quite.
Six words not enough for a.
Never lived up to my potential.
Didn't fit in then, still don't.
I write stories. They come true.
I still make coffee for two.

2 Match the famous people (*a–e*) to the six-word life stories (*1–5*).

a) Bill Gates
b) Julius Caesar
c) Agatha Christie
d) Martin Luther King
e) Princess Diana

1 Kept you guessing till the end.
2 My dream came true at last.
3 Died young and beautiful, loved forever.
4 I connected people and got rich.
5 I came, I saw, I conquered.

3 Work with a partner. Write six-word stories for three famous people. Read them to another pair. Can they guess whose stories they are?

Reading

1 What do you know about Michael Jackson's life and career? Read the extract from his obituary on page 37. Which of your facts were mentioned?

2 Work with your partner. Discuss whether these statements are true or false, according to the obituary. Find evidence.

a) He is undoubtedly the best pop performer who has ever lived.
b) He broke a musical record.
c) He was loved as a performer by all types of people.
d) He enjoyed publicity.
e) He had plastic surgery on his face.
f) He died during his last concert tour.

3 Complete the glossary on page 37 with the highlighted words in the obituary extract.

4 Which of these six-word stories best describes Michael Jackson's life for you? Why?

a) I was always young at heart.
b) My sad life made others happy.
c) Earned the title: King of Pop.

Michael Jackson

He liked to be known as the King of Pop, and only a handful of performers – Presley, Sinatra, the Beatles – could challenge Michael Jackson for the title of most successful popular music entertainer of all time. Although ill health
5 dogged his career in later years, the sheer scale of Jackson's achievements remains undiminished. With sales of about 53 million copies, *Thriller*, his magnum opus, released in 1982, remains by far the best-selling album ever released. His total record sales were estimated by his Sony Music label to be
10 in excess of 750 million. These staggering figures mark only some of the peaks of a career begun at the age of five.

Quite why Jackson should have been so phenomenally successful is difficult fully to explain. Musically, he was not a great innovator like Elvis Presley or Bob Dylan, nor
15 was he a role model for a generation like the Beatles or the Rolling Stones had been before him. But he emerged as a spectacularly talented all-rounder at a time when pop music was taking over as the world's primary mainstream entertainment. He was as good a dancer as he was a singer
20 and he employed the new technology to make videos that were as full of stylish impact as his music. The appeal of his impossibly slick and electrifying song-and-dance routines transcended barriers of age, race, class and nationality. Above all, Jackson was a stringent perfectionist.

25 However, he did not react well to the relentless barrage of (frequently prurient) media attention which was generated by success on such a grand scale. In Santa Barbara county, California, Jackson built himself a fantasy ranch called Neverland – a reference both to J. M. Barrie's *Peter Pan*
30 (perhaps significantly, the boy who never grew up), and to Elvis Presley's Graceland home in Memphis, Tennessee – where he created a zoo, a miniature railway and a Ferris wheel. But as he became an increasingly reclusive and secretive figure, so reports of his eccentricities became ever
35 more lurid and fantastic. He was known to have kept snakes and a pet chimpanzee called Bubbles who, it was said, slept in the same room as Jackson. He was photographed wearing a face mask, to ward off germs, and sleeping in
45 an oxygen chamber, a practice which he apparently believed would help to prolong his life to 150. He was
50 known to have had a nose job and a cleft put in his chin, but Jackson categorically denied persistent
55 allegations that he had had his whole face restructured and his skin tinted a shade lighter than its natural tone. As he got
60 older, though, his features became oddly contorted and he took on a distinctly unhealthy pallor.
65 Jackson's last years were marked chiefly by stories of financial difficulties brought on by
70 years of extravagant spending. He moved out of Neverland and at the time of his death was living with his children in a mansion in Bel Air, Los Angeles, which he was renting for $100,000 a month. His fans
75 remained loyal, however. The singer's death came only weeks before he was due to begin an unprecedented series of 50 concerts in London. When the performances were announced there was a strong suggestion that they might be Jackson's last, and that he would retire when they were
80 over. The dates sold out at once. Ominously, the first four concerts, beginning on 13th July, were postponed because Jackson needed more time to rehearse. The pop star had come to look increasingly frail and had long been erratic in his behaviour. What his true character
85 was like is difficult to say, it being heavily camouflaged by music industry public relations hype and lurid media speculation. He had spent almost his entire life in the showbusiness spotlight.

Glossary
a) _____ adj: physically weak and unhealthy
b) _____ verb [T]: caused trouble over a long period
c) _____ adj: impressive and seemingly without effort
d) _____ adj: considered normal and accepted by most people
e) _____ noun [U]: publicity designed to interest or influence people
f) _____ adj: living alone and avoiding other people
g) _____ adj: extremely surprising
h) _____ noun [C]: statements that someone did something wrong or illegal
i) _____ adj: never having happened or existed before
j) _____ adj: changing often, not following a regular pattern

Grammar

The future as seen from the past

Events that took place
He **would / was to** become the greatest entertainer of all time.

Events that did not take place
He **was to have given** a series of concerts.

Future plans in the past
He **was going / was planning** to retire. He **had been planning / had been thinking of** retiring.

Imminent events in the past
He was **(just) about to / due to** retire. He was **on the point / on the verge** of retiring.

---

1 Read the sentences about Michael Jackson and answer the questions.

a) *He <u>was to have given</u> a series of concerts in London.*
b) *'Thriller', released in 1982, <u>was to become</u> the best-selling album of all time.*
c) *Later, he <u>would suffer</u> financial problems.*

Which of the sentences express …

1 a future event, as seen from the past, that took place?
2 a future event, as seen from the past, that did not take place?

Are the sentences formal or informal in register?

2 Complete the sentences with the verbs in brackets in an appropriate form, to express the future as seen from the past. Which events took place and which didn't?

a) Jackson _____ (suffer) from ill health at the end of his career.
b) He _____ (release) a new album, but he fell out with his business partner.
c) The relentless media attention _____ (cause) Jackson to become a reclusive figure.
d) Jackson _____ (retire) from his career after the series of concerts.

3 Underline the correct alternatives about events that did not take place.

a) I was going **to get / to getting** married, but I realised he was the wrong person for me.
b) I had been hoping **of seeing / to see** the concert, but I got flu and had to give away my ticket.
c) I was just about **studying / to study** in the USA when my grant fell through and I had to call it off.
d) I had been thinking **of going / to go** into medicine, but I changed my mind and trained as a lawyer instead.
e) I was on the point **of winning / to win** the race, but I tripped over and came last.
f) I was planning **to buy / of buying** a car, but I failed my driving test.
g) I was on the verge **to give up / of giving up** waiting when the bus finally came.
h) I was due **to move / for moving** house, but the landlord put the rent up so I decided against it.

Is the register more or less formal than the sentences in Exercise 2? Which sentences refer more to intentions, and which refer more to imminent events?

4 Complete the sentences in a suitable way.

a) I was planning _____ , but it was sold out.
b) I was on the verge _____ , but I decided it was too expensive.
c) I had been hoping _____ , but my grades weren't good enough.
d) I was thinking _____ , but I was too tired.
e) I was just about _____ , when the phone rang.
f) I was going _____ , but a friend persuaded me not to.
g) I was on the point _____ , but I decided the salary was too low.

Are any of the sentences true for you? Discuss with a partner.

5 Grammar *Extra* 4, Part 1 page 136. Read the explanations and do Exercise 1.

Vocabulary

1 Work with a partner. Discuss the difference between the types of story in the box.

> anecdote   fable   fairy tale   legend   myth   news story   short story   whodunnit

In which type of story would you expect to find each of the following sentences?

a) Once upon a time, in a faraway kingdom, there lived a beautiful princess.

b) Have I told you about the time when I fell into the river?

c) Long ago, there lived a brave warrior and his band of soldiers.

d) 'Let's return to the scene of the crime and see if we can't find any more clues,' the inspector said.

e) At 92, Muriel felt she had achieved all she could in life.

f) And the moral is: pride goes before a fall.

g) Reports are coming in of a forest fire which is spreading rapidly in northern counties.

h) Athena, daughter of Zeus, was the goddess of wisdom and warfare.

2 Tell your partner about one of the types of story in Exercise 1 you have heard recently.

3 Read the definition of an *urban myth* on the left. Read the urban myth on page 129. Do you believe it? Do you know any others?

Urban myth

An urban myth is a funny, scary, sad or educational story which is supposed to be true. However, you'll never hear them told by the person they actually happened to. Every time an urban myth is retold it changes slightly.

Listening

1 🌐 1.29 Listen to Simon talking about his favourite book when he was a child. What kind of book is it? Why does he like it?

2 Work with your partner. Try to complete the sentences about the book in Exercise 1.

a) The story is set …

b) The characters are …

c) It tells the story of …

d) The main character is …

e) Basically the book is about …

f) The villain is …

g) They have all sorts of …

h) In the end …

i) He enjoyed the book because …

j) Now the book …

Listen again and check your answers.

3 If you have read this book, did you enjoy it? Why? / Why not? If you have not read it, does it appeal to you? Why? / Why not?

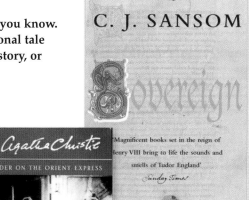

Speaking: anecdote

You are going to tell your partner about a story you know. It could be a favourite children's story, a traditional tale from your country, or the plot of a novel, short story, or film or television programme.

- Ask yourself the questions below.
- Think about *what* to say and *how* to say it.
- Tell your partner about the story.

Note: You can use the past simple tense or the present simple tense to tell a story.

a) What kind of story is it?

b) Where and when did you read, hear or see it?

c) What is the story about?

d) Where and when is the story set?

e) Who are the characters?

f) What is the plot of the story?

g) What happens at the end?

h) Why do you like it?

Listening

1 Work with a partner. Read the definition of the word *con*. Then look at the pictures (*1–4*) and discuss what con they might illustrate.

> **con¹** /kɒn/ noun [C] ★
> **1** *informal* a dishonest plan or method for making someone give you money = TRICK: *The insurance scheme was just a big con.*
> **2** *very informal* a PRISONER
> **con²** /kɒn/ verb [T] *informal* to make someone believe something that is not true, especially in order to get money from them = TRICK: *He conned them into believing he was ill.* ♦ *She was conned out of her life savings.*

2 🌐 1.30–1.33 Listen to the four stories of the pictures (*1–4*). Were you correct?

3 Listen again and answer these questions for each person (*1–4*) in the stories.
   a) What deception is described?
   b) Why did the person fall for it?
   c) How did they feel about being conned?

What would you have done in the situations described? Tell your partner.

Vocabulary

1 Work with your partner. Complete the sentences with words or phrases from the box. Use a dictionary if necessary.

> | a cock-and-bull story | end of story | a long story | an old wives' tale |
> | a sob story | tales | the story of my life | to cut a long story short |

   a) They say that eating carrots helps you see in the dark, but personally I think it's just _____ .
   b) I said you can't borrow my car, and I mean it. _____ .
   c) We lost our luggage at the airport, and had to fill in various forms and keep phoning up the airline. But anyway, _____ , we managed to get it back in the end.
   d) 'Mummy, Ella hit the cat.' 'Don't tell _____ about your sister, Mia.'
   e) I'm afraid you can't believe everything Karen says. She's always got _____ about how badly people have treated her.
   f) When he arrived late he told me _____ about being trapped in a lift and then being rescued by a news reporter and being interviewed on television.
   g) I didn't get the job – they told me I didn't have enough experience. But that's _____ , I'm afraid.
   h) 'So how come you managed to persuade your father to lend you the car?' 'Well, it's _____ .'

2 Work with your partner. Discuss which expressions (*a–h*) in Exercise 1 relate to …
   1 a myth or superstition.
   2 a silly story that is hard to believe.
   3 a story told to get someone else into trouble.
   4 a sad story designed to elicit sympathy.
   5 a story that you don't want to tell in detail.
   6 a detailed or complicated story.
   7 an attempt to stop discussion or argument about something.
   8 something unfortunate that often happens to someone.

3 Work with your partner. Write a short conversation containing one or more of the expressions in Exercise 1. Read it aloud to the class, missing out the expression(s). Can other people guess what they were?

Pronunciation

Weak and strong forms of auxiliary verbs

Have (/həv/) you … ?
Yes, I **have** (/hæv/). / No, I **haven't** (/'hævənt/).

Do (/də/) you … ?
Yes, I **do** (/du:/). / No, I **don't** (/dəʊnt/).

Can (/kən/) you … ?
Yes, I **can** (/kæn/). / No, I **can't** (/ka:nt/).

Are (/ə/) you … ?
Yes, we **are** (/a:/). / No, we **aren't** (/a:nt/).

See *Phonetic symbols* on page 159.

1 Read these extracts from the conversations in Listening, Exercise 2. How are the underlined words pronounced?

1 Q: So, <u>have</u> you ever been conned?
   A: I'm ashamed to say I <u>have</u>, actually.

2 Q: <u>Do</u> you have any experiences of being conned?
   A: I <u>do</u>, actually.

🌐 1.34 **Listen and check your ideas. Then answer these questions.**

a) Which words carry the main stress in each sentence? Why are the words pronounced differently in each exchange?

b) What is the pronunciation of *actually*?

Practise reading the exchanges aloud with a partner.

2 Work with your partner. Decide how the auxiliary verbs are pronounced in these exchanges.

a) A: So, do you ever go in for competitions?
    B: I have to say I don't, actually.

b) A: So, are you good at managing your time?
    B: I'm pleased to say I am, actually.

c) A: So, can you cook well?
    B: I'm proud to say I can.

d) A: Can you speak Chinese?
    B: I'm afraid I can't, actually.

🌐 1.35 **Listen and check your answers. Practise reading the exchanges with your partner.**

3 Ask your partner the questions in Exercise 2. Give true answers. Then ask more questions beginning *Do you ever … ?, Have you ever … ?, Are you … ?, Can you … ?*

Vocabulary & Speaking

Deception and belief synonyms

gullible	=	naïve
swallow	=	fall for
unscrupulous	=	dishonest
trick	=	con
make out	=	pretend
astute	=	streetwise
plausible	=	credible
sceptical	=	cynical

1 Read the situations and complete the sentences with words and phrases from the box.

> con   fall for   fishy   get taken for a ride   naïve   plausible   sceptical   unfaithful

a) I let the second-hand car salesman _____ me into believing that the sound that the engine makes was in fact a fault. I shouldn't have been so gullible.

b) You can't take Laura in – she's too streetwise to _____ any cock-and-bull story.

c) He made out he was a police officer and just needed to check my passport. How was I to know he was a con-man? His story seemed completely _____ to me.

d) You have to be really on the ball and astute if you don't want to _____ . There are some really unscrupulous people out there.

e) Did you really swallow that sob story about his daughter? I can't believe you were so _____ .

f) He led me to believe he wanted to marry me. Little did I realise he already had a wife and children back home. It's made me more _____ about men, I'm afraid.

g) 'I thought that investment deal sounded a bit _____ .' 'Yes, I should have realised. The trouble with me is, I'm too trusting – I take everyone at their word.'

h) Unbeknownst to Tim, his girlfriend is two-timing him. He can't seem to find a woman who isn't _____ to him.

2 Underline the correct alternatives.

a) Are you a(n) **gullible / plausible / unfaithful** person or are you more sceptical?

b) Have you ever been **tricked / made out / swallowed** into handing over money to a stranger?

c) Can you think of a **trusting / plausible / naïve** excuse for forgetting an appointment?

d) Have you ever **made out / taken in / conned** you were ill when you didn't want to go somewhere?

e) Would you ever **fall for / make out / two-time** a boyfriend or girlfriend behind their back?

f) Can you remember **being taken in / swallowed / led to believe** by a sob story?

g) Do you tend to take politicians **for a ride / at their word / in** when they make promises?

h) Were you **more naïve / fishier / more plausible** when you were younger?

Work with your partner. Ask and answer the questions.

Reading

1 Look at the cartoons on page 43. Do you get the jokes? Do you have similar jokes in your country?

2 Read an extract from a book on humour. Choose the best title, *a*, *b* or *c*.

    a) Elements of humour   b) Humour across frontiers c) The world's funniest jokes

We often hear it said that 'the -ese have no sense of humour'. Strictly speaking, this must be untrue, since all people laugh, therefore something must have tickled their sense of incongruity. What is obvious is that different peoples laugh at different things. The dry, subtle, humorous English professor could be regarded as eccentric or

5 weird by an Arab or a Japanese. The cleverest of French puns is lost on a Burmese. A Swiss friend of mine was offended by an earthy Spanish joke that had me in stitches.

    So, is there such a thing as a 'national' sense of humour? It is certainly the case that there is such a thing as 'international' humour – that is to say, some types of humour and some jokes gain international acceptance. In particular, this is true of slapstick, age-old in its use and laughed at

10 by Europeans, Americans, Africans and Asians alike. It is very much in evidence, for example, on Japanese television. There seems, too, to be a general love of witnessing violence, and visual humour seems to cross frontiers well. There are also 'international' jokes, repeated across borders, such as the one about who must jump first out of an aeroplane, elephant jokes, restaurant jokes, and hilarious stories about golfers.

15   Even in the area of international jokes, however, a distinct national flavour emerges. Take, for example, the old gag about the journalists who organised a competition to write an article about elephants. The titles were as follows:

ENGLISHMAN: Hunting elephants in British East Africa

FRENCHMAN: The love life of elephants in French Equatorial Africa

20 **AMERICAN**: How to breed bigger and better elephants

RUSSIAN: How we sent an elephant to the moon

SWEDE: Elephants and the welfare state

SPANIARD: Techniques of elephant fighting

FINN: What elephants think about Finland

25 This joke, which pokes fun at various national characteristics or weaknesses, has as its punchline the Finns' preoccupation with what other people think of them. In Helsinki, however, an alternative punchline was suggested:

NORWEGIAN: Norway and Norway's mountains

The Finns, Swedes and Danes find this absolutely side-splitting, whereas the

30 Norwegians, who consider themselves a humorous people, simply cannot see the joke. Can you?

Glossary

a) _____ adj: saying funny things in a serious way

b) _____ adj: having a sense of humour

c) _____ noun [C]: jokes involving a play on words

d) _____ adj: direct and possibly offensive

e) _____ verb phrase: make someone laugh

f) _____ noun [U]: humour based on physical actions, e.g. falling over

g) _____ noun [C]: joke

h) _____ verb phrase: make unkind jokes about s.o. / s.th.

i) _____ noun [C]: last line of a joke

j) _____ adj: very funny

3 Find evidence from the extract to support these statements. What examples does the writer give?

    a) All nations have a sense of humour.

    b) Jokes from one country are sometimes not understood in another.

    c) Sometimes jokes from another country can be seen as rude.

    d) Some elements of humour are universal.

    e) Different nationalities prefer different types of humour.

    f) Some jokes involve laughing at foreigners.

4 Complete the glossary using words in the extract.

5 Work with your partner. Discuss these questions.

    a) Do you agree with the writer's opinions on international humour?

    b) What sort of sense of humour do people of your nationality have?

Grammar

Discourse markers in writing

I love TV comedy shows, **particularly** *The Simpsons*.

for example, *Friends*.

or **at any rate**, cartoon shows.

and film comedies, **too**.

1 Match each discourse marker in the box with one highlighted in the extract on page 42 with a similar meaning.

then	in addition	to be accurate	say	particularly	in other words

2 Where in the sentences could you put the discourse markers in brackets? Change the punctuation where necessary.

a) Why do different nationalities laugh at different things? (so)
b) Some writers, Oscar Wilde, are famous for their wit. (for example)
c) Many nationalities enjoy puns, the English. (in particular)
d) What is universal about humour? (then)
e) The Americans love slapstick. Europeans find it hilarious. (too)
f) Slapstick leaves me cold. I don't find it in the least amusing. (in other words)

3 Look at these pairs of sentences. What is the difference in each pair?

a) 1 Some nationalities, **such as** the Finns, find this joke absolutely side-splitting.
　　2 Some nationalities, **namely** the Finns, find this joke absolutely side-splitting.

b) 1 The dry English professor could be regarded as eccentric, **or at least** slightly weird.
　　2 The dry English professor could be regarded as slightly weird, **not to say** eccentric.

c) 1 The Danes find this hilarious; the Norwegians, **by contrast**, simply do not see the joke.
　　2 The Danes find this hilarious; the Norwegians, **likewise**, are vastly amused by it.

Match each discourse marker in bold with one in the box with a similar meaning.

or at any rate	including	similarly	viz	on the other hand	or even

'Waiter, what's this fly doing in my soup?'
'I think it's the breast stroke, sir.'

4 Underline the best discourse marker.

a) I find puns, **particularly / that is to say / such as** jokes involving a play on words, very amusing.
b) I love classic comedies, **in other words / on the other hand / in particular** the films of Woody Allen.
c) I don't often tell jokes – **at any rate / on the other hand / namely**, not in a group.
d) I like subtle jokes rather than more earthy ones; my family, **say / similarly / by contrast**, tend to have a rather dry sense of humour.
e) I can only tell jokes in two languages, **including / in particular / namely** my own language and English.

Are any of the statements are true for you? Compare your answers with a partner.

5 Grammar *Extra* 4, Part 2 page 136. Read the explanations and do Exercise 2.

'Waiter, what kind of soup is this?'
'It's bean soup.'
'Never mind what it's been. What is it now?'

Listening & Speaking

1 1.36–1.39 Listen to the four jokes and write down the punch line. Did you get the joke?

2 Listen again and respond to each one using the expressions in the box.

It's hilarious.	It's quite funny.	I find it a bit offensive.
It leaves me cold.	I find it mildly amusing.	I don't get it.

3 Work with your partner. Student A: look at page 130. Student B: look at page 131. Read the joke and try to remember it. Then close your book and tell it without looking. Does your partner get the joke?

4 Do you think the jokes are funny? Do you have any similar jokes in your country? Tell a joke you know to your partner. Do they get it?

Useful phrases

1 🌐 1.40 **Listen to the conversation between two friends and answer these questions.**

    a) What two problems did the speaker have?

    b) Has anything like this ever happened to you or anyone you know?

2 **Listen again and number the useful phrases in the order that you hear them.**

  ☐ What a relief! I bet you were pleased!

  ☐ I'm not surprised!

  ☐ Oh no!

  ☐ Oh, good!

  ☐ Right.

  ☐ Oh, how scary! You must have been terrified!

  ☐ Oh, what a nightmare! That must have been awful!

  ☐ Oh, lovely!

  ☐1☐ Really?

3 **Work with a partner. Discuss which part of the story each useful phrase in Exercise 2 was in response to. Check your answers against the Recordings on pages 149–150.**

Which of the useful phrases express …

  a) interest?   b) sympathy?   c) gladness?   d) agreement?

4 **Match the useful phrases in the box to the categories in Exercise 3.**

a) Uhuh.	d) Poor you!	g) How awful!
b) I don't blame you!	e) What a shame!	h) Oh, wow!
c) Lucky you!	f) Quite right!	i) Fantastic!

🌐 1.41 **Listen and repeat the intonation of the responses.**

5 🌐 1.42–1.46 **Listen to extracts from five stories. What happened in each one? Listen again and respond with appropriate useful phrases.**

6 **Think of an anecdote beginning with one of the following sentences.**

Have I told you about the time when …
- I went skiing / sailing / fishing for the first time?
- I lost my handbag / keys / mobile phone / luggage on holiday?
- I went to a café / bar / restaurant without my wallet?

Tell your partner your story. Your partner should respond using appropriate phrases.

Writing *Extra*

Descriptive narrative

1 What are some of your earliest memories as a child? Tell a partner.

2 Read the narrative about a childhood memory. Does it have a happy or a sad ending?

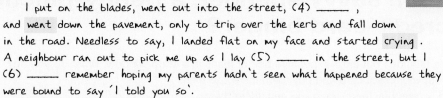

I remember the day when I got my first pair of rollerblades. I was about eight or nine at the time. I remember I had been asking my parents for ages to get me a pair but they had said no, saying they were too dangerous. Finally, when my birthday came I went downstairs to find a huge parcel on the kitchen table.
(1) _____ , I took off the wrapping paper and (2) _____ found that it contained a pair of brand new roller blades. (3) _____ .

I put on the blades, went out into the street, (4) _____ , and went down the pavement, only to trip over the kerb and fall down in the road. Needless to say, I landed flat on my face and started crying. A neighbour ran out to pick me up as I lay (5) _____ in the street, but I (6) _____ remember hoping my parents hadn't seen what happened because they were bound to say 'I told you so'.

Eventually, however, I had to go back home, carrying the blades which were badly damaged, and (7) _____ admit what had happened. (8) _____ , they didn't tell me off, and didn't say anything about the blades. My elbows and knees were hurt and I had bruises all over, and holes in the knees of my new trousers. It didn't put me off rollerblading though, and I eventually became quite good at it. I don't know what happened to the blades – I suppose my parents gave them away or maybe they are still there up there somewhere in my parents' attic.

3 Replace the highlighted words and phrases in the narrative in Exercise 2 with the ones in the box (*a–j*)

a)	clutching	f)	howling at the top of my voice
b)	must have been	g)	one of my most vivid childhood memories is
c)	pestering	h)	proficient
d)	quite badly grazed	i)	refused point blank
e)	tore	j)	went hurtling

4 Complete the spaces (*1–8*) in the story with these extra words and phrases (*a–h*), to add interest.

a)	sheepishly	e)	to my delight
b)	with my heart beating	f)	which was quite steeply inclined
c)	sprawled	g)	I could hardly contain my excitement
d)	distinctly	h)	to my relief

5 You are going to write about a childhood memory, for example:
- your first day at school or in a new house.
- a time you got lost or got into trouble.
- a birthday or a time you got a special present.
- a visit, outing, holiday or celebration.
- a memorable meeting.
- The first time you did something – for example, go the cinema, the zoo, the dentist's.

Write the story using vivid expressions. Give details of what happened and how you felt.

Exchange stories with your partner. Can they suggest how to make it more detailed or vivid?

5 Bargain

Grammar Prepositions in relative clauses. Articles
Vocabulary Spending and saving. Economising. Discussing prices
Useful phrases Negotiating, haggling, making a deal

Reading & Vocabulary

1 What have you bought in the last twenty-four hours? Tell a partner.

2 Do the quiz. Then compare and discuss your answers with your partner.

Are you a savvy spender, a penny-pincher or a credit-card binger?

1 You see a fabulous but ultra-expensive pair of jeans in a shop window. What do you do?
  a) Get out your credit card and buy them there and then.
  b) Save up and buy them when you can afford them.
  c) Forget them – you refuse on principle to pay exorbitant prices for things you don't need.

2 Your laptop is starting to play up and it's time to buy a new one. What's your solution?
  a) Buy the latest and most expensive model in the shops.
  b) Work out your spending limit and shop around for the best deal.
  c) Make do with your old one and wait for the sales.

3 How do you go about supermarket food shopping?
  a) Pile up your trolley with impulse buys and treats.
  b) Compile a careful list of what you need to buy and stick to it.
  c) Only select discounted products and budget brands, and bulk buy on special offers.

4 It's your mother's birthday. What do you get her?
  a) Hit the cash point and treat her to a slap-up meal at the best restaurant in town.
  b) Buy her a reasonably-priced, good quality screwdriver set – she's been needing one for ages.
  c) Dig out that unwanted vase you got for your birthday and recycle it as a present.

5 Your friend invites you on a last-minute beach holiday but you're broke. What's your reaction?
  a) Say yes immediately, and worry about paying for it later. You only live once!
  b) Make a down-payment now, put the rest on your credit card, and work out a schedule for paying it off.
  c) Who needs a holiday? You're happy enough staying in and watching TV.

Glossary

a) _____ noun [C]: a sum of money given to start paying for something
b) _____ verb [I]: manage with what is available
c) _____ verb [T]: buy a large number of the same item cheaply at the same time
d) _____ verb [I]: go wrong and cause difficulties
e) _____ adj: large and expensive (of a meal)
f) _____ verb [I]: go to several shops before buying
g) _____ noun [C]: items you buy without planning ahead

3 Turn to page 130. Check your scores and read the spending profiles. Is your profile an accurate description of your spending habits? Why? / Why not?

4 Complete the glossary using words and phrases from the quiz.

5 Look at the words and phrases. Circle the word or phrase in each group which has a different meaning from the other two. Use a dictionary if necessary.
  a) budget / pay over the odds / economise
  b) run up a bill / live within your means / get into debt
  c) save up / clear a debt / pay off a debt
  d) frugal / generous / thrifty
  e) broke / short of money / tight-fisted
  f) overdrawn / in the red / extravagant

6 Write five sentences describing your spending habits or those of someone you know. Read your sentences to your partner. Ask questions to find out more information.

Listening

1 **2.01** Listen to six people being interviewed about their shopping habits for a survey. Which question (*a–i*) are they each answering?

a) Do you enjoy shopping?
b) What's your earliest shopping memory?
c) What's your favourite shop?
d) What was your most extravagant purchase?
e) What was your last big purchase?
f) Who does the food shopping in your household?
g) What's the next thing you're planning to buy?
h) Are you an impulsive shopper?
i) What was your best ever bargain?

2 Listen again to the six people in Exercise 1 and make notes on their answers. Then choose three of the questions to ask a partner.

Grammar

Prepositions in relative clauses

Formal
She's the person **from whom I'm buying the flat.**

That's the flat **into which I'm moving.**

Informal
She's the person **(that / who) I'm buying the flat from.**

That's the flat **(that / which) I'm moving into.**

Of in non-defining relative clauses
My friends, **many of whom are in debt / all of whom are broke**, often want me to lend them money.

I bought several souvenirs, the **most expensive of which / the first of which is this necklace.**

1 Look at the pairs of sentences. Which sentence sounds more natural and how are the sentences different in register?

a) 1 When I go shopping, I pick the produce I like the look of.
   2 When I go shopping, I pick the produce of which I like the look.

b) 1 Are you the person I should speak to about opening a bank account?
   2 Are you the person to whom I should speak about opening a bank account?

In which sentences could you use the relative pronouns *that* or *who*? Is it more or less common to miss them out when speaking?

2 Rewrite the sentences to make them more informal.

a) The supermarket at which I do my shopping is very cheap.
b) I have a good friend with whom I like to go shopping.
c) At the moment, there is nothing for which I am saving up.
d) I never buy clothes in which I don't feel comfortable.
e) Being tight-fisted is something of which my friends would never accuse me.
f) I can't remember the last person to whom I gave a present.
g) The last thing for which I wrote out a cheque was very expensive.

Are any of the sentences true for you? Discuss with your partner.

3 Look at the pair of sentences. Underline the relative clause in *b*).

a) I bought loads of clothes in the sale. I'll probably never wear most of them.
b) I bought loads of clothes in the sale, most of which I'll probably never wear.

Is it a defining or non-defining relative clause? How do you know?
Can *which* be replaced by *that*?

4 Rewrite the sentences to include a non-defining relative clause, as in sentence *b*) in Exercise 3.

a) I earn $200 a week. I spend half of it on rent.
b) I have several close friends. None of my close friends enjoys shopping.
c) There are several restaurants near my house. The nicest restaurant is beyond my price range.
d) My mobile phone bills are quite high. I got the latest bill last week.
e) The people in my class can't afford to go out for a slap-up meal. The majority of them are students.

5 Write true sentences about shops or restaurants in your neighbourhood, using a similar non-defining relative clause. Compare with your partner.

6 **Grammar Extra 5, Part 1** page 138. Read the explanations and do Exercise 1.

Reading & Vocabulary

1 Do you think you could survive on £1 a day? What would you stop buying and what would you cut back on? Tell a partner.

2 Read the article on page 49 about someone who decided to take up the challenge of surviving on £1 a day. What economies did she make?

3 Choose the best alternative to complete the statements. Find evidence to support your choices.

  a) Kath Kelly **wasted a lot of money / bought too many luxury items** before taking up the challenge.
  b) She took up the challenge in order to **pay off her overdraft / be able to buy a wedding present for her brother.**
  c) Her friends **were sceptical about her plan / encouraged her to take up the challenge.**
  d) She **stopped socialising / found alternative ways of socialising.**
  e) She changed her eating habits by **making economies / eating less.**
  f) The hardest part of the challenge was **cutting back on basic necessities / changing her travel habits.**
  g) At the end of the year, she **reverted to old habits / had changed her attitude to spending.**

4 Complete these sentences from the article. Then check your answers.

  a) I earned enough to get _____ .
  b) I desperately wanted to save _____ and buy him something special.
  c) I told only a select few friends who, in truth, could have done with cutting _____ themselves.
  d) I opted _____ invitations to the pub.
  e) I resisted the urge to purge everything in my food cupboard in case it came _____ useful.
  f) My main challenge, however, was getting _____ .

  Look at the phrasal verbs in the sentences. Write questions using three of the phrasal verbs. Ask and answer with your partner.

5 Could you do what Kath Kelly did? Do you agree with her conclusions?

Listening

1 🌐 2.02 Listen to an extract from a radio programme in which the speaker gives some money-saving tips. Answer these questions.

  a) What are the tips?
  b) What benefits are mentioned for each tip?

  What do you think of the tips? Would they work for you? Discuss with your partner.

2 Work with your partner. Write a tip to send in to the programme. Use one of these money-saving ideas, or your own idea.

  • walk/cycle to the station/work
  • take a packed lunch to work
  • have picnics instead of going to cafés
  • make your own clothes, cards and presents
  • shop online
  • avoid the 'buy one get one free' trap

  Use the prompts to help.

  My top tip for saving money is to …   *My suggestion is to …*
  It really makes sense to …   *You can make huge savings by …*

  Read your tip to the class. Which of the ideas presented in class would work for you? Can you think of other ways to save money?

How I lived on £1 a day for a year

BY KATH KELLY

The average young woman spends £289 a week – £15,028 a year – on stuff, according to statistics. As a forty-something teacher on a reasonable salary, I earned enough to get by. Yet I was permanently peering over the precipice of my overdraft, spending whatever I wanted without a thought for the future. I squandered thousands, not on exotic holidays or expensive cars, but on the mundane items that we think we need: lunches out, coffees, toiletries and make-up, socialising, phone calls. Then one day I saw an American lady on a TV chat show explaining how she had lived on 'just necessities' for a year. It was an epiphany for me. I realised I didn't need to spend all the money I did. Perhaps I was just rebelling against my thrifty upbringing and what I had viewed as a dreary way of life. But enough was enough. It had to stop.

My brother's wedding was a year away and that was another incentive. I desperately wanted to save up and buy him something lavish. So I made a decision – I would survive on an average of £1 a day for a whole year. Mind you, I didn't want to tell everyone what I was doing. Maybe it was pride or embarrassment, or the niggling worry that they would think I was a cheapskate. So I told only a select few friends who, in truth, could have done with cutting back themselves. 'A pound a day?' they spluttered, over their third glass of Merlot and bag of Doritos. 'Maybe in Bangladesh,' they scoffed. 'Maybe on food alone. But what about wine and phone bills? Coffee and make-up? Clothes and transport?' 'I'll prove you all wrong,' I insisted.

In my previous existence, I would eat out twice a week, read glossy magazines over a latte at Starbucks, scour upmarket shops for new clothes, and socialise most nights with my friends. But now all this was gone. Lunch was cold, wretched leftovers in a lunchbox. I opted out of invitations to the pub, or would turn up late and order a glass of water. I didn't want to spend the year scrounging off my friends, so time and again I'd drag them to a bench in a park, with a flask of coffee and a rug – and a few doughnuts if we were lucky.

I quickly became obsessed with food bargains and well-acquainted with supermarket discount shelves. I resisted the urge to purge everything in my food cupboard in case it came in useful during the year, and became an expert at making perishables last: storing red cabbages in the dark so they kept longer; cooking in a wok to use as little oil as possible; blending left-over veg into soup. On top of this, I'd gorge on tasters at organic stores and buffet food at university evening lectures. And in warmer months I'd pick blackberries, apples and hazelnuts in the countryside.

As for entertainment, I raided discarded newspapers for coupons for free cinema tickets, offered myself up to trainee hairdressers and signed up for one-off gym trial days and pool sessions. And life's necessities proved easy enough to come by, too – there are always free samples of shampoo, toothpaste and washing-up liquid in magazines, and I even organised clothes swap parties with my friends. My main challenge, though, was getting around. Buses – my previous staple, as I didn't own a car – were too expensive, so I cycled or walked everywhere, whatever the weather, though venturing further afield did prove trickier.

Of course, looking back, there were countless times I wanted to put my head in my hands and weep. I recall how depressing it was choosing between an apple or a carrot, because I couldn't afford both. But over the course of the year I learnt so much about myself and others. Pre-challenge, I thought I was an independent person, in control of my life. I was wrong. So many people – like my former self – are constantly in debt, living beyond their means and in fear of not earning enough. But if we could open our eyes we'd see there is a more satisfying way to live. With all the money I saved, I could afford to splash out on a lavish gift for my brother and his wife (though admittedly I did hitchhike to the wedding in a second-hand dress). And now the challenge is over, living frugally has become second nature to me. I think carefully before I buy a coffee or clothes and have eaten out only once. In fact, four months on, I probably still spend less than £5 a day – a miserly sum to most people, but an absolute fortune to me.

Glossary

squander verb [T]: to waste
dreary adj: boring and dull
cheapskate noun [C]: someone who does not like to spend money
upmarket adj: very expensive, fashionable
scrounge off verb [T]: get something you want by asking someone for it instead of paying for it yourself
purge verb [T]: to remove a bad or unpleasant condition
gorge on verb [T]: have as much of enjoyable experience as you want
one-off adj: happening, made, or done, only once
splash out verb [T]: buy something expensive
miserly adj: a very small amount

Reading & Listening

1   Read the tips on bargaining from a tourist guide. Which one is false?

   - Shop around before you make a purchase to get an idea of the average price of whatever it is you want to buy.
   - Be prepared to drive a hard bargain – sellers expect it.
   - Try to appear casual and indifferent while browsing in shops and markets. Never show enthusiasm for the item you want to buy, as the seller may react by jacking up the price.
   - Start the bargaining process by proposing a price considerably lower than the asking price. A good rule of thumb is to halve the price and work upwards from that.
   - Try to find and point out as many flaws as possible in the product so you can get a better price for it.
   - If the price proposed by the seller is still unacceptable and outside your budget, pretend to walk away. Usually, you will be called back again, and the price you offer may be accepted by the shopkeeper.
   - Avoid paying with small change, as this may annoy the seller. Larger denominations are preferable.

2   🌐 2.03 Listen to Marina and Bill discussing their experiences of bargaining. Do they discuss a) bargaining abroad? b) bargaining in their own country? c) both situations?

3   Read a summary of the conversation. Cross out any factual errors.

▲ Bill and Marina

> Marina saw a rug in Turkey. She really wanted it and it was reasonably priced, but she decided to bargain for it. She did not start by offering a very low price because she was afraid she might lose the rug. In the end, she was able to knock down the seller's price and bought the rug.

> Bill does not like bargaining. He believes that the sellers do not enjoy it either. Generally, he has been unsuccessful in his experiences of bargaining when abroad. However, he feels that his experience of bargaining in England have been more successful.

Listen again and check. Then rewrite the summary correctly.

4   How do you feel about bargaining? Have you had any similar experiences? Tell a partner.

Pronunciation

Weak forms of common words

> Try to find and point out as many flaws as possible in the product so you can get a better price for it.

1   Which sound occurs in the words in red in the bargaining tip on the left?

Are the words in red stressed or unstressed? Practise saying the sentence with your partner, stressing the sounds in bold.

2   How is *to* pronounced in each of the sentences below?
   a)   Be prepared <u>to</u> drive a hard bargain.
   b)   Try <u>to</u> appear casual and indifferent while browsing in the shops.

   🌐 2.04 Listen and check your ideas.

What is the pronunciation of *to* before a) a consonant sound? b) a vowel sound?

3   Work with your partner. Practise reading the other bargaining tips from Reading & Listening Exercise 1, paying attention to the pronunciation of *to* and weak forms.

Vocabulary

1   Put the words and phrases in the box into two groups: *cheap* or *expensive*.

> affordable   budget   daylight robbery   discounted   exorbitant   lavish
> low-cost   no-frills   overpriced   a rip-off

2   Work with a partner. Discuss these questions about the words and phrases in Exercise 1.
   a)   Which are more informal in register?
   b)   Which have negative connotations?
   c)   Which two could not be used before a noun?

3   Underline the best alternative in the shopping tips.
   a)   If you want to find **budget / discounted** accommodation, go to …
   b)   If you want a(n) **lavish / overpriced** meal, a good place to eat out is …
   c)   The best place to buy **low-cost / budget** souvenirs is …
   d)   Be prepared to pay **exorbitant / lavish** prices for …
   e)   A good place to find **affordable / no-frills** clothes is …
   f)   A good **no-frills / discounted** airline is …
   g)   Try to avoid shopping **in / at** … It's a complete **rip-off / daylight robbery**.

   Complete the shopping tips to make them true for a visitor to your town or country.
   Tell your partner.

Speaking: anecdote

You are going to tell your partner about a purchase you have made recently.
•   Ask yourself the questions below.
•   Think about *what* to say and *how* to say it.
•   Tell your partner about the purchase.

a)   What did you decide to buy and why?
b)   Was it an impulse buy or had you shopped around?
c)   Who did you go shopping with?
d)   Where did you look for the item?
e)   Where did you find the item?
f)   What was the item like?
g)   How expensive was it?
h)   Did you pay in cash or by credit card?
i)   How pleased were you with the purchase?
j)   How do you use the item now?
k)   With hindsight, was it a good purchase?

1 What is the meaning of the English proverb 'One man's meat is another man's poison'? Do you have similar proverb in your country?

2 Read the article and think of a good way to complete the title.

One man's rubbish ...

Move over, eBay – a website where members advertise free unwanted goods is helping to keep tonnes of waste out of landfill sites.

Like so many fads, it started in America. In May 2003, Deron
5 Beal, a 36-year-old professional recycler, was looking for a
way to get rid of surplus office supplies in Tucson, Arizona. He
recalls: 'The Salvation Army didn't want my junk so I thought:
'How can I get this stuff not put in a hole in the ground?' We
have some beautiful desert landscape out here and no-one
10 wants to see it ruined with landfills. That led me to start the
first group, and it worked so well I thought: 'Hang on, anyone
could do this. Think of a nifty name and it might take off! And
did it!'

That clever moniker was Freecycling, a grassroots non-profit
15 movement that has now stretched its web to more than 50
countries. Every day, the movement is responsible for keeping
more than 200 tonnes of waste a day out of landfill sites across
the globe. In the UK, it is estimated that 122,000 members will
exchange some 45,000 items this month alone.

20 The system's beauty is in its simplicity. You sign up to an
email list via the site Freecycle.org and receive regular missives
from people in your area looking to rid themselves of unwanted
belongings, or alternatively, looking to find particular items.
Or you can choose not to sign up to email postings and view
25 messages online. No money changes hands and you do not
have to exchange anything with the person you receive the
item from. Unlike eBay, the responsibility for picking up the
item in question lies with the person receiving it, meaning
the givers do not have to put themselves out.

30 Ripe for abuse, you might think. Surely some unscrupulous
soul will use the system to pick up valuable goods from
philanthropically or environmentally-minded people? Fine, say
Freecycle's advocates – if it keeps waste out of landfills, who
cares? 'When you Freecycle, for example, a sofa, you haven't
35 just saved the waste that goes into the landfill, but also all the
raw materials that would be required to make another sofa,' says
Beal. 'The ratio is about 20:1, so if you have a 200lb sofa you
are effectively saving two tonnes in raw materials.' 'The goal is
to make it easier to give something away than it is to throw it
40 away, and I believe that's possible,' he says. 'There's a whole lot
of potential there that we haven't even started to test.'

What's on offer

- Second-hand washable nappies
- 30 used video tapes
45 - A didgeridoo
- A fake grass carpet
- A large model railway set
- 200 padded envelopes
- 50ml ice-cream scoops
50 - A book on Edwardian fashion
- 6 stiff white collars
- A heart-shaped fizzy bath tablet

3 Read the article again. Answer the questions with a partner.

a) What was the founder of Freecycle's original aim?

b) How can you find out what's on offer on Freecycle?

c) What benefits are there of Freecycling an item?

4 Complete the glossary using words or phrases from the article.

5 Work with your partner. Discuss these questions.

a) Would you want to take any of the items on offer?

b) What three items would you like to get rid of or advertise for at the moment?

Glossary

a) _____ verb [I]: make room for

b) _____ noun [C]: short-lived fashions

c) _____ adj: not needed

d) _____ adj: run and used by ordinary people

e) _____ noun [U]: advantage

f) _____ noun [C]: emails

g) _____ verb [T]: throw away, give away or sell

h) _____ verb [I]: help others even if it causes difficulties for yourself

i) _____ adj: willing to do things that are unfair, dishonest or illegal

j) _____ noun [C]: supporters

Grammar

Articles

Use *a/an* before singular nouns:

a bed / **an** idea

I need **a** room.

Use *some* / no article before plural and uncountable nouns:

things / **some** things

furniture / **some** furniture

I need (**some**) accommodation.

Use *the* before singular, plural and uncountable nouns:

the bed / **the** idea / **the** furniture / **the** things

I'm very pleased with **the** curtains.

How much is **the** accommodation?

---

1 Read the Freecycle email exchange. What furniture is Harry going to collect?

> Hi, I have furniture I need to get rid of (sofa-bed, and bookshelves) as I'm giving my bedroom makeover. May be of use to someone? It's all in good condition. Cheers, Mike.
>
> Hi Mike,
> If furniture is still available, I'd be very grateful for it, as I'm moving house and starting from scratch in new accommodation. Could you give me information about sofa-bed? What size is it, and what colour? Also, I'm in dire need of wardrobe if you happen to have one. Cheers, Harry.
>
> Hi Harry,
> Yes, it's all still available. Sofa-bed is king-size. Sorry, I don't have wardrobe but I do have chest of drawers, if that's any use. You're welcome to come and collect stuff if you have van. Mike.
>
> Hi – Yes, I'm still interested in everything, including chest of drawers. I'll contact you again as soon as I've got hold of van to pick things up. Thanks a lot! H.

2 Correct the emails by adding the missing articles.

a / an (x 7)   some (x 3)   the (x 6)

Delete the alternatives below that are incorrect. Then find examples in the text.

- If something is unknown to the speaker, the listener or both, use **a(n) / some / the / –**.
- If something is known to both speaker and listener, use **a(n) / some / the / –**.

3 Write a posting for Freecycle offering an item or items. Exchange postings with a partner and write an email reply.

4 Complete the sentences with *a, an, the,* or put a dash (–) if no article is necessary.
a) What time do you have _____ dinner? When did you last go out to _____ special dinner?
b) Do you ever travel by _____ train? When did you last take _____ train?
c) When is _____ next long weekend? What are you doing _____ next weekend?
d) What is your view of _____ internet shopping? How often do you use _____ internet?
e) What is the countryside like _____ north of your town? What is it like in _____ north of your country?
f) Do you think _____ English are friendly? Why do you want to speak _____ English?

Work with your partner. Ask and answer the questions.

5 Cross out the alternative in each sentence which is *not* possible.
a) I'd like a (coffee / cake / juice / beer / bread / chocolate), please.
b) I might go to the (bank / cinema / gym / theatre / shops / work) after the lesson.
c) This time tomorrow I'll probably be at (school / university / supermarket / home).
d) I would be interested in working for the (army / police / business / media / government / press).
e) I don't like (rock music / jazz / seventeenth-century Italian classical music / music of Beethoven).
f) Most of the (people I know / people / people in my country / people here) speak English.
g) I love (the pasta / fresh pasta / the pasta you make / all kinds of pasta).

Underline alternatives to make the sentences true for you. Discuss with your partner.

6 Grammar *Extra* 5, Part 2 page 138. Read the explanations and do Exercise 2.

Useful phrases

1 🌐 2.05 **Listen to a conversation between a customer and a market stall holder. Answer the questions.**

a) What does the customer want to buy?
b) How does she try to get a reduction?
c) What is the final outcome?

2 **Work with a partner. Complete the useful phrases.**

a) It's a bit more than _____ pay.
b) Could you give me _____ , do you think?
c) The _____ is, it's a little bit chipped.
d) I'm afraid it's still a bit _____ .
e) I think _____ , thanks.
f) Is that your _____ ?
g) Okay, I _____ .

Listen again and check your answers.

3 **Read the first line of three conversations in which people negotiate a solution to a problem. Answer the questions (1–3) with your partner.**

> a) Fiona: Well, it's a lovely room, and the location is ideal. It's just that I was really looking for something that's furnished, particularly as the rent is rather high ...

> b) Brian: Yes, I really like the flat, and I'm very interested. The only problem is, I don't have enough for a month's deposit at the moment ...

> c) Patrick: I wanted to have a word with you about my essay. I know the deadline is the end of next week, but the thing is, I've had quite a lot to deal with recently ...

1 What is the situation in each case?
2 Underline the expressions the speakers use to introduce the problem.
3 Try to guess how the conversations will continue.

🌐 2.06–2.08 **Listen to the conversations (1–3). Were your predictions correct?**

4 **Match the sentence halves from the conversations.**

a) Supposing I were to
b) I don't have any objections to
c) That sounds like
d) There shouldn't be
e) I was wondering
f) In principle I'm prepared to
g) How would it be if
h) I should be able

1 any problems.
2 I handed it in next Monday?
3 if I could ask for an extension?
4 grant you an extension.
5 to have it done by then.
6 put in some furniture?
7 a good compromise.
8 deferring the deposit.

Which sentences express a) a request? b) a proposal? c) agreement?

5 **Work with your partner. Student A: turn to page 130. Student B: turn to page 131. Improvise conversations for the two situations.**

Vocabulary *Extra*

British and American English

1 Which variety or varieties of English have you studied? Which do you prefer? Discuss with a partner.

2 Read the two adverts below. What are they advertising? Do you ever shop like this?

> Shopping has gotten a whole lot easier with <u>shoppingexperience.com</u>, the world's largest online catalog. Why travel to your local mall when, from the comfort of your own home, you can access literally hundreds of your favorite stores selling thousands of products from diapers to cellphones, from baby strollers to drapes? Once you've gotten the <u>shoppingexperience.com</u> habit, you'll never need to go downtown to do your shopping again.

> Shopping has just got so much easier with <u>shoppingexperience.com</u>, the world's largest online catalogue. Why travel to your local shopping centre when, from the comfort of your own home, you can access literally hundreds of your favourite shops selling thousands of products from nappies to mobile phones, from prams to curtains? Once you've got the <u>shoppingexperience.com</u> habit, you'll never need to go to into town to do your shopping again.

Which text is written in American English and which in British English? How do you know? Underline differences in vocabulary and spelling.

3 Look at the words in the box. How would you rewrite these words in British English?

> center   color   a driver's license   gray   organize   pedaling
> TV program   traveled

4 Work with your partner. Discuss the different meanings of these words in British and American English.

> college   gas   holiday   public school   school   subway

Read the dictionary extracts on the right and check your ideas.

5 Work with your partner. Discuss whether the sentences below were said by a British or American English speaker.

a) After I graduate from high school, I want to go to school in France.
b) I went to a state school as my parents couldn't afford to send me to a public school.
c) At college I majored in math, and graduated summa cum laude last year.
d) I use public transportation because the cost of gas is too high.
e) We're hoping to go on holiday to Vancouver in the autumn.
f) The quickest way to the drugstore is to take the subway. It's only two stops away.

6 Read these American sentences (*a–f*). Change them to British English by substituting the words in bold with their British equivalents.

a) I usually take the **elevator** if I have to go higher than the **second floor**.
b) I love **French fries** and **potato chips** but I'm not so fond of **candy** or **cookies**.
c) My **mom** and dad live in an **apartment building**, so they don't have a **back yard**.
d) **On** weekends, I like to **take a walk** in the countryside or go to the **movies**.
e) I hate **standing in line** and it makes me **mad** if people **cut in**.
f) I always **wash up** before I have a meal.

Which of the sentences are true of you? Discuss with your partner.

7 Check your own dictionary. How does it show information about British and American English?

Differences between British and American English: college

In the UK, a **college** usually means a place where students over the age of 16 are trained in a particular subject or skill, earning a qualification that is not usually an academic degree. People studying for an academic degree go to a **university**. In the US, a **college** is a place where students can earn a bachelor's degree (=first degree), and a university offers both bachelor's degrees and advanced degrees.

Differences between British and American English: gas

In the UK, **gas** usually refers to a clear substance like air that is burned to cook food or to heat your house: *a gas boiler*. Gas can also have this meaning in the US, but when American speakers say **gas** they are usually referring to a type of liquid fuel that is used to produce power in cars: *We'd better get gas on our way out of town*. In the UK, you call this fuel **petrol**.

Differences between British and American English: holiday

In the UK, a **holiday**, often called your holidays, is a period of time during which you do not go to school or work, and usually you go to a place away from home to relax: *Where are you going for your holiday?* American speakers call this period a **vacation**. In the US, **holiday** refers to a single day fixed by law when people do not have to go to school or work: *I forgot that Monday's a holiday*. In the UK, this is usually called a **bank holiday**. Both American and English speakers also call this a **public holiday**. When American speakers say **the holidays** or the **holiday season**, they are referring to the period of time that includes Christmas, Hanukkah, and New Year's Day: *Have you got any special plans for the holidays?*

Differences between British and American English: school

In both the UK and the US, **school** usually means a place where children are taught from the age of four or five until they are 18. American speakers also use **school** to refer to a university. In the UK, you say that children are **at school** during the day: *The kids are at school until 3.00*. In the US, you usually say they are **in school**, but American speakers also use **in school** when they mean studying at a school or university rather than having a job: *She's still in school, but she's graduating in the spring*.

Differences between British and American English: subway

In the UK, a **subway** is an underground tunnel that people can walk through to get to the other side of a busy road: *It's safest to use the subway to get from the car park to the museum*. In the US, this is called an **underpass**. A **subway** in the US is an underground railway in a city: *Take the subway to 14th Street*.

6 Mind

Grammar Verbs of the senses. Participle clauses
Vocabulary Verbs of seeing. Collocations with *mind*
Useful phrases Making appropriate requests

Speaking

How much do you know about your brain? Decide if these statements are true or false.

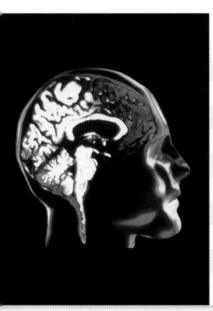

The Human Brain

a) On average, the adult brain weighs 2.8kg in a man and 2.2kg in a woman.

b) The brain floats in a liquid in the skull.

c) 50% of the average human brain is water.

d) Your brain is uniformly pink in colour.

e) The human adult brain uses up to 25% of the blood's oxygen supply.

f) We only use 10% of our brains.

g) Your brain cannot feel pain.

h) Your brain is more active watching TV than it is sleeping.

i) We yawn more when our brains are not being stimulated.

j) The human brain continues to send out electrical signals for up to 37 hours following death.

Check your answers on page 130.

Listening

1 Work with a partner. Label the games in the photos. Order them from oldest to the most recent. What is the aim of each game? Which do you like playing?

2 🔊 2.09 Listen to four people answering questions about some of the games in the photos. Which question (*a, b, c* or *d*) was each of them asked?
   a) Do you do or play any of these games on a regular basis?
   b) Which of them do you think requires most brain power?
   c) Which of them do you think are a waste of time?
   d) Which of them did you use to play as a child?

3 Listen again and make notes on the people's answers in Exercise 2. Then compare your notes with your partner. Do you disagree with anything they said?

▲ 1 _____

▲ 2 _____   ▲ 3 _____   ▲ 4 _____   ▲ 5 _____

Reading & Speaking

1 Work with a partner. Look at the words in the box. Which have negative connotations? Write a definition for one of the words with negative connotations and read it to the class. Can they guess the word?

> decay   decline   fit   growth   inactivity   lack   loss   stretching   training

2 Use six of the words in the box in Exercise 1 to complete the article about brain training.

Everyone knows keeping fit is important, but what a lot of people forget is that your brain needs exercise as well. A (1) _____ in memory or motor skills is usually the result of (2) _____ and/or a (3) _____ of mental exercise and stimulation. In the first twenty or thirty years of life, your brain, under a constant barrage of stimuli (your teachers, your parents, your friends, all trying to teach you new things, not all of which are going to help you in life, but there we go), undergoes incredible growth, with neurons multiplying and connecting at incredible rates. All of this, however, disappears when you settle into the comfort of routine,

a regular job, regular meals, regular friends, etc.

At which point the (4) _____ sets in! But it doesn't have to. You can keep your brain (5) _____ without having to go back to school and by doing far more pleasurable activities than working out how long it takes the milkman to deliver 212 pints of milk if his milk float goes at 2 mph... Just turn to the double spread we've dedicated to brain (6) _____ in this month's issue. It'll boost your memory and powers of observation, improve your reflexes, make you more creative and increase your popularity. The last one's not true. I was just seeing if you were concentrating!

3 Work with your partner. Discuss these questions.

a) Choose two adjectives from the box to describe the article in Exercise 2.

> censorious   chatty   critical   familiar   funny   hard-hitting   informal
> sarcastic   serious

b) Where do you think the article might come from?
c) Has it inspired you to do some brain training?

4 Check your brain power by answering as many of the questions in the quiz as you can in three minutes.

Calculate your brain power

1 What was the day and date you started this course?

2 What were the grammar focuses in Unit 4 of this book?

3 What was your teacher wearing last lesson? (The more detail you give the more points you get.)

4 How many Rs are there in this sentence?
   Red rhinoceroses are a rarity in Rochester although they have been observed in Rome.

5 How many circles do you have to move to turn this triangle upside down?

6 Complete this chart so that all the vertical and horizontal columns add up to 9.

5		2	
	3	2	
1		0	
			1

7 Study these words for one minute, then close your book and write them down.

> sold   rare   very   today   tree   about
> radio   paint   book   tried   mix   next
> brief   could   dish

Check your answers on page 131. Did you score better or worse than you expected? Compare your scores with your partner.

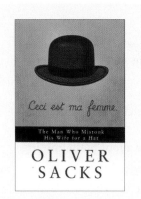

Ceci est ma femme.

The Man Who Mistook His Wife for a Hat

OLIVER SACKS

The Man Who Mistook His Wife for a Hat is the title of a book concerning malfunctions of the brain. It was written by the neurologist Dr Oliver Sacks. The title of the book is also the title of one of the cases.

Reading

1 **Work with a partner. Look at the book on the left. Discuss these questions.**

a) Have you read or heard about this book or Dr Oliver Sacks?

b) What do you think the case is about?

2 **Read four extracts from the case on page 59. Label the extracts (1–4) with the headings in the box.**

The doctor's examination	The doctor's first impression
The diagnosis	The patient

3 **Read the extracts again. Work with your partner. Discuss these questions.**

a) What were Dr P.'s first symptoms? Why did he consult an ophthalmologist? Was the ophthalmologist able to help him?

b) What did Dr Sacks notice about Dr P.'s eyes when they first met?

c) Was Dr P. aware that he didn't see normally? Why? / Why not? How *did* Dr P. see?

d) How do you think Dr P. would describe a book or a mobile telephone? What might he mistake them for?

e) What advice did Dr Sacks give the patient? This book was written more than 20 years ago. Would you expect this kind of advice today?

f) Look at these titles of other case histories from the book. What do you think the problem was in these cases? Check your answers by reading the case file cards on page 131.

The Lost Mariner   *The Phantom Finger*   *The Dog Beneath The Skin*

Vocabulary

1 **Look at the highlighted verbs in the extract. Try to guess the meaning from context and complete the glossary.**

> **Glossary**
>
> a) _____ verb [I]: look steadily at something for a long time
>
> b) _____ verb [T]: notice
>
> c) _____ verb [I/T]: move suddenly and quickly
>
> d) _____ verb [T]: spend time looking at something
>
> e) _____ verb [T]: know what something is when you see it again
>
> f) _____ verb [I/T]: look at or over something quickly to get a general impression
>
> g) _____ verb [T]: to look closely or analytically at something
>
> h) _____ verb [T]: to become aware of someone or something using your eyes

2 *Observe, recognise* and *see* **have more than one meaning. Look at these sentences and match the verbs (1–6) to the meanings (a–f).**

a) I recognise I'm not perfect.

b) I see what you mean.

c) You should observe the customs of the country you are visiting.

d) Are you still seeing Peter?

e) 'That wasn't very clever,' he observed.

f) As I see it, she's making a big mistake.

1 understand

2 date someone

3 admit

4 follow/obey a law/rule

5 have an opinion

6 comment

3 **How would you translate *observe, recognise* and *see* into your own language? Do the translations have multiple meanings?**

4 **Write a paragraph using *observe, recognise* and *see*. Use each word once. Show it to your partner and ask them to work out the meanings of the verbs you have used.**

THE MAN WHO MISTOOK HIS WIFE FOR A HAT

1) _____

Dr P. was a musician of distinction, well-known for many years as a singer, and then at the local School of Music, as a teacher. It was here, in relation to his students, that certain strange problems were
5 first observed. Sometimes a student would present himself, and Dr P. would not recognise him; or, specifically, would not recognise his face. The moment the student spoke, he would be recognised by his voice. Such incidents multiplied, causing
10 embarrassment, perplexity, fear – and, sometimes, comedy. For not only did Dr P. increasingly fail to see faces, but he saw faces when there were no faces to see: genially, when in the street, he might pat the heads of water-hydrants and parking-meters, taking these to
15 be the heads of children; he would amiably address carved knobs on the furniture and be astounded when they did not reply.

The notion of there being 'something the matter' did not emerge until some three years later, when
20 diabetes developed. Well aware that diabetes could affect his eyes, Dr P. consulted an ophthalmologist, who took a careful history and examined his eyes closely. 'There's nothing the matter with your eyes,' the doctor concluded. 'But there is trouble with the
25 visual parts of your brain. You don't need my help, you must see a neurologist.' And so, as a result of this referral, Dr P. came to me.

2) _____

It was obvious within a few seconds of meeting him that there was no trace of dementia in the ordinary
30 sense. He was a man of great cultivation and charm, who talked well and fluently, with imagination and humour. I couldn't think why he had been referred to our clinic.

And yet there was something a bit odd. He faced
35 me as he spoke, was oriented towards me, and yet there was something the matter – it was difficult to formulate. He faced me with his ears, I came to think, but not with his eyes. These, instead of looking, gazing, at me, 'taking me in', in the normal way,
40 made sudden strange fixations – on my nose, on my right ear, down to my chin, up to my right eye – as if noting (even studying) these individual features, but not seeing my whole face, its changing expressions, 'me', as a whole. I am not sure I fully realised this at
45 the time – there was just a teasing strangeness, some failure in the normal interplay of gaze and expression. He saw me, he scanned me and yet …

'What seems to be the matter?' I asked him at length.

'Nothing that I know of,' he replied with a smile,
50 'but people seem to think there's something wrong with my eyes.'

'But you don't recognise any visual problems?'

'No, not directly, but I occasionally make mistakes.'

3) _____

55 He saw all right, but what did he see? I opened out a copy of the *National Geographic* Magazine, and asked him to describe some pictures in it.

His responses here were very curious. His eyes would dart from one thing to another, picking up
60 tiny features, individual features, as they had done with my face. A striking brightness, a colour, a shape would arrest his attention and elicit comment – but in no case did he get the scene-as-a-whole. 'What is this?' I asked, holding up a glove.

65 'May I examine it?' he asked, and, taking it from me, he proceeded to examine it.

'A continuous surface,' he announced at last, 'infolded on itself. It appears to have' – he hesitated – 'five outpouchings, if this is the word.'

70 'Yes,' I said cautiously. 'You have given me a description. Now tell me what it is.'

'A container of some sort?'

'Yes,' I said, 'and what would it contain?' 'It would contain its contents!' said Dr P., with a laugh. 'There
75 are many possibilities. It could be a change-purse, for example, for coins of five sizes. It could …'

I interrupted the barmy flow. 'Does it not look familiar? Do you think it might contain, might fit, a part of your body?'

80 No light of recognition dawned on his face. No child would have the power to see and speak of 'a continuous surface … infolded on itself', but any child, any infant, would immediately know a glove as a glove, see it as familiar, as going with a hand. Dr
85 P. didn't. He saw nothing as familiar. Visually, he was lost in a world of lifeless abstractions.

4) _____

'Well, Dr Sacks,' he said to me. 'You find me an interesting case, I perceive. Can you tell me what you find wrong, make recommendations?'

90 'I can't tell you what I find wrong,' I replied, 'but I'll say what I find right. You are a wonderful musician, and music is your life. What I would prescribe, in a case such as yours, is a life which consists entirely of music. Music has been the centre, now make it the
95 whole, of your life.'

Listening

1 **Work with a partner. Discuss these questions.**

a) How many senses have we got?
b) Which do you think is most important to you in your everyday life?
c) Which would you be able to cope best without?
d) Which sense triggers the most memories?
e) Have you ever lost the use of one of your senses temporarily?
f) Do you think any of your senses is especially well-developed?
g) Which sense do we most take for granted?

2 2.10–2.14 **Listen to Mike, Maria, Helen, Nick and Petra answering some of the questions in Exercise 1. Which question is each person answering? Which senses do they mention? Compare your notes with your partner. Were the speakers' answers similar to yours?**

Grammar

Verbs of the senses

see, feel, taste, smell, hear, sense

I **can't see** without my glasses.
I'**m seeing** Liam tomorrow.

I think I **can hear** the phone.
I **must be hearing** things. My phone's turned off.

1 **Work with your partner. Look at the verbs in the box. Which can a) only be used with a stative meaning (i.e. to refer to an ability or a sensation)?, b) only be dynamic (i.e. to refer to an action), c) be used with a stative or dynamic meaning.**

| feel hear listen look see sense smell taste touch watch |

2 **Complete these extracts from the speakers' answers in Listening, Exercise 2 with the correct form of some of the verbs in the box in Exercise 1. Some of the verbs are used more than once. You may need to add a modal verb or a negative.**

a) … if you're blind, if you _____ , then although you can lead a full life and all that, I think it does make you more vulnerable …
b) … I would really hate it if I _____ what things or people looked like …
c) … I read this article about a man who'd gone deaf and then his hearing was restored to him, and he spoke about how isolating it can be if you _____ .
d) … he really missed _____ to music, that was the worst part, he said. That and not being able to _____ his wife's voice.
e) … I _____ the palm trees, _____ the food, _____ the sun on my skin …
f) … they _____ the vibrations of the drums, even though they _____ them.
g) … I'm really sensitive to things like gas leaks and anything that _____ bad …
h) … I really miss the subtler smells in the kitchen. It affects my taste too. Everything _____ so bland.

2.15 **Listen and check your answers.**

3 **What modal auxiliaries were used in the sentences in Exercise 2? Were they used with a stative or a dynamic meaning? What other verb phrase was used with the same meaning?**

4 **Work with your partner. Look at the pairs of sentences below and discuss the difference in meaning of the verbs in italics.**

1A I *can see* John. He's just over there, standing next to the bar.
1B I'*m seeing* John tomorrow. I'll let him know what we've decided.

2A I *could hear* strange sounds coming from downstairs, so I decided to go and investigate.
2B I'*ve been hearing* great things about you recently. You must be doing really well.

3A I'*m not feeling* very well. I think I'm going to go and lie down for a while.
3B That heater's really good! I *can feel* the heat from here.

4A I'*m just tasting* the soup to see if I need to add any more salt.
4B I really *can't taste* the difference between butter and margarine.

5 **Pay careful attention to what's going on around you, both inside and outside the class. Write down what you can hear, smell and touch. Compare your answers with the class.**

6 Grammar *Extra 6, Part 1* page 138. Read the explanations and do Exercise 1

Reading & Vocabulary

1   Work in small groups. Discuss these questions.

a) Have you ever had a pet? What was it? How long did you have it for?
b) Why do you think people keep unusual pets such as spiders and chameleons?
c) Do you think pets serve a useful function? If so, what?
d) Do you think some people get too attached to their pets?

2   Match the problems (a–e) to the definitions (1–5).

a)	nervous breakdown	1	hostile action taken towards trespassers
b)	addiction	2	the condition of doing or consuming something habitually and being unable to give it up
c)	separation anxiety	3	a loss of mental health and strength
d)	phobia	4	a state of uneasiness brought about by the absence of a person or thing
e)	territorial aggression	5	an irrational fear or hatred of something

Which of these problems do you think are more common in animals and which in humans?

3   Read this pet case history and decide which of the problems in Exercise 2 Willy was probably suffering from.

The Canine Cruncher

The day Mr X took delivery of his new van was the day his dog decided to start out on a new career. Previously a docile creature, Willy the cross-bred terrier turned into Lex Flex, the Canine Cruncher, in the time
5   it took his owner to eat a three-course meal.

Having left his trusty companion to keep an eye on the smart new van, Mr X returned from lunch to find that his new mode of transport had been completely remodelled. What had been a sturdy, dependable
10   method of delivering frozen foods around the city centre would now not have looked out of place by a beach on a hot summer's day. The roof had been torn back as if with a tin opener, an air-conditioning system had been thoughtfully provided by the removal
15   of the windscreen and the seats had been given a new look, which might have been described as 'ripped and tattered'. Exhausted by all his hard work, Willy was having a quick nap when his owner reappeared.

Speechless, Mr X rushed towards his hound with
20   his arms outstretched. Waking up with a jump, Willy sat up to greet his owner and barked with excitement. However, being a modest sort of dog and not thinking it necessary for his devoted owner to thank him so profusely, he bounded through the shattered
25   windscreen and took off down the street. Mr X's voice could be heard fading into the distance behind him as he raced away. Overcome with emotion, the van owner returned to survey the full extent of the new design.

These days it's not uncommon to see Mr X driving
30   round the streets of the city looking for his absent friend. Numbed by the efficiency of his new air-conditioning system, he's often spotted scouring the streets between deliveries, under the protection of a
35   warm blanket.

4   Work with a partner and discuss the meanings of these expressions in the case history.

a) a docile creature (line 3)
b) ripped and tattered (lines 16–17)
c) a quick nap (line 18)
d) fading into the distance (line 26)
e) overcome with emotion (line 27)
f) he's often spotted (line 32)

5   The case history contains a lot of descriptive language. However, the actual events of the story can be summarised in a few sentences. Write as short a factual account of the story as you can.

Participle clauses

Participle clauses are formed using:

A present participle
Seeing the dog, she braked sharply.

A past participle
Encouraged to write from an early age, she published her first book when she was 12.

A perfect participle
Having seen the house, she knew it wasn't worth the price they were asking.

1 Make three sentences using one clause from each box: A, B and C.

A	a) Having left his trusty companion to keep an eye on the smart new van,
	b) Waking up with a jump,
	c) Numbed by the efficiency of his new air-conditioning system,
B	d) he's often spotted scouring the streets between deliveries,
	e) Willy sat up to greet his owner
	f) Mr X returned from lunch to find
C	g) and barked with excitement.
	h) that his new mode of transport had been completely remodelled.
	i) under the protection of a warm blanket.

Now check your answers.

2 Work with a partner. Look at the participle clauses in box *A* in Exercise 1 and answer these questions.

a) Which contains: a present participle? a past participle? a perfect participle?

b) What is the subject of each participle clause?

c) Look at the sentences below and answer the questions.

1 *Exhausted by all his hard work, Willy was having a quick nap when ...*
2 *Willy was exhausted by all his hard work, so he was having a quick nap when ...*

- Which sentence, *1* or *2*, is more likely to be spoken?
- Which was used in the pet case history on page 61?
- What has been added to sentence *2* to replace the participle clause?

3 Rewrite these sentences using participle clauses.

a) When I finished university I went on a long holiday.

b) Because I live on my own, I don't really do a lot of cooking.

c) I don't eat sweets because I'm on a diet.

d) I like to spend the weekends relaxing as I'm tired after a long week at work.

Are these sentences true for you, for anyone you know or anyone in your class?

4 Look at this sentence. What word is missing and where should it go?

However, being a modest sort of dog and thinking it necessary for his devoted owner to thank him so profusely, he bounded through the shattered windscreen and took off down the street.

Now check your answer in the pet case history on page 61.

5 Work with your partner. Look at these sentences and add *not* where necessary.

a) Discouraged by the long climb ahead of them, they set off at dawn.

b) Wanting to offend people, they decided to extend the guest list to include both family and friends.

c) Having completed the form, please send it, with a photograph, to the address below.

d) Knowing that arriving on time would make a very bad impression, he left with plenty of time to spare.

6 Rephrase your answers to Exercise 5 without using participle clauses. You may need to add linking words.

a) *They were not discouraged by the long climb ahead of them, and they set off at dawn.*

7 Grammar *Extra 6, Part 2* page 138. Read the explanations and do Exercise 2.

Vocabulary

1 Work with a partner. How many collocations with the word *mind* do you know?

2 Look at the collocations in the sentences (*a–j*). How many of your collocations from Exercise 1 are in the list? Look at the collocations again. Is *mind* a verb or a noun in each one?

a) Have a nice trip. **Mind how you** go on the roads, they're terrible at this time of day!

b) They pay really well. **Mind you**, they can afford to.

c) I wish Bill would **mind his own business**. He's always asking awkward questions.

d) Jen's invited me to go on holiday with her, but I'm **in two minds about** going.

e) A good night out will help you **take your mind off** your exams.

f) Could you **mind** the cat while I'm away?

g) I'll go **out of my mind** with boredom if I have to stay in this job.

h) **Great minds think alike**, but fools never differ!

i) Do you believe that healing is a question of **mind over matter**?

j) Holidays are **the last thing on my mind** at the moment.

3 Match the collocations (*a–j*) in Exercise 2 to one of the definitions (*1–10*).

1 the least important problem to deal with at the moment

2 make you stop worrying or thinking about something

3 be careful

4 to look after something or someone for a short time

5 to add a comment that makes something you've already said less strong or general

6 (humorous) used for saying that you are both very clever when you and another person have the same idea

7 to be uncertain about something or to have difficulty in making a decision

8 not interfere in other people's affairs

9 mad, insane

10 the belief that our minds are stronger than our bodies and that we can control pain or other unpleasant situations through mind power

Which of the collocations would you like to learn? Write a sentence for each of them to help you remember.

Pronunciation

1 🌐 2.16 Listen to a conversation between three people and answer these questions.

a) What do you think the relationship is between them?

b) What do you think they're talking about?

2 Look at these sentences from the conversation in Exercise 1. Complete them with collocations with *mind*.

a) _____ budging up a bit?   c) _____ your own business!

b) ... _____ not sitting there?   d) _____ , Nicholas will.

Listen again and check your answers.

3 How do the speakers pronounce the underlined sections?

a) Woul<u>d you</u> mind …

b) <u>Do you</u> mind …

c) Min<u>d you</u> …

4 Work with your partner and discuss these questions. Think carefully about the pronunciation of the underlined sections.

a) <u>Do you</u> mind if people keep you waiting?

b) Would <u>you</u> mind if someone borrowed something of yours without asking?

c) When was the last time you spoke your mind? <u>Did you</u> offend anyone?

d) <u>Do you</u> find it difficult to make up your mind?

Useful phrases

1 Work with a partner. Look at the requests (*1–8*). Order them from the most polite to the most informal.

1   Do you mind if I smoke?
2   Okay if we pick you up at six?
3   Would you mind lending me a fiver?
4   Can I copy your homework?
5   May I have my book back, please?
6   Give me a pen!
7   Please sign here.
8   Would you mind awfully if I asked you to write that report again?

2 Match the requests (*1–8*) in Exercise 1 to the most appropriate response (*a–h*). Note that some of the responses can be matched with more than one request.

a) I'm cool with that.
b) I hope you're joking!
c) What book?
d) Er, I don't think you can here actually.
e) What do you mean, sign?
f) Anything else?
g) It depends.
h) Er, well, to be honest, I'm not really comfortable with that.

    ◉ 2.17 Listen and check your answers. Did any of the responses seem inappropriate?

3 ◉ 2.18 Listen to the complete conversations. Do the speakers know each other well? Are they just acquaintances or are they complete strangers? What is the request in each?

4 Work with your partner. Look at the pictures (*a–c*). Act out one of the situations.

Change partners. Choose another situation and change the relationship between the speakers. Act out the conversation in front of the class. Can they guess the relationship between you?

5 Work in small groups. Discuss these questions.

a) What other useful phrases do you know for replying to requests?
b) Do you find it difficult to say no? What tactics do you use to avoid saying no outright? What tactics were used in the conversations?
c) What excuses have you made to get out of doing something?
d) What sorts of requests get on your nerves?

6 Write down a request. Think of at least six ways of making this request. Ask everyone in the class your request but vary the way you make it.

7 Work with your class. Discuss these questions.

a) How successful were you in making your request?
b) Which manner of making your request was the most successful?
c) What was the politest negative response you heard?
d) What was the most common response?

Writing *Extra*

Emails making and declining requests

1 Work with a partner. Read the emails below and decide...
a) who the sender might be   b) what requests were made of them.

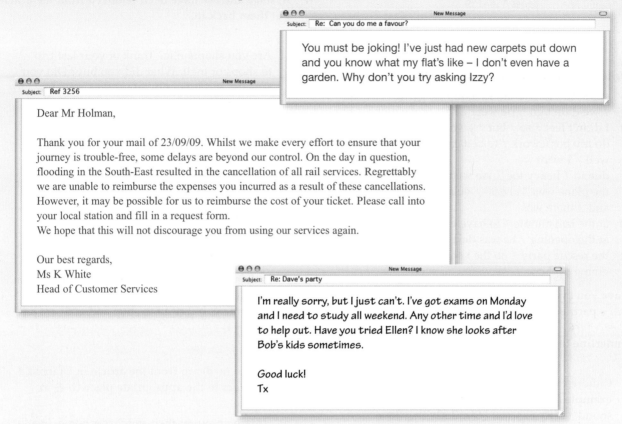

Subject: Re: Can you do me a favour?

You must be joking! I've just had new carpets put down and you know what my flat's like – I don't even have a garden. Why don't you try asking Izzy?

Subject: Ref 3256

Dear Mr Holman,

Thank you for your mail of 23/09/09. Whilst we make every effort to ensure that your journey is trouble-free, some delays are beyond our control. On the day in question, flooding in the South-East resulted in the cancellation of all rail services. Regrettably we are unable to reimburse the expenses you incurred as a result of these cancellations. However, it may be possible for us to reimburse the cost of your ticket. Please call into your local station and fill in a request form.
We hope that this will not discourage you from using our services again.

Our best regards,
Ms K White
Head of Customer Services

Subject: Re: Dave's party

I'm really sorry, but I just can't. I've got exams on Monday and I need to study all weekend. Any other time and I'd love to help out. Have you tried Ellen? I know she looks after Bob's kids sometimes.

Good luck!
Tx

2 Look at the emails again. Underline the phrases used...
a) to refuse the requests   b) to soften the refusal.

3 Read the emails. Which one would you find the most difficult to refuse? Why?

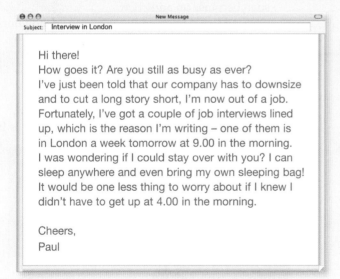

Subject: Interview in London

Hi there!
How goes it? Are you still as busy as ever?
I've just been told that our company has to downsize and to cut a long story short, I'm now out of a job. Fortunately, I've got a couple of job interviews lined up, which is the reason I'm writing – one of them is in London a week tomorrow at 9.00 in the morning. I was wondering if I could stay over with you? I can sleep anywhere and even bring my own sleeping bag! It would be one less thing to worry about if I knew I didn't have to get up at 4.00 in the morning.

Cheers,
Paul

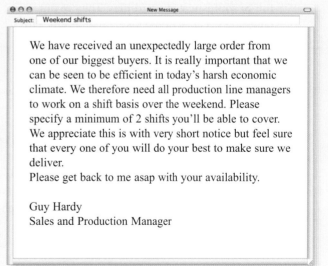

Subject: Weekend shifts

We have received an unexpectedly large order from one of our biggest buyers. It is really important that we can be seen to be efficient in today's harsh economic climate. We therefore need all production line managers to work on a shift basis over the weekend. Please specify a minimum of 2 shifts you'll be able to cover. We appreciate this is with very short notice but feel sure that every one of you will do your best to make sure we deliver.
Please get back to me asap with your availability.

Guy Hardy
Sales and Production Manager

4 Work with your partner. Write a reply to one of the two emails refusing the request and explaining why. Use the expressions you underlined in Exercise 2 to help you.

5 Exchange your email with other students in the class and answer these questions.
a) Which email are they replying to?
b) Which reply was the most inventive?
c) Which excuses were the most unbelievable and which were the most likely?

Review B

▶ Grammar *Extra* pages 136–139

Grammar

1 Write the sentences in the correct order.

a) supposed to / to the seaside / be going / the car / we didn't go / We were / so / broke down / but

b) I didn't feel / so / but / going to / last night / do my homework / to bed early / I was / very well / I went

c) due to / heavy fog / We were / by six hours / the plane was / at 8.30 / delayed / leave / but / and / there was

d) at the last minute / to have met / the minister / at the opening / he was delayed / I was / but

e) the rescue party / on the verge of / when / giving up hope / We were / arrived

Have you ever found yourself in a similar situation? Tell a partner about it.

2 Underline the correct alternative.

Children will laugh at almost anything, (1) **for example / not to say,** a funny face or a strange sound. (2) **By contrast / Similarly** they love slapstick and farce, things (3) **including / such as** people walking into doors or falling into holes on the street. They will even laugh at things they don't really understand, (4) **strictly speaking / that is to say**, jokes aimed at adults full of sophisticated word play. They're not laughing because of the joke, (5) or **at any rate / particularly**, not because of the content of the joke, but because everyone else is laughing, and they simply want to join in.

Do you agree with the text? Why? / Why not?

3 Work with your partner. Choose the correct alternative. Sometimes both alternatives are possible.

a) I once bought a pair of expensive, designer jeans **that / which** I really couldn't afford.

b) My best friend is the kind of person **who / which** shops until they drop.

c) On Sunday I went for a day out shopping with my family, **that / which** was good fun, but not a good use of my time.

d) I found a real bargain **that / who** I couldn't let slip through my fingers.

e) We were greeted by one of those super-efficient sales people **who / that** scares the customers off by being over-helpful.

Are any of the sentences above true for you? Tell your partner.

4 *A, some* and *the* have been removed from the article. Put them back in.

Are you shopaholic? Think of your last trip to shops or mall. What did you buy? Did you take list and buy only things you came for? Or did you come home laden down with lots of new – but totally unessential – items? There's very little difference between treating yourself to something new and compulsive shopping. Difference lies in your attitude to shopping. Compulsive shopper can't stop thinking about shopping. (1) They think about it all time and only really find relief when they are actually in shop, choosing their next purchase. (2) As addiction grows, so does deceit. (3) It could be anything, CDs, new pair of shoes, expensive make-up. Men are just as vulnerable as women. Men tend to buy electronic goods or sports equipment, but need to shop and guilt are just same. (4)

5 Sentences (*a–d*) are from the article in Exercise 4. Match them to the appropriate place (*1–4*) in the article.

a) Having brought their purchases home, they'll hide them in the back of the wardrobe.

b) Feeling guilty about the money they've spent, they'll lie about the price.

c) Finding pleasure in spending money, shopping soon becomes an addiction.

d) Once addicted to shopping, they can spend hours at the mall, comparing prices and specifications.

Underline the participle clauses. Rewrite them as full clauses.

6 Work with your partner. Look at the photos (1–3). Which sense is being used in each photo? What is it being used for?

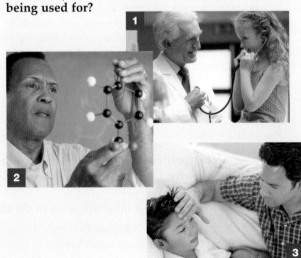

Vocabulary

1 Complete the expressions with *story* or *tale(s)*.

a) He told me some cock-and-bull _____ about the dog having eaten his homework.

b) I hate it when the kids tell _____ about each other.

c) A: So, what happened?
   B: Don't ask! It's a long _____ !

d) I'm sorry, it just won't work out. End of _____ .

e) I'm sorry, but you can't expect me to swallow yet another sob _____ about how awful her family is!

f) Yes, well, to cut a long _____ short, we had to go to the party in our shorts and T-shirts.

g) A: So, did you see the concert?
   B: No, we arrived too late – again. All the tickets had sold out – _____ of my life!

Do you have similar expressions in your language?

2 Complete the adjectives then answer the questions below.

a) g_ll_ bl_   e) tr_st_ng

b) pl_ _ s_bl_   f) f_shy

c) n_ _ v_   g) _nf_ _ thf_l

d) sc_pt_c_l

Choose three adjectives and write definitions for them. Use the expressions in the box to help you.

take someone in   take someone for a ride   trick
lead someone to believe   take someone at their word
swallow a story   two-time   make out   con   fall for

Read your definitions to the class. Can they guess what adjective it is?

3 Complete the sentences with the phrases in the box.

bulk buy   down-payment   impulse buys
over the odds   shop around   slap-up
within your means

a) Last week I went for a _____ meal with my family.

b) I don't think it makes sense to _____ – especially not with food – you end up throwing most of it away.

c) We made a _____ on a house last week! It's our first home, I'm so excited!

d) I always _____ before buying anything, from a television to a loaf of bread.

e) I try not to make _____ – but it's so difficult to resist the temptation, especially when it comes to shoes.

f) I never pay _____ for anything – I just don't have enough money!

g) I think it's really important to try and live _____ . Taking out loans and buying stuff with your credit card all the time is just asking for trouble.

Are any of the sentences true for you? Tell your partner.

4 Complete the questions with a preposition.

a) How much money do you need a month to get _____ ?

b) How much do you usually run _____ in bills for your phone and other services?

c) Do you think it's better to pay _____ a credit card bill in one go, or in instalments? Why?

d) Are you saving _____ for anything special at the moment?

e) If you are, does that mean you have to cut _____ on your spending?

5 Look at the verbs in the box. Which would you (or your eyes) do when you …

dart   examine   gaze   observe   recognise   scan

a) look through a newspaper to find a particular piece of information?

b) look hurriedly around a room to find your keys or mobile phone as you are about to leave to go out?

c) look for a long time into the eyes of someone you love?

d) look carefully at a contract or official document?

e) see someone you know in a crowd?

f) watch something interesting take place, without being directly involved?

Have you done any of these things recently? Tell your partner about what you were doing and why.

Pronunciation

1 Look at some words from Units 4–6. Say the words and add them to the table.

addiction   aggression   competition
disappointment   eccentric   economise   emotion
exorbitant   extravagant   necessities   observation
recognise   side-splitting   sheepishly
superstition   sympathy

A: ☐▢▢	B: ▢☐▢	C: ▢☐▢▢	D: ▢▢☐▢
	addiction		

2 Underline the stressed syllables.

🌐 2.19 **Listen, check and repeat.**

7 Digital

Grammar Complex sentences. Speculating about the future
Vocabulary Compound nouns. Informal expressions
Useful phrases Discussing implications

Speaking

Work with a partner. Look at the photos and discuss these questions.

a) What's the difference between the two mobile phones?
b) Which one would be more expensive to buy? Why?
c) How long have you had your mobile phone and why did you choose it?
d) Would you like to upgrade it? Why? / Why not?

Reading

1   Work in small groups. Discuss ...

a)   the functions a mobile phone could perform ten years ago.
b)   the extra functions it can perform today.
c)   other functions you think it might be able to perform in ten years' time.

2   Read the article about mobile phones in the future on page 69. As you read, tick (✓) the functions you came up with in Exercise 1 and write an asterisk (*) next to the ones you didn't mention.

When you've finished, compare your notes with your partner. Which functions would you find most useful? And least useful? Do any of the developments described in the article worry you?

3   Sentences (a–f) are from the article. Match them to the appropriate places (1–6) in the article.

a)   What we do need is better mobiles and more intelligence.
b)   It is your entertainment centre when away from home.
c)   On a typical day it will start work even before you wake.
d)   – it's more like a remote control for your life.
e)   With its understanding of almost all aspects of your life,
f)   such as transport updates from major providers.

4   Do you think the future lies in mobile phones? Or do you think another device will take its place?

The future of mobile phones

A remote control for your life

In the near future, your mobile phone will be so powerful it'll guide you through your whole life, *says William Webb*.

▲ **Mobile phone with integrated projector**

Your mobile is now much more than just a communication device [1]. You still call it a 'mobile' from habit, but it is an organiser, entertainment device, payment device and security
5 centre, all developed and manufactured by engineers.

[2] Because it knows your travel schedule it can check for problems on the roads or with the trains and adjust the time it wakes you up accordingly, giving you the best route into work. It can control your
10 home, re-programming the central heating if you need to get up earlier and providing remote alerts if the home security system is triggered. It is your payment system – just by placing the phone near a sensor on a barrier, like the Oyster Card® readers in use on London
15 transport, you can pay for tickets for journeys or buy items in shops. With an understanding of location, the mobile can also provide directions, or even alert the user to friends or family in the vicinity.

[3] As well as holding all your music files, as
20 some phones today are able to do, it will work with your home entertainment system while you sleep to find programmes that will interest you and download them as a podcast to watch on the train or in other spare moments. It will intelligently work out what to

25 do with incoming phone calls and messages. Because it knows your diary it will also know, for example, to direct voice calls to voicemail when you are in a meeting, perhaps providing a discrete text summary of the caller and the nature of their call.

30 [4] many new services become possible. For example, a 'Good Food' meal planning service could send daily suggestions for your evening meal based on learned preferences, previous selections made and the likely contents of your refrigerator. The latter might
35 work by uploading the bill from the weekly grocery shop and then removing those items it deduces have been used for meals earlier in the week.

So what will this apparently massive change in our relationships with our mobiles require in the way
40 of new technology or extra expenditure? Actually, surprisingly little. Now that we have widespread cellular coverage, with high-speed data networks in many homes, offices and points of congregation such as coffee shops, we have all we need to get a signal
45 to the mobile.

[5] Mobiles will continue to get steadily better, with higher resolution touchscreens, speech recognition that really works and much greater memory and storage capabilities. Increasingly
50 intelligent software will be running on these mobiles, and also on home and wide-area networks, able to learn behaviour, predict needs and integrate with a growing number of databases, [6]. So, instead of the train company just sending you a text to tell you
55 of delays, your mobile will analyse it in conjunction with your travel plans and modify those plans if needs be.

This evolution will be a slow but steady one as every few years mobiles get slightly better, intelligent
60 software evolves and the various providers of all the necessary input data – such as transport organisations and shops – gradually make the data available in formats that become increasingly useful.

Ten years ago the mobile was purely a device for
65 making voice calls. Now it is a camera, MP3 player, organiser and texting device. This is only the start of an evolution that will turn it into our trusted and indispensable companion in life.

Glossary
device noun [C]: a machine or piece of equipment that does a particular thing
trigger verb [T]: to make a machine or piece of equipment start to work
Oyster Card® noun [C]: an electronic card used to pay for journeys on London transport
podcast noun [C]: a multimedia file, such as a radio programme or music video, that can be downloaded from the internet and played
indispensable adj: difficult or impossible to exist or do something without

Vocabulary & Listening

1 Work with a partner. Look at the compound nouns in the box. Match them to these patterns.

    1   adjective + noun   2   noun + noun

> card reader   cellular coverage   central heating   communication device
> data network   evening meal   grocery shopping   home entertainment system
> mobile phone   payment system   remote alert   remote control   security centre
> speech recognition   travel schedule   voice call   voicemail

2 Match these definitions to five of the compound nouns in Exercise 1.

    a) a system which is used to protect your home and alert you to any intruders
    b) a device you use to listen to music or radio shows, or to watch films or TV programmes
    c) a system for storing and retrieving messages left, for example, on your phone
    d) supper or dinner
    e) the act of going out to buy food

3 Work with your partner. Take turns to explain five of the remaining compound nouns in the box in Exercise 1. Do not use either component of the compound noun.

    A: You can programme it to keep your house warm.
    B: Central heating.

4 Work with your partner. Look at the photos for a new prototype mobile phone. What feature do you think each photo is showing?

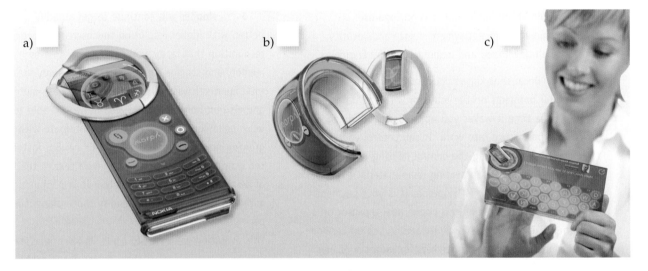

a)   b)   c)

5 🔊 2.20 Listen and number the photos in the order they are described. Were your guesses in Exercise 4 correct?

6 Complete the summaries of the main functions with the words in the box.

> earpiece   keyboard   keypad   music player   touch screen   wristband

    1   The _____ is the phone itself, whilst the silver hoop, which looks like it should be part of a pendant , is actually the _____ .
    2   … it can open out into a fairly traditional phone size and shape with all the familiar features: _____ , camera, _____ . The earpiece can be worn separately or clipped onto the phone and the phone brought up to your ear.
    3   … it also folds out even further and the transparent _____ converts into a full size qwerty _____ or an interactive map.

Listen again and check. What other features and functions are mentioned?

7 Compare your answers with your partner. Which innovation or innovations do you think would be most popular? Why?

Grammar

Complex sentences

Simple, one clause sentence
Your phone can re-programme the central heating.

Complex, multi-clause sentence
It can control your home, re-programming the central heating and alerting you if the home security system is activated.

1 Work with a partner. Look at this sentence from the article on page 69. How many clauses does it contain? Are the underlined clauses…
a) main clauses?   b) subordinate clauses?

Because it knows your travel schedule, / <u>it can check for problems on the roads …</u> / <u>and adjust the time it wakes you up accordingly,</u> / giving you the best route into work.

Break the sentence down into simple one-clause sentences.

a) It knows _____ .   c) It adjusts _____ .
b) It checks _____ .   d) It gives _____ .

2 Compare the original sentence in Exercise 1 with the shorter sentences. Circle any differences in the longer sentence and find examples of …

a) use of linkers.
b) dropping subject pronouns and auxiliaries.
c) use of participle clauses.

What is the advantage of the longer sentence?

3 Put the words in the correct order to form complex sentences.

a) when I can't find it. / when I call it, / or whistling, / where I've left it / I'd like to see a mobile that answers me / to let me know / maybe by beeping
b) giving me the best directions to get there /or text me, / and making sure I'm never late. / My ideal phone would call me, / to remind me about important appointments,
c) voice recognition is really important for me, / without my having to press any buttons. / Because I use my phone in the car, / I gave it / and my ideal phone would be able to follow the instructions

Underline the main clauses. Which feature appeals to you most? Why?

4 Write a multi-clause sentence explaining what you'd like from your mobile phone. Compare your sentences with the class.

5 Grammar *Extra* 7, Part 1 page 140. Read the explanations and do Exercise 1.

Pronunciation

1 Look at the words in the box. Say the words and add them to the table according to their pronunciation.

| ~~familiar~~   interactive   jewellery   prototype   recognition   technology   traditional   transparent |

A: □ ☐ □	B: ☐ □ □	C: □ ☐ □ □	D: □ □ ☐ □
/ə/   /ə/
familiar			

Look at the words again and write /ə/ above the unstressed syllables where appropriate.

2 🌐 2.21 Listen and check your answers to Exercise 1. Listen again and repeat the sentences.

Reading

1 Match the phenomena in the box to the definitions (*a–f*).

| force field   invisibility   precognition   telepathy   teleportation   time travel |

a) sending someone or something from one place to another instantaneously
b) a barrier, made of energy or charged particles, that protects a person, object or area from attack
c) the concept of being able to visit the past or the future
d) the state of an object or person that cannot be seen
e) the ability of people to be able to communicate directly with each other's minds
f) the ability to know what will happen in the future

Which of these phenomena do you think ...

• only exist in science fiction?   • will exist one day?   • already exist?

2 Read the article on page 73 about physicist Professor Michio Kaku's ideas and see if he agrees with your answers.

3 Work with a partner. Discuss these questions. Refer back to the article if necessary.

a) What is the difference between Class I, Class II and Class III impossibilities?
b) Which class does each of the phenomena in the box in Exercise 1 fit into?
c) Are you surprised by any of the Professor's predictions?
d) Do you think you will live to see any of these 'impossibilities' come into being?

4 Complete the words in the glossary with words or phrases from the article.

> **Glossary**
> a) *hierarchy* noun [C]: a series of things arranged according to their importance
> b) _____ adj: capable of being achieved
> c) _____ noun [C]: thousands of years
> d) _____ noun [C]: a device used in hospitals for creating images of internal organs
> e) _____ noun [C]: small metal or carbon objects through which electricity flows
> f) _____ noun [U]: a man-made material with unusual properties
> g) _____ noun [C]: hypothetical tunnel in space
> h) _____ adj: that cannot be imagined

5 Work in small groups. Look at the Class I impossibilities again. Which do you think would ...

a) be most useful to mankind? Why?
b) have the most dramatic impact on our way of life? Why?

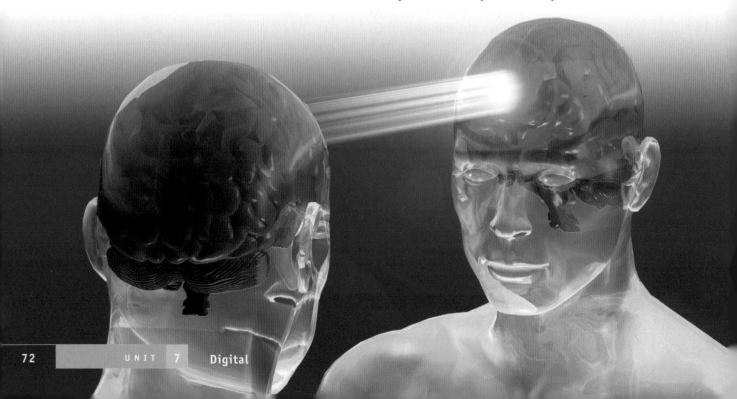

Teleportation and force fields possible within decades

says Professor Michio Kaku

Teleportation and force fields could become scientific realities within decades, and time travel will also be possible in the future, according to one of the world's leading physicists.

Michio Kaku is a highly-regarded physicist and one of the world's leading authorities
5 **on string theory (essentially an attempt to discover a 'theory of everything' combining all of the known physical forces).**

Professor Michio Kaku of City University in New York has studied a range of scientific 'impossibilities' and concluded that most will almost certainly be achieved as our knowledge expands. Applying the rule that unless something breaks a law of physics 'then
10 it's not only possible, it is sure to be built someday', Prof Kaku has established a hierarchy of 'impossibilities', separating those phenomena that are sure to remain science fiction from those which are likely to become reality at some point in the future. Teleportation, telepathy, force fields and invisibility are Class I impossibilities, meaning they are likely to be realisable within a few decades or at most a century. Class II impossibilities may take
15 centuries or millennia to perfect, while Class III impossibilities are truly impossible.

Class I

Teleportation is likely to be achieved through 'quantum entanglement', a property that allows connections to be formed – and information transmitted – between particles many miles apart. Applying the process to larger objects like people is just a scientific 'engineering problem', that is likely to be solved in time, Prof Kaku writes in his new
20 book, *Physics of the Impossible*. Similarly, telepathy will be made possible by improved MRI machines that can effectively read minds, and electrodes that can then pass the information into the brains of other humans. Invisibility will probably be achieved using a recently built 'metamaterial' capable of bending light rays, he argues. Alien life will most likely be discovered within decades as our ability to analyse the universe improves.

Class II

25 Time travel is a Class II impossibility because, while it need not break the laws of physics, science still has major knowledge gaps to cross to make it a reality, Prof Kaku believes. 'What makes them (Class II impossibilities) so difficult is that they generally require vast amounts of energy, and their underlying physics is not totally understood,' he writes in this week's *New Scientist* magazine. The research of Stephen Hawking, Albert Einstein and
30 the physicist Kip Thorne has shown that time travel is theoretically possible, but no-one has yet found a way to produce the energy necessary to keep a 'wormhole' open. 'This technology is only achievable for a civilisation significantly more advanced than ours,' Prof Kaku writes. Parallel universes and travelling faster than the speed of light are also Class II impossibilities, he argues.

Class III

35 The only two science fiction phenomena which Prof Kaku believes are truly impossible – Class III impossibilities – are perpetual motion machines and telling the future (precognition), both of which break the fundamental laws of modern physics. 'In considering what the future may hold, then, we should keep an open mind to Class I and Class II impossibilities,' Prof Kaku writes. 'What is unthinkable today might not be
40 forbidden in a few decades or centuries.'

Grammar

Speculating about the future

Modals

Teleportation **will** / **may** / **might** / **could** / **should** be possible within the next 50 years.

Adverbs with *will* and *won't*

Invisibility devices **will (almost) certainly** / **definitely** / **easily** / **probably** be perfected within our lifetime.

Invisibility devices **(almost) certainly** / **definitely** / **probably won't** be perfected within our lifetime.

Adverbs with *may*, *might* or *could*

Time travel **may possibly** / **(very) well** / **easily** be a reality for our grandchildren.

Phrases

It is **sure to** / **bound to** / **(highly) likely to** / **(highly) unlikely to** happen in the next ten years.

---

1 **Work with a partner. Look at the verbs and phrases in bold in the predictions (a–c). Match them to the three categories (1–3).**

a) Teleportation and force fields **could** become scientific realities within decades.
b) Time travel **will definitely** be possible in the future.
c) Telepathy, force fields and invisibility **are likely to** become reality at some point in the future.

1 certain (you are sure this will happen)
2 fairly confident (you are almost sure this will happen)
3 uncertain (you think it's possible but you aren't sure)

Make the sentences (a–c) negative. What do you notice about the position of *definitely* **in sentence** *b*?

Which predictions do you agree with? The ones in the original sentences or the ones in the negative sentences you just wrote?

2 **Look at the phrases in the box. Which could be used to replace**

a) *could?*   b) *will definitely?*   c) *are likely to?*

> could easily   is bound to   is sure to   may   may very well   might   should
> will almost certainly   will probably

3 **Rewrite the sentences using the words in brackets.**

a) Computers are sure to become more intelligent than humans one day. (definitely)
b) A cure for cancer could easily be within our reach in the next decade. (highly likely)
c) The Earth will eventually be destroyed by overpopulation. (sure)
d) It may well become possible to engineer food crops that grow in space. (we should)
e) Men could soon be incubating babies using artificial wombs. (will)
f) Low-lying countries like the Maldives and Mauritius may soon be under water as sea levels rise. (likely)
g) Organ donors are likely to become things of the past, thanks to advances in stem cell technology. (easily)
h) The next generation of computer whizzkids will be travelling to India and China to look for work. (bound)

Change the sentences you don't agree with. Compare your new sentences with your partner.

4 **Grammar *Extra* 7, Part 2** page 140. Read the explanations and do Exercise 2.

5 **Work in small groups. What will the world be like in twenty years' time? Make predictions about the following topics. Use a variety of forms from Exercise 1.**

- the kinds of jobs available to young people
- the size and shape of your home town
- new gadgets and appliances in your home
- the kind of food we'll be eating and the kinds of clothes we'll be wearing
- changes to the way people meet, date and fall in love

Share your ideas with the class. Whose predictions are the ...

- most conservative?   • most outlandish?

Listening & Vocabulary

1   **2.22 Listen to two people on a radio show discussing the gadget in the photo. Answer these questions.**

   a)   What exactly is the gadget? What can it do?
   b)   How do the two people feel about it?

2   **Listen again and make notes on …**

   a)   the arguments put forward in favour of the device.
   b)   the arguments put forward against the device.

3   **Look at the extracts (*a–f*) from the radio show in Exercise 1. Who is speaking each time: the man or the woman? What do the words and expressions in bold mean?**

   a)   … what trendy new gadget are you going to **wow** us with today … ?
   b)   … books have **gone digital**.
   c)   You've been reading too much **hype**!
   d)   … I really don't think any device, no matter how **slick** and quick and easy to use, can possibly replace a much-loved book …
   e)   Not to speak of the mountains and mountains of newspapers **trashed** every single day …
   f)   … you're definitely **sold on the idea** …

4   **Work in small groups. Discuss these questions.**

   a)   Who does the device appeal to? Would you like to try it? Why? / Why not?
   b)   Do you think it'll become as popular as MP3 players?
   c)   Do you think paper books will disappear from our bookshelves? Why? / Why not? If they did, how would that affect your everyday life and the world around you?

Speaking

1   **Work in small groups. Discuss these questions. Prepare to justify your choices to the rest of the class.**

   a)   What do you think were the top five scientific breakthroughs of the last century? Write them in order of importance.
   b)   What do you think will be the top five scientific breakthroughs of our present century? Again, write them in order of importance.

2   **Present your lists to the class. Then discuss these questions.**

   a)   Which of the past breakthroughs has had the biggest effect on your life and lifestyle?
   b)   Which could you happily live without?
   c)   Which future breakthrough will have the greatest impact on life as we know it?

Useful phrases

1 Work with a partner. Look at this list of decisions. Discuss what the future implications of each decision might be.

- getting a tattoo done
- choosing which university to go to
- leaving your job
- having plastic surgery
- dyeing your hair bright blue
- standing for election

Are you an impulsive decision-maker or do you usually consider all the implications beforehand? Give examples of decisions you've had to take recently to your partner.

2 🌐 2.23–2.26 Listen to the conversations (1–4). What decisions are the people talking about? Match the conversations to the pictures (a–d).

3 Look at the extracts (a–i). Which conversation (1, 2, 3 or 4) do they come from?

a) … it's **not such a big deal**, is it?
b) Once I've had a chance **to think it through properly** …
c) … once you've done it, **there's no going back** …
d) … I should stop **dithering** all the time …
e) … I obviously hadn't **thought through all the possible consequences**.
f) … I keep **going round and round in circles** …
g) … why don't you **sleep on it**?
h) … **it isn't the end of the world** …
i) … You know, **what's done is done** and all that.

Listen again and check.

4 Look at the useful phrases in bold in Exercise 3. Which useful phrases mean …

1 to consider something carefully?
2 not very important?
3 a decision cannot be reversed?
4 to waste time being unable to make a decision?
5 to postpone making a decision?

5 Work with your partner. Student A: look at page 131 and read about the situation. Student B: look at page 132 and read about the situation. You are going to take it in turns to help your partner discuss a difficult decision. Use the useful phrases in Exercise 3.

Vocabulary *Extra*

Acronyms and collocations

1 Work with a partner. Look at the acronyms and abbreviations in the box and answer the questions.

a) Do you know what the letters stand for?
b) Do you know how to say them in English?
c) Do you use the same acronyms in your language?

> 3G DVD GPS MP3 PC PDA PIN Wi-Fi

Match them to their definitions on the right.

2 Match the gadgets and systems in the box in Exercise 1 to the tasks (1–10). Some can be matched with more than one task.

1	connecting to the internet	6	watching a movie
2	checking your email	7	texting
3	instant messaging	8	playing games
4	downloading a podcast	9	finding your way around
5	paying for goods and services	10	keeping up with the news

How many of the gadgets or systems do you use at least once a day? What for?

3 Read the article and find out the difference between a *digital native* and a *digital immigrant*. Which are you? Compare your answer with your partner.

Digital technology has been part of everyday life for many years now, so logically there's a whole generation of individuals for whom concepts such as the internet and wireless technology are just humdrum, because they've never lived in a world where they didn't exist. These are the so-called **digital natives**, generally anyone born from 1980 onwards. **Digital immigrants** are their antithesis, being the folks born earlier who, either reluctantly or enthusiastically, have adapted to the digital world and incorporated its tools into their lives.

Observation of contrasts such as these has led to what is referred to as **digital nativism**, the idea that those who have grown up in the digital world have an advantage, not only in terms of using technology, but also because of enhanced cognitive skills developing from a multi-tasking, 'always-on' way of life.

4 Work with your partner. Look at the words in the box and answer these questions.

a) Which (if any) do not collocate with *digital*?
b) What does each collocation in a) mean?
c) What did we have before the digital version?

> banking broadcasting camera display entertainment friend
> images learning library life shopping sleep technology
> thermometer TV universe world

Look at the words in the box again. How many can you combine with *cyber*, *e-*, or *online*?

5 Tell your partner how you would update the technology you use in your everyday life if money were no object. What could you live without?

Acronyms

1 _____ , stands for personal computer.

2 _____ stands for global positioning system – most frequently used in satnavs (satellite navigation systems) in cars, coaches and taxis.

3 _____ stands for MPeg audio player 3, a method of reducing the size of a computer file that contains sound, especially music, so that it can be sent quickly by email or over the internet.

4 _____ stands for digital versatile disk.

5 The _____ stands for wireless, the _____ does not actually stand for anything but simply creates a catchy name with the rhyme. It echoes the use of hi-fi used for high fidelity music systems.

6 _____ stands for personal digital assistant – otherwise known as a palmtop computer.

7 _____ is a personal identification number, used most frequently with bank cards to get cash from an ATM machine.

8 _____ stands for third generation, a technology that gives you a high-speed connection to the internet, video and multimedia on your mobile phone.

---

cyber- /ˈsaɪbə(r)/ prefix relating to computers and the Internet: used with some adjectives and nouns

digital /ˈdɪdʒɪt(ə)l/ adj ★★
1 storing information such as sound or pictures as numbers or electronic signals: *a digital recording* ♦ *digital technology* → ANALOGUE 1
2 a digital clock or instrument shows information as a row of numbers: *a digital watch/barometer*
4 relating to or used in E-COMMERCE (=buying and selling goods on the Internet): *Digital music sales continue to rise.*

e- /iː/ prefix on or using the Internet: used with some nouns for making new words: *e-business* ♦ *e-learning* ♦ *e-finance*

online /ˈɒnlaɪn/ adj ★★
1 COMPUTING connected to or available through a computer or a computer NETWORK (=a group of connected computers), especially the Internet: *an online bookshop* ♦ *companies with an online ordering service*

8 Law

Grammar Paraphrasing. Using modals to talk about the past. Inversion after *neither / nor, so / such*
Vocabulary Legal vocabulary. Collocations with *law*. Formal vocabulary
Useful phrases Expressing surprise or disbelief

Reading

1 Read the article about some blunders made in real-life courtrooms. What did the lawyer really want to say?

> The following exchanges all occurred in American courts of law. The questions put to those in the witness stand are accompanied in some instances with the responses by the quick-witted – and usually exasperated – witnesses.
>
> ☞ *'And the youngest son, the 20-year-old, how old is he?'*
> ☞ *'Was it you or your younger brother who was killed in the war?'*
> ☞ *'You say the stairs went down to the basement?' 'Yes.' 'Did they also go up?'*
> ☞ *'Are you qualified to give a urine sample?' 'I have been since early childhood.'*
> ☞ *'All your responses must be oral, okay? What school did you go to?' 'Oral.'*
> ☞ *'Now, doctor, isn't it true that when a person dies in his sleep, he doesn't know about it until the next morning?'*
> ☞ *'Were you present when your picture was taken?'*

2 Work with a partner. Think of a good title for the article. Compare your title with the rest of the class. Whose title is the best?

Vocabulary

1 The words and phrases in the box are all connected to the theme of law. Work with your partner and categorise them under the headings in the table.

arson   attorney   award damages   barrister   community service
cross-examine   embezzlement   fine   libel   manslaughter
prison sentence   probation   return a verdict   solitary confinement   speeding
sue   suspended sentence   the accused   to sentence   weigh up the evidence

Crimes	Punishments	People	Legal processes

2 Complete these sentences with words and phrases from Exercise 1.
   a) Slander is when you say something about someone which isn't true. _____ is when you publish it, and that's when people generally take action.
   b) If a person is on trial the press must refer to them as _____ .
   c) You _____ someone to claim money from them if they have harmed you in some way.
   d) The jury has to listen to the case, _____ and then _____ .
   e) A '_____' is the person who represents you in court.
   f) _____ can be anything from teaching kids to play football to cutting the grass. Obviously, it's not paid.
   g) Once the prosecution has questioned a witness, the defence have the possibility to _____ him or her.

3 Choose another three words or phrases from Exercise 1 and write three sentences like the ones in Exercise 2. Give them to your partner to complete.

Listening & Grammar

Paraphrasing

Paraphrasing is expressing the same thing using different words.

A strange case was brought before the court.

The case which was brought before the court was **a strange one**.

It was **a strange case** that was brought before the court.

1   🌐 2.27–2.29 **Listen to three conversations about crimes. Which of the crimes in Vocabulary, Exercise 1 are the speakers talking about?**

2   **Look at the sentences. Which of the conversations (1–3) do they come from?**
a) The verdict we returned was unanimous – guilty.
b) That's a lesson I won't forget in a hurry.
c) The best person to ask is Fred MacIntyre.
d) It was fascinating, seeing how a court works.
e) It's been almost three weeks since they published the article.

3   **There is always more than one way of saying something. Paraphrase the sentences (a–e) in Exercise 2 starting with the words given.**

1   We …
2   I …
3   Fred MacIntyre …
4   Seeing …
5   They …

Compare your answers with a partner. Are there any differences between your sentences?

4   **Look at the picture and read about a court case in Wales. Rewrite each sentence twice, starting with the words given.**

a) A recent court case was held in Wales.
  1   It was …
  2   Wales …

b) In the witness box stood a Welshman who was accused of shoplifting.
  1   A Welshman …
  2   Accused …

c) He was defended by a Welsh lawyer.
  1   Defending …
  2   The lawyer …

d) Towards the end of the trial the lawyer asked the judge if he could speak to the jury in Welsh.
  1   'May I …
  2   The lawyer …

e) The judge agreed because he didn't wish to appear biased towards English.
  1   Not wishing …
  2   In order not to …

f) The jury returned a verdict of not guilty.
  1   A verdict …
  2   Not guilty …

g) The judge was puzzled as the defendant was obviously guilty.
  1   What puzzled the judge …
  2   The defendant …

h) The judge didn't speak Welsh so he hadn't understood what the lawyer had said.
  1   Not being able …
  2   As the judge …

The lawyer had said to the jury 'The prosecutor is English, the prosecution counsel is English, the judge is English. But the prisoner is Welsh, I'm Welsh and you're Welsh. Do your duty.'

5   **Use the sentences you have written in Exercise 4 to write an account of the court case for the 'News in Brief' section of a newspaper. Make any changes or additions that you think are necessary.**

Compare your story with the one on page 132. What differences are there?

6   Grammar *Extra* 8, Part 1 page 140. Read the explanations and do Exercise 1.

Speaking & Listening

1   Put the crimes in the box in order of seriousness. Compare your answers with a
    partner and decide what punishment should be given for each crime.

> graffiti   identity theft   inciting violence   internet piracy   littering
> pollution crimes   shoplifting   spreading computer viruses
> tax evasion   texting and driving

"I'm in for forgery."

2   🔊 2.30–2.35 Six people were asked what punishment they would give people guilty
    of some of the crimes in Exercise 1. Listen and answer these questions.

    a)   Which crime is each person (1–6) talking about?
    b)   What punishments do the speakers suggest?

3   Listen again and answer these questions.

    a)   Which speaker, in your opinion, has a more lenient approach?
    b)   Which punishment do you think would be the most effective?
    c)   Which speaker holds views most similar to your own?

4   Work in small groups. Discuss these questions.

    a)   Do you think punishment is an effective deterrent to crime? If yes, what sort of
         punishments do you think are most effective? If not, how would you prevent crime?
    b)   Can you think of any cases that have been in the press recently? What was the
         crime? What was the punishment?

5   Work with your partner. Read each case and discuss the questions that follow.

Case one

A driver swerves to avoid a little girl
crossing the road. The driver goes off
the road and injures a pedestrian.

a)   What is the driver guilty of, if anything?
b)   Who should pay for the pedestrian's
     medical expenses?
c)   Who should pay for the damage
     done to the car?

Case two

A footballer trips up an opponent
deliberately. The opponent breaks
a leg and is unable to play football
again. He sues the other footballer
for a lifetime of lost earnings.

a)   Should the footballer pay?
     Why? / Why not?

6   Turn to page 132 and read the rulings for the two cases. Do you agree with the judge?
    Do you think the rulings are fair? Do you think these rulings would be possible in
    your country?

Listening

1 **Work with a partner. Discuss these questions.**

a) Have you ever had anything stolen? If you have, what was it? Did you get it back? Were you insured? Was the thief caught?

b) If you haven't, what would cause you the most inconvenience if it was stolen? Why?

2 2.36 **Listen to Anne telling Tim about a time she had something stolen. Answer the questions.**

a) What was stolen?
b) Who stole it?
c) Was she insured against theft?
d) What happened in the end?

3 **Listen again. Are these statements true or false?**

▲ Anne and Tim

a) Anne's car was stolen by a band of car thieves.
b) Her insurance documents had disappeared from the car.
c) Her insurance didn't cover accidents after theft.
d) She had read the contract carefully before signing it.
e) She thought something fishy was going on with the insurers.
f) Her friend finds it difficult to believe the story.
g) Her insurance company paid up in the end.
h) She split up with her boyfriend.

4 **Work with your partner and answer these questions.**

a) What would you say were the three most important points in Anne's story?
b) What details do you think made the story more interesting or dramatic?
c) Do you think there's any truth in Anne's conspiracy theory?

Pronunciation

1 **Work with your partner. Look at the extracts from the conversation in Listening, Exercise 2. Are the underlined consonants pronounced or are they silent?**

a) a bran_d_ new car
b) they jus_t_ didn'_t_ wan_t_ to pay up
c) secon_d_-hand
d) wha_t_ did you do?

e) they sai_d_ it didn'_t_ matter
f) I was insure_d_ against theft
g) I ough_t_ to have done
h) you coul_d_ have aske_d_ a friend

2 2.37 **Listen and check your answers. Then match the two halves of the pronunciation rules.**

a) When a word ending in consonant + /t/ or /d/ is followed by a word starting with a consonant other than /t/ or /d/ …
b) When a word ending in /t/ or /d/ is followed by a word starting with a vowel …
c) When a word ending in /t/ or /d/ is followed by a word starting with /t/ or /d/ …

1   we only pronounce the /t/ or /d/ in the second word.
2   we often drop the /t/ or /d/.
3   the /t/ or /d/ is always pronounced.

Find examples for each rule in the extracts in Exercise 1.

3 **Look at these questions. Work with your partner and decide how the final /t/ and /d/ sounds are pronounced.**

a) Why is it important to read everything you sign?
b) When was the last time you signed an official document? Are you sure you read it all before signing?
c) Have you ever had to go to a police station? What for?

Discuss your answers to the questions.

Grammar

Using modal verbs to talk about the past

modal + infinitive
He **couldn't / wouldn't** drive.

modal + *have* + past participle
I **should / ought to have** checked.

They **might / could / may have taken** them.

They **wouldn't have dared.**

That **can't / must have happened.**

1 Work with a partner. Underline the modal verbs in the sentences (*a–j*). Match them to the functions (*1–3*) below.

a) The insurance company wouldn't pay up.
b) I couldn't believe it when I saw it!
c) You really should have read it before signing it.
d) I suppose with hindsight I ought to have done.
e) Couldn't you have asked your boyfriend to check it over for you?
f) They're standard forms so I thought I'd be all right.
g) They might have simply ticked the box themselves to save them having to pay out the equivalent of £8,000.
h) They wouldn't have dared do something like that, surely?
i) You must have been upset at the time.
j) They can't have just stolen the documents like that!

1 reporting speech or thought
2 speculating / making deductions
3 commenting / criticising

2 Look at these sentences. In two of them the modal verb is being used incorrectly. Correct the sentences which are wrong.

a) Anne mustn't have been very happy when she found her car had been stolen.
b) Her boyfriend must have worked hard to win the case.
c) The boys can't have known how to drive very well.
d) Anne can have made a mistake about the insurance company.

3 Rewrite these sentences using an appropriate modal verb phrase.

a) I believe they stole the documents.
b) It's possible that they changed the original contract.
c) You were a bit silly signing a contract without reading it first.
d) I think it's possible that you were wrong.
e) The garage owner had the opportunity to take the documents.
f) The boys' parents refused to take any responsibility for the boys' actions.

4 Work with your partner. Look at the photos (*1–3*). What do you think happened? Write sentences with *might have, could have, must have* or *can't have*.

Compare your answers with the rest of the class. Who came up with the most original explanation? And the most realistic?

5 Work with your partner. Think of something …

a) you should have done last weekend, but you didn't.
b) you could have done last night, but you didn't.

Tell your partner why you didn't do these things. Do you wish you had? How would things have been different if you had done these things?

6 Grammar *Extra* 8, Part 2 page 140. Read the explanations and do Exercise 2.

Vocabulary

1 Match the collocations with *law* (*a–i*) to their meanings (*1–9*).

a) against the law
b) a law unto herself
c) by law
d) in trouble with the law
e) law-abiding
f) my word is law
g) no-one is above the law
h) take the law into one's own hands
i) laying down the law

1 suspected of having committed a crime
2 she doesn't follow rules
3 we are all equal in the eyes of the law
4 take revenge without using the legal system
5 bossing people about
6 what I say must be respected
7 illegal
8 obeying and respecting the law
9 legally

2 Complete these sentences with the collocations in Exercise 1.

a) Policeman: You were doing 160 kilometres per hour.
   Prince: Yes, but do you know who I am?
   Policeman: Yes, but _____ .
b) After years as a _____ citizen, John decided to rob a bank and flee the country.
c) There was a constable here earlier. I think Mark's _____ again!
d) I was tempted to _____ and wring his neck.
e) 'Do this! Do that! Be back by 10!' My father was always _____ .
f) You can never tell what Ruth's going to do. She's _____ .
g) I'm the boss and _____ .
h) Most Europeans are required _____ to carry ID cards.
i) In some countries it's _____ to chew gum.

3 How many of the collocations in Exercise 2 are similar in your language? In English we talk about making and breaking laws as if they were material objects. Do you use the same metaphors in your language?

Speaking

1 Work in small groups. Look at these proposals for laws and discuss with your group which would affect you personally. Which of these laws do you think would make the world a better place?

a) No-one should work more than a 32-hour week.
b) Politicians should only be allowed to serve for a maximum of eight years and then be made to work in the real world.
c) All major cities should provide free Wi-Fi access in all public places.
d) Families should not be allowed to have more than one car.

2 Are there any laws in your country that you would like to change or introduce?

Reading

1 Read a real-life legal anecdote and decide which is the best title for it, *a, b* or *c*.

a) It pays to do your homework   b) Honesty is the best policy   c) Crime doesn't pay

A prominent Canberra barrister, Ian Byrne, appeared for an Italian who was seeking worker's compensation for an injury which he claimed he received at work.

5   It was alleged on his behalf that he had difficulty in moving, bending and even walking. He could not lift any heavy article, nor could he indulge in his hobbies of gardening and tennis. So severe was the injury that he was practically
10 housebound.

Prior to the trial the respondent insurance company engaged a loss assessor to follow the applicant Italian, photograph him when he was unaware, and report with a view to giving
15 evidence at the trial.

Eventually the application came on for hearing. Ian Byrne put his client (whom I shall call Bruno) in the witness box. He told his story of pain and suffering. He showed
20 that he had severe limitation of movement and could not bend or carry weights because of his unfortunate injury.

At the end of his examination Ian Byrne's opponent, a somewhat inexperienced Counsel,
25 sprang to his feet, enthusiasm gleaming in his eyes, and said 'Your Worship, I have here nearly 350 metres of film which shows this man Bruno bricklaying, lifting weights, concreting, vaulting a fence, working on his own house and even
30 running. I would ask leave of Your Worship to run the film before I begin to cross-examine the applicant.'

The film was then run. It showed the applicant running, making a brick wall, carrying
35 wheelbarrow loads of bricks, picking up slabs of concrete, climbing up and down ladders, digging in the garden and running behind a lawnmower. Further, it depicted the applicant's home and his small truck with his name clearly

40 marked on the door, and also showed him wearing a red cardigan which he was wearing in the witness box. At the finish of the screening the enthusiastic Counsel for the insurance company commenced his cross-examination.

45   'You saw that film?'

'Yes,' said Bruno.

'There is nothing wrong with your back at all, is there?'

'Yes,' said Bruno. 'Everything that I said
50 before is true. That was not me in the picture. That was my brother.'

'But,' exploded Counsel. 'That was your house, wasn't it?'

'Yeah,' said Bruno.

55   'And the same cardigan you've got on today is the one shown in the film?'

'Yeah,' said Bruno, 'I lent it to my brother. He is very good to me. He helps me round the house, he paints, he cements the paths, he
60 mows the lawns.'

'But,' said learned Counsel, 'His Worship has seen the film and he knows it is you.'

'It is not me. It's my brother.'

In due course Ian Byrne called the brother,
65 and when he walked into Court it was obvious to all that he was the identical twin of the applicant; and after a few questions it was obvious that he was the one in the film doing all the physical acts.

70   The angry Counsel for the defendant had the applicant recalled and said to him, 'You have tried to deceive the Court. You and your brother knew he was being photographed.'

'Yes,' said the applicant, 'we thought it was
75 funny.'

(From The Oxford Book of Legal Anecdotes)

Glossary
a) _____ verb [I]: showed
b) _____ adj: well-known
c) _____ conj: in addition
d) _____ verb [T]: to trick
e) _____ adv: before
f) _____ verb [I]: said
g) _____ adj: very bad
h) _____ verb [I]: asking for
i) _____ verb [I]: enjoy
j) _____ verb [T]: employed
k) _____ verb [I]: started
l) _____ phrase: later

2 Read the anecodote again and find formal words or phrases to complete the glossary.

3 Work with a partner. Complete the sentences.
a) Bruno was in court because …
b) He was photographed in order to …
c) The lawyer representing the insurance company didn't know …
d) When Bruno's brother walked into the courtroom the lawyer felt …
e) After the court case …

Compare your answers with the class.

Grammar

Inversion after neither / nor, so / such

They weren't hungry, **nor were they** thirsty.

He wasn't seeking recognition and **neither did he** appreciate it when it came.

So disgusted **was he** by the service, he decided to complain.

Such was the weather that even the most daring windsurfers stayed at home.

1 Look at these sentences. Which come from the anecdote on page 84?

a) He could not bend or move easily, **neither** could he walk without assistance.

b) He could not lift any heavy article, **nor** could he indulge in his hobbies of gardening and tennis.

c) **So severe** was the injury that he was practically housebound.

d) **Such** was the nature of his injury that he could no longer work.

2 Look at the sentences in Exercise 1 again. What do you notice about the position of the verb and the subject after *nor*, *neither*, *so* (+ adj) and *such*?

3 Rewrite the sentences in Exercise 1 using the words given.

a) He couldn't move, bend or …   c) His injury was …

b) He couldn't lift heavy objects or …   d) The nature of his injury meant …

Which form of the sentence is more formal? The one in Exercise 1 or the one you have just written?

4 Match the sentence beginnings (*a–d*) to the endings (*1–4*).

a) They didn't release the prisoner

b) He isn't young and he isn't good-looking either,

c) They were so happy with the results

d) There was such an outcry over the new proposals

1 but he is very popular.

2 that they have recommended the company to all their colleagues.

3 and they didn't let the family see him.

4 that the government is having to reconsider its plans.

5 Rewrite the sentences in Exercise 4 using inversion. Make any other changes that are necessary.

They didn't release the prisoner, nor did they let his family see him.

6 Work with a partner. Look again at the sentences you wrote in Exercise 5. Invent a context for each of the sentences.

Vocabulary

1 The anecdote on page 84 contains a lot of formal vocabulary. Use some of the formal words and phrases from the glossary on page 84 to complete the newspaper headlines. Make any changes necessary to the verbs.

a Mayor caught in bribe scandal ____ election

b ____ flooding hits southern France. Hundreds left homeless over night

c ____ politician loses driving licence in drink driving scandal

d Shock photos ____ banker as tropical playboy

e Number of refugees ____ asylum in Europe grows

f Internet users ____ by online scams

2 Work with your partner. Look at the headlines in Exercise 1 again. Which stories are about a law being broken? What do you think happened? Do you know of any other stories in the news at the moment that involve laws being passed or broken?

Useful phrases

1 🌐 2.38 **Listen to two colleagues discussing some news. Answer the questions.**

a) What's the news?   b) What's their reaction to the news?

2 **Listen again and complete the conversation with the useful phrases in the box.**

> Who'd have thought it   Did I hear you right   I never
> You don't expect me to believe that   you've got to be kidding   you never can tell

A: Have you heard about Bainbridge?

B: No, what?

A: He's been arrested!

B: What? (1) _____ ? Arrested? But he **wouldn't hurt a fly**. What are they charging him with?

A: Embezzlement.

B: Come on, (2) _____ . Embezzlement? Old Bainbridge? (3) _____ , do you?

A: Well, that's what they're saying. Seems it's been going on for some time as well. Hundreds of thousands they're talking about.

B: Well, (4) _____ ! (5) _____ ? But what did he do with all the cash? I mean, he hardly **lives in the lap of luxury**, does he?

A: Ah well, it seems **you can't judge a book by its cover**. Apparently he'd bought himself a house in the south of France ... and a sports car to go with it.

B: Wow! Well, it just goes to show, (6) _____ ...

A: Yeah, but it's always the quiet ones, isn't it? **Still waters run deep** and all that ...

What do the missing useful phrases have in common? Do you have the same expressions in your language?

Look at the four idiomatic expressions in bold. What do they mean?

3 🌐 2.39 **Listen to extracts from four conversations. What's the news in each one?**

4 **Listen again and make a note of the useful phrases used to express surprise or disbelief. Can you think of any other useful phrases used to show surprise or disbelief?**

5 **Work with a partner. Take it in turns to break one of the pieces of news from the list below. Respond using useful phrases from Exercises 2 and 3.**

a) You're quitting your job/studies and going to work for a charity in Africa.

b) Your grandad has just won a million on the lottery.

c) Your boss/teacher has published a best-selling novel under a pseudonym.

d) The government is going to prohibit the use of mobile phones on public transport.

e) Your boss is going to give everyone a massive pay rise and three weeks' holiday.

f) Your college has just announced they're going to abolish written exams.

News stories

1 Work with a partner. Student A: read article a. Student B: read article b. Tell each other about your article. Decide which one was published first.

a

TRAIN STATION SPREADS LOVE

A SIGN informing rail passengers kissing is welcome has been put up at a train station days after it was BANNED at another stop.

The notice at the entrance to High Wycombe station in Buckinghamshire shows a cartoon couple in a pink heart sharing an embrace and tells customers 'Kissing welcome here!'

Smooching

It was put up after news earlier this week that smooching had been outlawed at a passenger drop-off point at Warrington Bank Quay Station in Cheshire because it holds up commuters.

No-kissing signs appeared in the taxi rank, forcing couples to only use 'designated areas' for a quick kiss.

But in High Wycombe, passion is being encouraged by train operator Chiltern Railways who state on the poster: 'Unlike other train companies, we would never dream of banning kissing at our stations.'

b

Kissing banned at railway station

Couples have been banned from kissing at Warrington Bank Quay Station

No-kissing signs have appeared in the taxi rank at Warrington Bank Quay Station, forcing  lovers to use designated areas only.

The signs were erected after concerns that passionate embraces were causing delays for commuters with more passengers being attracted there.

Warrington Bank Quay is believed to be the first in the country to put up such signs.

The no-kissing signs are part of the £650,000 station refurbishment funded by Virgin Trains, Network Rail, the Northwest Regional Development Agency and the Department for Transport.

2 Work with your partner. Which article do you think was published in the popular press? And which in a quality newspaper? Look at the notes explaining the difference between the two and check your ideas.

Quality press

Newspapers which are generally aimed at the 'educated classes'. News is reported in a formal style. The items reported are generally of a serious nature and cover issues of national and global interest. Examples of British quality newspapers include *The Times*, *The Independent* and *The Guardian*.

POPULAR PRESS

Newspapers which contain bold headlines and large photographs. The writing style is informal; sentences are short and dramatic vocabulary, exclamation marks and capital letters are used to grab the reader's attention, especially in the headlines. British popular newspapers include *The Sun*, *The Mirror* and *The News of the World*.

3 Match the phrases (a–d) from the articles in Exercise 1 to the phrases (1–4) with similar meanings.

a) held up   1   a passionate embrace
b) a quick kiss   2   erected
c) put up   3   an intimate farewell
d) smooching   4   were causing delays

Can you find more examples of differences in style between the two stories?

4 Work with your partner. Look again at article b in Exercise 1. Rewrite it in the style of a popular newspaper. Use no more than 100 words.

9 Night

Grammar Concessive clauses and adverbials. Regrets and past conditionals
Vocabulary Times of day and night. Expressions with *night*
Useful phrases Making and responding to invitations

Reading & Speaking

1 Do the quiz and check your answers on page 132.

Are you a lark or an owl?

1 The alarm clock goes off and it's time to get up. What do you do?
  a) Leap out of bed, ready to start the day.
  b) Press the snooze button and doze for just a few more minutes.
  c) Put a pillow over your head and go back to sleep.

2 You have a day off tomorrow and no commitments. What time do you plan to get up?
  a) As early as possible, and definitely before 7.00.
  b) Probably sometime between 7.00 and 9.00.
  c) Why get up? You will sleep in as long as possible.

3 You have to take an important exam. When are your mental powers at their peak?
  a) First thing in the morning.
  b) Anytime between mid-morning and mid-afternoon.
  c) Last thing at night.

4 A friend has invited you for a work-out in the gym between 9.00 and 10.00 p.m. How will you perform?
  a) Very poorly. You will struggle to keep your eyes open.
  b) Reasonably, as long as you can go home and wind down straight afterwards.
  c) Very well. And then you'll invite your friend to go out on the town – the night is still young!

5 When is your normal bedtime?
  a) You're usually tucked up and fast asleep by 10.00 at the latest.
  b) You generally call it a night around 11.00.
  c) You're still up and wide awake well after midnight.

6 You've been invited to an all-night party. How do you respond?
  a) Sounds like your idea of hell. You'd much rather have an early night and get some beauty sleep.
  b) You go along and stay until about one or two in the morning.
  c) You arrive at midnight and are still going strong as the sun comes up.

2 Work with a partner. Discuss the meaning of the highlighted words and phrases. Check in a dictionary if necessary.

3 Compare your answers to the quiz in Exercise 1 in small groups. How does your energy pattern compare and fit in with those of your friends or family members?

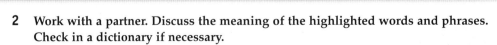

Vocabulary & Speaking

1   Work with a partner. Put these times of day in chronological order.

> at dawn   at dusk   mid-afternoon   mid-morning   at midday
> at midnight   at sunrise   at sunset

2   When are these times? Discuss with your partner. Which phrases are literary in style?

> at noon   at twilight   at daybreak   at nightfall   in the middle of the night
> at the crack of dawn   in the wee small hours   first thing in the morning
> last thing at night

3   Work with your partner. Tell each other about the following:
   • your favourite time of day
   • when you usually feel most and least alert
   • what you generally do first thing in the morning and last thing at night
   • the last time you got up at the crack of dawn
   • being woken up in the wee small hours / in the middle of the night

Listening

1   Work in small groups. Discuss what the words and phrases in the box mean.

> body clock   circadian rhythms   jet lag   nocturnal and diurnal creatures

 3.01 Listen to a radio show in which these words are discussed, and check if you are right.

2   Read the sentences and decide if they are true or false, according to the radio programme in Exercise 1.
   a)   The normal circadian rhythm is twenty-four hours in length.
   b)   Nocturnal animals do not live according to circadian rhythms.
   c)   A body clock is responsive to changes in the environment.
   d)   A body clock changes our feelings of tiredness and wakefulness.
   e)   People are born with individual differences in their circadian rhythms.
   f)   Young children need more sleep than adolescents.
   g)   Older adults tend to get up later than younger adults.
   h)   Jet lag is caused by lack of sleep.

Listen again and check your answers. Is there anything that surprises you about what the scientist said?

Reading

1 **Read the profiles from a sleep website. Are you like any of these people?**

How well do you sleep?

▶ Sleep-related problems
▶ Insomnia
▶ Apnea

A As a journalist I tend to work long hours and so I rarely get more than five or six hours sleep a night. I'm often up at the
5 crack of dawn to chase breaking news, and then working late into the night keeping the blog up to date. I'm an energetic sort of person most of the time and late
10 nights don't normally bother me. That said, I find the only way I can function properly is by taking regular power naps throughout the day. I usually drop off straight away – even so, I can generally only get away with fifteen or twenty minutes
15 at a time before the phone rings and I have to go off on some assignment. Napping just takes the edge off the tiredness and means I'm less groggy and more alert, which is absolutely essential in my line of work.

▲ Pete

B I have real problems getting
20 to sleep at night. I do all the things you're supposed to do – wind down slowly, only go to bed when you're tired, etc., etc. But try as I might to get off to sleep,
25 I'll invariably be tossing and turning for ages, then getting up to busy myself with various chores to try and tire myself out.

▲ Penny

And then, when I do eventually drop off, I tend to
30 wake up at the slightest sound and lie awake for hours worrying. I've tried all sorts of remedies – prescription drugs and over-the-counter medication – but even though the sleeping pills have some effect, I'm wary of becoming too reliant on them as I don't know what the long-term
35 effects are. Lack of sleep is also making me incredibly run down. I'm really at my wits' end – I just can't remember when I last got a decent night's sleep.

C I'm the annoying sort of person who sleeps like a log. I'm
40 normally so exhausted by the end of the day that I never have any problems dropping off – in fact, I generally go out like a light as soon as my head hits the
45 pillow. I'll sleep anywhere – in a hotel, on a plane, on a friend's mattress, on a sofa, even – and I

▲ Amy

can sleep through a thunderstorm, a wild party in the next door house, anything. All the same, I need a good
50 eight hours' sleep to recharge my batteries otherwise I tend to spend the next day yawning and I have even been known to snap at people. Normally I wake up feeling refreshed and revitalised.

D Apparently I snore heavily
55 (I've never actually heard myself so I wouldn't know). It drives my wife mad, particularly as she's a light sleeper herself. It causes quite a bit of friction because
60 when I snore my wife prods or kicks me to wake me up and then I can't get off to sleep again. Or she'll move into the spare room

▲ Joe

and then she'll complain the next day that she didn't
65 get a wink of sleep. I've tried sleeping on my side and using a raised pillow but in spite of my efforts, none of it has done any good. My wife keeps going on at me to lose weight – I'm not convinced it will make any difference, though. Much as I'd like to stop snoring, I
70 tend to think if you're a snorer, that's just the way you are and you're never going to change.

Glossary

a) _____ verb [I]: relax to conserve energy
b) _____ verb phrase [I]: had a sleepless night
c) _____ noun [C]: siestas
d) _____ adj: wide awake
e) _____ verb [I]: sleeps soundly
f) _____ noun [C]: person who wakes up regularly
g) _____ verb [I]: go to sleep
h) _____ verb [I]: fall asleep immediately
i) _____ adj: drowsy
j) _____ verb [I]: relax

2 **Read the profiles again. Which person or people (Pete, Penny, Amy or Joe) …**

a) can only sleep for short stretches?
b) mentions health problems as a result of sleep deprivation?
c) can get short-tempered if they don't get enough sleep?
d) experiences relationship difficulties because of their sleep habits?
e) needs to sleep to cope with work commitments?
f) have/has experimented with different ways of solving their sleep problems?
g) wants to change their sleeping habits?
h) normally have/has no problems sleeping?

3 **Complete the glossary with the highlighted words and phrases from the profiles.**

4 **Work with a partner. What advice would you give these sleepers? Compare in small groups.**

Grammar

Concessive clauses and adverbials

Even though / Although I tried hard, I couldn't get to sleep.

Despite / In spite of my efforts, / Much as I'd like to, I couldn't get to sleep.

I tried hard. **Even so / Yet / However / That said, I couldn't get to sleep.**

I tried hard. I couldn't get to sleep, **though. / All the same,** I couldn't get to sleep.

Try as I might, I couldn't get to sleep.

Strange as it may seem, I couldn't get to sleep.

---

1 Read the sentences (*a–d*). Are they the same or different in meaning?

  a) I slept for ten hours, **yet** I still felt tired the next day.
  b) **Although** I slept for ten hours, I still felt tired the next day.
  c) I slept for ten hours. **However**, I still felt tired the next day.
  d) **Despite** sleeping for ten hours, I still felt tired the next day.

2 Underline eight concessive clauses or adverbials in the profiles on page 90 that express a similar contrast. Which two are more formal in register?

3 Rewrite the sentences using the words in brackets.

  a) Despite going to bed early, I was still groggy the next day. (Even though)
  b) I don't usually oversleep. All the same, I prefer to set the alarm clock. (though)
  c) The bed was very uncomfortable. Nevertheless, I slept like a log. (In spite of)
  d) I'd like to get by on six hours a night but I can't manage on less than seven. (Much as)
  e) Although I'm normally an early riser, I like to have a lie-in on Sundays. (That said)

4 Reorder the underlined words to make concessive clauses.

  a) <u>was / as / exhausted / I</u>, I couldn't get off to sleep.
  b) <u>may / strange / seem / it / as</u>, I can't get by on less than ten hours sleep a night.
  c) <u>it / be / as / may / hard</u>, we need to get up at the crack of dawn tomorrow.
  d) <u>might / try / I / as</u>, I couldn't wake him up.

5 Read the posting to a website. What is the person's problem?

Does anyone have any suggestions as to what to do about persistently noisy neighbours? The people in the flat above mine have their music on at full blast till the small hours most nights and it's driving me mad. (1) _____ my polite requests to them to turn the music down, so far they haven't taken a blind bit of notice. I've tried using ear plugs, I've tried banging on the wall – all to no avail, (2) _____ . My boyfriend thinks I'm being unreasonable. (3) _____ , I do think everyone is entitled to a good night's sleep! Patient (4) _____ I am normally, I'm at my wits' end – can anyone help?

Complete the posting with appropriate words or phrases.

Have you ever been in a similar situation? If so, what did you do? What advice would you give to the writer?

6 Work with a partner. Write a similar posting for one of these problems. Use at least three different concessive clauses.

- I keep oversleeping in the morning.
- I'm always drowsy in the afternoon.
- I always wake up at five in the morning and can't get back to sleep.

Show your posting to another pair. What advice do they have?

7 Grammar *Extra* 9, Part 1 page 142. Read the explanations and do Exercise 1.

▲ James

▲ Rosie

▲ Phillip

Listening & Pronunciation

1 🌐 **3.02–3.04 Listen to three friends, James, Rosie and Phillip, describing experiences of staying up all night. For each person, make notes on the following questions.**

a) Where did the experience take place?
b) What did the person do during the night?
c) Did they enjoy the experience? Why? / Why not?

Which of the nights would you *most* and *least* like to have shared? Why? Discuss with a partner.

2 🌐 **3.05 Listen to some extracts from the experiences in Exercise 1 and complete the sentences with adverbs. Sometimes there is more than one adverb in a sentence.**

a) I had this one unforgettable night up in the mountains – in Nepal it was _____ .
b) The hours just passed, you know, just conversing about the sky _____ .
c) It's _____ manic. The whole experience is crazy.
d) So there's _____ no point in going to bed because everyone's up anyway.
e) It was _____ worth it.
f) _____ there were about, I think about twenty people in front of us.
g) We were going to go and see this show – _____ our hero.
h) We slept out the whole night and spent the whole night there and didn't even get to see the show, _____ .
i) We were _____ upset.

3 Which adverbs in the sentences (*a–i*) in Exercise 2 …

1 add emphasis?
2 express regret?
3 suggest that something is obvious?
4 express surprise?
5 emphasise the main point, not specific details?
6 stress exact details ?
7 add an afterthought?

4 How many syllables are there in each of the adverbs in the box? Practise saying each of the words.

> actually   basically   especially   eventually   generally   ironically   literally
> particularly   practically   usually

🌐 **3.06 Listen and check.**

5 Write true sentences about your experience of parties, concerts or festivals using some of the adverbs in Exercise 4. Practise reading them aloud to your partner.

Speaking: anecdote

You are going to tell your partner about a time you stayed up late or all night, for example: working a night shift, travelling overnight, attending a party or festival, writing an essay or revising for an exam.

- Ask yourself the questions below.
- Think about *what* to say and *how* to say it.
- Tell your partner about the night.

a) Where and when did the experience take place?
b) Why did you stay up all night?
c) Who were you with?
d) What happened during the night?
e) What did you see, hear or do?
f) What feelings did you experience?
g) How did you feel at the end of the night?
h) Was it a worthwhile experience?

Speaking

1 **Match the two halves of the proverbs about night.**

a) Wait for the night
b) If you befriend a mosquito,
c) No matter how long the night,
d) Red sky at night, shepherds' delight;
e) If in doubt about what is right,
f) He who does not lose his way by night,
g) At night all cats
h) The road to Heaven is well signposted,
i) The night hides a world,

1 will not lose his way by day. (Nigerian)
2 but reveals a universe. (Iranian)
3 are grey. (Dutch)
4 but it is badly lit at night. (Irish)
5 before saying that the day has been beautiful. (Bengali)
6 it will still attack you at night. (African)
7 red sky in the morning, shepherds' warning. (English)
8 consult your pillow overnight. (Mexican)
9 the dawn will break. (African)

2 **Work with a partner. Discuss these questions about the proverbs in Exercise 1.**

a) Are there any proverbs you don't understand?
b) Which do you like best, and why?
c) Do you have similar sayings in your own country?

3 **Work with your partner. Complete the sentences to create proverbs of your own.**

a) No matter how long the journey, …
b) However good the teacher, …
c) Wherever you live, …
d) Even if …

Compare with another pair. Which proverbs do you like best?

Vocabulary

1 **Work with your partner. Complete the sentences with words from the box.**

> *nightcap   hen   long   overnight   stag   town*

a) I'm absolutely exhausted. I worked *all night* _____ yesterday.
b) 'Would you like *a* _____ before you go home?' 'I'd better not, I'm driving.'
c) We had *a night on the* _____ last night. We went clubbing and didn't get back till the small hours.
d) I'm going to get the _____ *sleeper* to Venice so I'll arrive first thing in the morning.
e) Magda and Peter are getting married next week. Magda's having her _____ *night* at Luigi's Night Club and Peter is going with some friends to Dublin at the weekend for his _____ *night*.

Discuss the meaning of the words and expressions in italics with your partner.

2 **Work with your partner. Choose one of these questions to discuss.**

a) Imagine you've just passed your final exams. Where would you go to have a night on the town? Who would you invite? What would you do?
b) Imagine your best friend is getting married and has asked you to organise his/her stag/hen night. What would you do?

Northern Lights

The aurora borealis is a fickle phenomenon. A week can pass without a flicker ... then bang! The Northern Lights come on like a celestial lava lamp. In the far north of Sweden, Nigel Tisdall is rewarded for his patience.

1) _____ In days of yore, when the fur-wrapped peoples of the Arctic looked up at the celestial disco we now know as the aurora borealis, they would see warriors with burning swords, shimmering shoals of fish and the spirits of the dead playing football with a walrus skull. Our modern eyes can't help but see more contemporary likenesses, yet this sense of wonder binds us through time like a heartbeat. The fleeting light show is so magnificent that my mind goes into overdrive as I try to burn the fast-changing shapes into my memory bank for ever. At the same time, a baser feeling is rising. Yes! I've done one of those thousand things we're all supposed to do before we die, as if life were just a shopping list of sensational experiences to be ticked off.

2) _____ Yet true travellers would have it no other way. Like going on safari, whale watching or fly-fishing, seeing the aurora is a beguiling marriage of sheer luck and the effort you make to be in the best place at the optimum time. The annoying thing is that the aurora is above us all the time, day in, day out – and in duplicate. Imagine a beautifully-coloured halo, ebbing and flowing in a circle above Alaska, northern Canada, Iceland, Arctic Scandinavia and the north coast of Siberia – with a mirror image, the aurora australis, looping over Antarctica.

3) _____ This means travellers have to be especially smart in their search for the clear, dark skies that are ideal conditions for a sensational sighting. Travelling close to the Arctic Circle in the winter months holds the key, preferably on dates when there isn't a full moon (a rival light source) and to locations beneath the auroral oval that are not only far from light pollution but also blessed with good weather. You can try to narrow the odds by looking for a 'sweet spot', which is why I am tramping the pristine snows of Abisko, 60 miles west of Kiruna in the far north of Sweden. Abisko is brazenly claimed to be 'the best place in the world' to see the aurora borealis. All this is rather galling as I sit in the Abisko Turiststation, nursing a frighteningly-priced beer and thinking, 'Okay, night sky ... bring it on.' Unfortunately there is a mighty blizzard outside. Yes, I do appreciate that this is the Arctic in winter – and, being British, I know all about meteorological disappointment. We have all lit the barbecue just seconds before the first raindrops fall ...

4) _____ Our arrival is timed for 10.30p.m.: 'magnetic midnight', when the local auroral activity should be at its most intense. Except it isn't. Everyone lolls around in the café as if some divine flight has been delayed – but as the small print says, sightings are not guaranteed. Our guide has a rule of thumb that if you stay at Abisko for three nights, you are certain to see the aurora (though he is offering no refunds) – but of course, silly time-poor me is trying to do it in two.

5) _____ It is far better to head north for an Arctic holiday packed full of adventures; then, should the Northern light bulbs also flash, well, that's a bonus. And so it is that, just when I am not desperately seeking them, the Northern Lights come to me. My sighting happens while we are out on a night snowmobile safari, and everyone skidoos to a halt as the heavens erupt in what looks like the prelude to a visitation by UFOs. Marching armies in shining armour, apocalyptic bonfires, bolts of silk in rainbow hues ... It is a brief encounter none of us will forget, sparking feelings of humility and euphoria. Yes, I know it is –5°C and we have to spend the night kipping on a block of ice but really, I don't care, because – hallelujah! – I have seen the Northern Lights. That leaves only another 999 things to do.

Glossary

a) _____ verb [I]: changing often and unexpectedly
b) _____ adj: gently shining and shaking
c) _____ adj: very brief
d) _____ adj: heavenly
e) _____ adj: annoying and unfair
f) _____ adj: wild and terrible, like the end of the world
g) _____ noun [C]: a simple, practical rule
h) _____ adj: perfectly clean
i) _____ adj: attractive and interesting

Reading

1 Read the traveller's account of a trip to Sweden to see the Northern Lights on page 94. Was the trip worthwhile? Why? / Why not?

2 Match the first lines (*a–e*) to the paragraphs (*1–5*) in the account.

a) The strength of auroral activity runs in 11-year cycles, and it is just our luck that we are currently in a trough.

b) It is, of course, courting disaster to set so much store by a natural phenomenon that is notoriously elusive.

c) There is a lesson here for all aurora chasers, and that is not to get fixated with this single goal.

d) Heavens above! The night sky is singing with colour.

e) The next night I take the chairlift up to the Aurora Sky Station.

3 Find evidence from the account to support these statements about the Northern Lights.

a) People's interpretation of them has changed over the years.

b) There are two kinds of aurora in the world.

c) It is not easy to see the Northern Lights.

d) Precise conditions are needed to be able to see them.

e) The experience of seeing them is awe-inspiring.

4 Complete the glossary with words and phrases from the account.

5 Would you like to go on a holiday like this? Why? / Why not? What three experiences would you like to have before you die?

Listening & Grammar

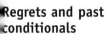

Regrets and past conditionals

I **wish I'd** / **If only I could have gone** for longer.

I**'d have liked** to go for longer.

I **regret** (not) going in the low season.

If I had stayed for longer, I**'d** / **could** / **might** have seen the sunrise.

If it hadn't been for the rain, I**'d have seen** the sunrise.

▲ Kieran

1 ◉ 3.07 Listen to Kieran talking about a trip to Machu Picchu. What was disappointing and rewarding about the experience?

2 ◉ 3.08 Listen again to extracts from the recording. Complete Kieran's sentences.

a) I _____ there in the low season …

b) I think if _____ those altitude pills, I _____ okay.

c) It's a pity _____ for longer.

3 Read the sentences about Kieran's regrets and underline the correct alternatives.

a) I wish I**'d gone** / **went** / **could have gone** in the low season.

b) I regret **taking** / **having taken** / **not taking** / **not having taken** altitude pills.

c) If you **came** / **'d come** / **would have come** with me, it **'d been** / **'d have been** / **might have been** more fun.

d) **If I'd been** / **Had I been** / **If I was** feeling well, I **'d** / **could** / **should** have got up to see the sunrise.

e) **But for** / **Except for** / **If it hadn't been for** the rain I **'d have had** / **'d** / **'d have** some photos now.

4 Rewrite the sentences, using the words in brackets.

a) I'm sorry I didn't go in the low season. (I wish)

b) What a pity I wasn't able to go with you. (I regret)

c) I didn't see the sunrise, which was a shame. (I would have liked)

d) It was packed with tourists, so I didn't get a feel for the atmosphere. (If)

e) If only I had taken some good photos! (It's a pity)

f) My altitude sickness meant I couldn't get up to see the sunrise. (But for)

g) It was a great experience, though – that's why I want to go again. (If)

5 Tell your partner about a holiday you have been on. Use the language in Exercises 3 and 4 to express things you regret, or things you were glad about.

6 **Grammar Extra 9, Part 2** page 142. Read the explanations and do the Exercise 2.

Useful phrases

1 Read the exchanges (*1–4*). What is the problem with B's responses?

1 A: What are you up to tomorrow night?
   B: Nothing.
2 A: Are you doing anything tonight?
   B: No.
3 A: Do you fancy coming to a jazz concert tonight?
   B: I don't like jazz.
4 A: I was wondering if you'd like to come round for a bite to eat this evening?
   B: Yes.

2 How could you improve the exchanges in Exercise 1 using the useful phrases (*a–f*)?

a) To be honest, I'm not very keen on …
b) No, what did you have in mind?
c) That sounds great!
d) I'd love to!
e) Nothing special – why do you ask?
f) That's really kind of you, but …

3 🌐 3.09 Listen to the exchanges and compare your answers with the recording. Then practise the exchanges with a partner.

4 Look at the responses to the invitation. Which one is more formal than the others?

I'm having some friends over for a barbecue on Sunday afternoon. You're very welcome to join us.

a) Thanks very much for asking, but I'm afraid I can't make Sunday afternoon.
b) I'd really like to, but I've got something on then. I'm going to my parents'.
c) I really appreciate the invitation, but unfortunately I have a prior engagement.
d) I'm tied up on Sunday, I'm afraid. Thanks anyway.

5 Complete the conversations (*1–3*) with useful phrases.

1 A: Hi, what _____ tonight?
   B: Actually, I'm up to _____ with work tonight.
   A: Oh, that's _____ . I just thought we might go out for a drink to celebrate the end of term.
   B: That _____ brilliant, but I'm afraid I've got to hand in a report first thing tomorrow morning. Thanks _____ .
   A: Never mind. Some _____ perhaps.

2 A: How about _____ sometime over the weekend to discuss the holiday?
   B: _____ good. My place or yours?
   A: You could come round here if you like. Would eleven on Sunday be _____ ?
   B: _____ , could we make it a bit later? Say, twelve-ish?
   A: That'd be _____ . See you around twelve on Sunday then.
   B: Cool. See you _____ .

3 A: We're having a party on Friday night, from about eight onwards. Do you _____ ?
   B: That'd be fab. Thanks! _____ bring anything?
   A: No, that's fine. Just yourself! And _____ a friend if you like.
   B: Great, see you on Friday then.
   A: Yeah, look _____ it.

🌐 3.10 Listen and compare your answers with the recordings. Then practise reading the conversations with your partner.

6 Work with your partner. Invite each other to do something tomorrow, on Friday evening and at the weekend. Accept or give an excuse if you turn down the invitation. If you accept, make clear arrangements to meet.

Vocabulary *Extra*

Phrasal verbs

1 Underline the verb and circle the particle in the phrasal verbs in the sentences (a–e). What is the general meaning of *up* and *off* in the phrasal verbs?

a) You're still up and wide awake well after midnight.

b) What time do you plan to get up?

c) Can you remember a time when you stayed up all night?

d) I am up and down all night until I eventually feel tired enough to drop off.

e) I generally start nodding off at about nine o'clock.

2 Work with a partner. Match the meaning of the phrasal verbs with *up* (a–e) in Exercise 1 to the dictionary extracts (1–5).

a) Do you always remember to **do up** your seatbelt before you travel by car?

b) Do you **tear up** letters when you've finished reading them?

c) Do you usually **tidy up** your bedroom before you leave the house?

d) When did you last **go up** to someone in the street to ask a question?

e) Do people ever ask you to **speak up** because they can't hear you?

Ask your partner the questions.

3 Find three more phrasal verbs in the dictionary extracts on the right and write sentences that are true for you. Compare your ideas with your partner.

4 Choose the correct particle from the box for each pair of sentences.

down	in	off	on	out

a) 1 If I run _____ of money, I usually ask a friend to lend me some.
   2 A lot of species of plants and animals are dying _____ in my country because of pollution.

b) 1 I tend to keep _____ working even if I feel tired.
   2 I'd like to stay _____ at school next year to study more English.

c) 1 Reading a bad review tends to put me _____ films.
   2 I used to like chocolate but now I've gone _____ it.

d) 1 I generally note _____ English words when I come across them.
   2 If I don't write things _____ on a list I tend to forget to do them.

e) 1 I like to lie _____ on Sunday mornings.
   2 Sometimes I sleep _____ till midday if I've had a late night the day before.

Are any of the sentences true for you? Discuss with your partner.

5 Work with your partner. Complete the sentences with the prepositions in the box.

up (x 2)	down	on	out

a) Can you cut _____ the cake so that there's a piece for everyone?

b) I'm afraid all the tickets for tonight's concert have sold _____ .

c) Can you put my name _____ for the trip to the museum on Sunday?

d) At the end of the boat trip, we tied _____ the boat and got out.

e) If you want to know what happens in the rest of the story, you'll have to read _____ to the end of the book.

6 Check your own dictionary. Look up meanings of one of the particles *in, on, off, out* or *down*. Choose three uses with different verbs to learn.

up¹ /ʌp/ adj, adv, preposition ★★★
1 moving near to sb/sth moving near to someone or something and then stopping: *One of the salespeople came up and asked if she could help.* ♦ **+to** *Two women ran up to us, shouting in Spanish.* ♦ *Just go up to him and say hello.*

2 increased in amount/level 6a. at or towards an increased number, level, or amount: *Total new car sales were up £3 million over last year.* ♦ **go up** *Fuel prices went up by 3 per cent.* ♦ **be up on sth** *Profits for August were slightly up on July's figure.* **6b.** becoming louder, stronger, or more active: *Billy, will you turn the volume on the TV up – I can't hear anything.* ♦ *Competition between the production groups is hotting up rapidly.*

3 in or into smaller parts divided or broken into small pieces or equal parts: *The prize money will be divided up among the team members.* ♦ *Divorce settlements often involve property that can't be split up easily.*

4 completely completely done or used so that there is nothing left: *Eat up all your dinner.* ♦ *I think it was selfish of me, using up all her free time like that.* ♦ *The stream dries up in summer.*

5 fastened fastened or closed completely: *She kept Albert's letters in a bundle tied up with ribbon.* ♦ *Did you lock the house up before you left?*

Review C

► Grammar *Extra* pages 140–143

Grammar

1 Rewrite these complex sentences as simple single-clause sentences. The number of single-clause sentences is in the brackets.

a) Having had a particularly stressful day at work, I got home, switched on the TV and promptly fell asleep! (4)

b) I really enjoy taking time out, maybe buying a newspaper and finding a quiet café where I can order a coffee and spend an hour or so quietly catching up with the news. (5)

c) After a long day of intensive study, I always try to do some sport in order to clear my mind and renew my energy levels. (3)

d) Going to the cinema really helps me unwind, taking my mind off my problems and letting me escape into another world for at least a couple of hours. (3)

e) Some people say that shopping is relaxing, but I just think it's another source of stress, often leading to over-spending, which in turn can cause financial problems. (4)

Write a complex sentence explaining what you like to do to relax. Show it to a partner.

2 Work with your partner. Look at the ideas below. Which do you think are a) highly likely to happen in the next ten years? b) may happen sometime but you don't know when? c) will probably never happen?

a) Your country's leader will be a woman.
b) Your home town will have doubled in size.
c) Cars will have become a luxury that only a few people can afford.
d) Chinese will have taken over as the world's number one most studied foreign language.
e) Water will have become the most precious commodity on Earth.

Write three or four sentences summarising your discussion. Use the words and expressions in the box.

> might well   could easily   bound to
> probably won't   almost certainly will   should
> to our minds   unlikely that

3 Write a second sentence that means the same as the first, using the words given.

a) A man contacted me.
   I _____ .

b) Strangely, he refused to tell me his name.
   The strange thing _____ .

c) He said he was an old friend of the family and that he had a message for me.
   What he did tell me _____ .

d) The message was from my father, who had disappeared five years ago.
   It was _____ .

e) He asked me to meet him outside the church at 6 o'clock so he could give it to me personally.
   In order to _____ .

f) I arrived at the church as the clock struck six.
   As _____ .

g) There was a dark figure standing in the doorway.
   A dark figure _____ .

h) The dark figure was my father!
   My _____ !

Work with your partner. Discuss what happened next. Write the next three sentences of the story.

4 Work with your partner. Read the story in Exercise 3 again. What do you think had happened to the father? Complete these sentences with some of your theories.

a) He must have …
b) He may well have …
c) He can't have …
d) He should have …
e) He might not have …
f) He wouldn't have …

5 Complete the sentences with words or expressions from the box.

> Despite having   Even so   even though   However
> in spite of   Try as I might

a) I could still hear the noise of the traffic outside, _____ I was wearing earplugs.

b) _____ had less than five hours sleep, I felt fresh and ready to start the day.

c) _____ , I just couldn't get to sleep.

d) I usually like to get to bed quite early. _____ , last night was an exception.

e) I managed to get a good night's sleep. _____ , all the noise.

f) I had a really good night's sleep. _____ I still couldn't get up when the alarm rang!

Which sentence best describes how you slept last night?

6 Write three things you wish you'd done yesterday. Write a sentence explaining how your day would have been different if you'd done them.

> I wish I'd got up earlier this morning. I could have finished all my work in the morning and then spent the afternoon doing some sport.

Compare your sentences with your partner.

Vocabulary

1 Match a word from column *A* to a word in column *B* to form compound nouns.

A	B
cellular	coverage
ear	pad
key	piece
music	player
touch	recognition
voice	screen

Match the compound nouns to the objects below.

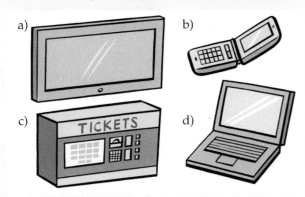

a)   b)   c) TICKETS   d)

Work with a partner. Think of five more compound nouns associated with objects or gadgets.

2 Complete the article with the words and phrases in the box. Make any changes that are necessary.

> wow   go digital   hype   slick   trash   sold

The manufacturers obviously thought we'd all be (1) _____ by this particular digital gadget. And with everything in the world (2) _____ , it doesn't surprise me that someone has produced a digital coffee machine as well. The (3) _____ claims that this (4) _____ machine is the latest must-have gadget for all modern kitchens. But I'm not (5) _____ on the idea. I love my old Italian coffee maker and its simple, functional shape. And I must admit that I was really pleased to find a review that completely (6) _____ the idea of the new digital version. But who knows, maybe the writer was just another old fogey like me?

Would you like to have a digital coffee maker? Why? / Why not?

3 Cross out the incorrect word in each line, and explain why it is incorrect.

a) embezzlement   libel   manslaughter   probation
b) the accused   arson   attorney   barrister
c) award damages   cross-examine   return a verdict   speeding
d) community service   to sentence   solitary confinement   suspended sentence

4 Complete the sentences with one word. The first letter has been provided for you.

a) He thinks that just because he's in a position of power, he's somehow a_____ the law and can do anything he wants.
b) We were really surprised when we heard the news. We'd always thought he was a very quiet, law-a_____ kind of person.
c) She may be a bit of a rebel, but she's never been in t_____ with the law.
d) There was no-one there to help them, so in the end they were forced to t_____ the law into their own hands.
e) Their father was far too lenient and it was always their mother who had to lay d_____ the law.
f) He's a real little despot. He marches around giving everybody orders and thinking that his w_____ is law!

Can you think of anybody in the news, or in your life, that matches the descriptions above? Tell your partner.

5 Choose expressions from the box to answer the questions below.

> dawn   dusk   mid-afternoon   mid-morning
> midday   midnight   sunrise   sunset   noon
> twilight   daybreak   nightfall
> the middle of the night   the crack of dawn
> the wee small hours   first thing in the morning
> last thing at night

a) What time is it now?
b) When did you last go to bed really late? What time was it?
c) When did you last get up very early? What time of day was it?
d) What time do you find you study best? Why?
e) When are you at your least productive? Why?
f) What time of day do you think is the most romantic? Why?

Pronunciation

1 Look at some words from Units 7–9. Say the words and add them to the table.

> adolescent   attorney   barrister   decision
> deprivation   digital   embezzlement
> entertainment   manslaughter   nocturnal
> pedestrian   probation   prominent   sensational
> situation   telepathy

A: □□□	B: □□□	C: □□□□	D: □□□□
			adolescent

2 Underline the stressed syllables.

🔊 3.11 **Listen, check and repeat.**

10 Footprints

Grammar Passive structures. Comparative structures
Vocabulary Ecological expressions. Expressions with *foot* or *feet*. Shoes
Useful phrases Persuasion and responding to persuasion

Reading & Speaking

1 Look at the quotations. What theme do they have in common?

> Take nothing but pictures.
> Leave nothing but footprints.
> Kill nothing but time.
> ~Motto of the Baltimore Grotto
> (caving society)~

> Tread lightly on the Earth.
> ~Australian aborigine motto~

2 Read the descriptions of a carbon footprint and an ecological footprint. What is the difference between the two?

What is a carbon footprint?

A carbon footprint is a way of measuring the environmental (1) _____ of human activities on the planet. It is a measure of the amount of carbon dioxide (CO_2), or (2) _____ , produced by a person, organisation or country as a result of burning (3) _____ such as coal, gas or oil. A carbon footprint is expressed in terms of tonnes of carbon produced over a given time period, usually a year. It takes into account both direct fuel (4) _____ , such as the energy a person uses in heating, lighting, transport and (5) _____ , and indirect fuel consumption, i.e. the energy consumed in producing goods or services a person uses. The average carbon footprint worldwide is around four tonnes (4,000 kilos) of carbon dioxide per person per year. The average UK (6) _____ produces more than double, over ten tonnes, while the average American produces twice this, close to twenty tonnes a year.

What is an ecological footprint?

An ecological footprint measures the total area of productive land and water and the global (7) _____ needed to support an individual or country. The component elements include the following: the land used to grow food, the land used to grow trees and biofuels, the land used to raise animals, and the areas of ocean used for fishing. However, the most important element is the land required to support the plant life needed to absorb CO_2 from the (8) _____ , in other words, areas such as the Amazon rainforest. It is expressed in global hectares, and can also be understood in terms of the number of planets that would be required to sustain the global population if everyone on earth had the same (9) _____ . Some calculations suggest that the ecological footprint of the average US citizen is equivalent to five planets, whereas a person in a (10) _____ such as Bangladesh or Mozambique would need only a quarter of a planet to sustain their lifestyle.

Complete the descriptions with words and phrases from the box.

| atmosphere | citizen | consumption | developing country | fossil fuels |
| greenhouse emissions | household appliances | impact | lifestyle | resources |

3 Work with a partner. Discuss these questions.
   a) Have you ever calculated your carbon footprint or your ecological footprint?
   b) Do you know what your country's carbon or ecological footprints are? Can you guess?
   c) Is it helpful to use measurements like this? Why? / Why not?

Vocabulary & Speaking

1 Do the lifestyle quiz. Score 2 for 'Usually', 1 for 'Sometimes' and 0 for 'Never'.

How eco-friendly is your lifestyle?

Tick how often you do these things.	Usually	Sometimes	Never
I walk, cycle or use public transport to go to work or college.	☐	☐	☐
I avoid flying where possible.	☐	☐	☐
I turn off lights when I leave a room.	☐	☐	☐
I use a laptop rather than a desktop computer.	☐	☐	☐
I keep my internet use to a minimum.	☐	☐	☐
I do not leave household appliances on stand-by.	☐	☐	☐
I do not leave my mobile phone charger plugged in.	☐	☐	☐
I do not leave the tap running when I brush my teeth.	☐	☐	☐
I do not spend more than two minutes in the shower.	☐	☐	☐
I recycle glass, tins and paper.	☐	☐	☐
I buy recycled paper and stationery.	☐	☐	☐
I re-use plastic carrier bags.	☐	☐	☐
I only buy what I really need.	☐	☐	☐
I buy locally-produced food where possible.	☐	☐	☐
I buy organic products.	☐	☐	☐
I buy products made from sustainable sources.	☐	☐	☐
I avoid eating meat or fish.	☐	☐	☐

2 Work with a partner. Add up your score and discuss these questions.

a) How did you score on the quiz? High scores are more eco-friendly.

b) In your opinion, which of the activities mentioned in the quiz is the most important in reducing a person's footprint?

3 Cross out the word or phrase in column *B* which does not collocate with the word in column *A*.

A	**B**
a) locally-grown	produce / fruit and vegetables / apples / meat
b) energy-efficient	washing machine / paper / dishwasher / fridge
c) solar-powered	emissions / central heating / car / house
d) recycled	paper / glass / central heating / plastic
e) organic	glass / cotton / meat / produce
f) sustainable	farming / development / forests / light bulbs
g) renewable	energy / resources / food / power

In what way are the items eco-friendly? Which of these items form a part of your lifestyle, or that of people you know?

Listening

1 3.12 Listen to Chloe and her mother, Barbara, discussing eco-friendly lifestyle choices. Answer these questions.

a) How are their attitudes different?

b) Which of the quiz topics do they mention?

Listen again. Note down the facts Chloe mentions to support her ideas.

2 Work with your partner. Discuss these questions.

a) Who do you agree with most in the conversation in Exercise 1, Chloe or her mother?

b) Would you consider making any changes in your lifestyle to reduce your footprint? Why? / Why not?

▲ Chloe and Barbara

Reading

1 Read the headline and look at the photos of the world's oldest footprints. Work with a partner. Discuss these questions.

a) Who might have made the earliest footprints?
b) Where and how long ago might they have been made?
c) How do you think they might have been preserved?
d) Why might they be lost forever?

2 Read the article and check your answers to the questions.

Man's earliest footprints may be lost forever

They are the world's oldest human tracks, a set of footprints pressed into volcanic ash that have lain perfectly preserved for more than three-and-a-half million years. Made by a group of
5 ancient apemen, the prints represent one of the most important sites in human evolutionary studies, for they show that our ancestors had already stopped walking on four legs and had become upright members of the primate world.
10 The Laetoli steps were discovered in 1976 by a team of scientists led by the late Mary Leakey, mother of conservationist Richard Leakey. They found a couple of prints that had been exposed by the wind and then uncovered a trail that led across an expanse of volcanic
15 ash, like footprints left behind by holidaymakers walking on a wet beach. The researchers could make out the arch of each foot, the big toe, even the heel. The prints had clearly been made by creatures who had long been adapted to walking on two legs. Yet tests showed the prints
20 had been made about 3.6 million years ago.

At that time, the area was populated by a short, small-brained species of apeman known as Australopithicus afarensis, an ancestor of modern human beings. Most scientists believe these were the creators of
25 the Laetoli footprints, individuals who may have been escaping an eruption of the nearby Sadiman volcano.

By studying the prints, scientists conclude that a smaller individual – presumed by Leakey to be a female – stopped in her tracks and glanced at some threat or sound to her
30 left. 'This motion, so intensely human, transcends time,' Leakey wrote in *National Geographic*. 'Three million, six hundred thousand years ago, a remote ancestor – just as you or I – experienced a moment of doubt.' It is this window on human behaviour that makes Laetoli so
35 important, say scientists.

But now the Laetoli steps in northern Tanzania are in danger of destruction. The footprints, although reburied ten years ago and covered by a special protective coating, are suffering storm erosion. A study presented
40 at an international conference last month warns that unless urgent action is taken, the site will suffer serious, irreparable damage, and the Laetoli steps – 'the rarest, oldest and most important evidence' documenting humans' ability to walk on two legs, will be lost to
45 civilisation.

Dr Charles Musiba of the University of Colorado, Denver, argues that building a museum over the footprints is the perfect solution. Palaeontologists agree that something must be done, but claim that constructing a
50 building over the steps in remote Laetoli is impossible and would only lead to further degradation. 'No matter how good the intentions, any attempt to preserve them in place is doomed to failure,' said one of the steps' discoverers, Tim White of the University of Berkeley, California.
55 'Laetoli is remote and inaccessible, and would require infrastructure currently not available or foreseeable to preserve these prints in place.'

3 Underline the correct alternative in each sentence.

a) The footprints were discovered by **a conservationist / scientists / holidaymakers**.
b) They were made by **the first modern human being / a female apeman / ancestors of modern humans**.
c) They are important because they indicate **when humans started to walk / that men are descended from apes / what early human feet looked like**.
d) The prints are under threat from **holidaymakers / storm erosion / volcanic ash**.
e) Experts agree that the footprints must be **kept in place / preserved / moved to a safer place**.

4 Discuss the meaning of the words and phrases highlighted in yellow with your partner. Use a dictionary to check your answers.

5 Work with your partner. Discuss these questions.

a) Does it matter if the footprints are lost? Why? / Why not?
b) Have you ever visited an important historical site? What were your impressions?

Passive structures

The footprints …

are pressed into volcanic ash.

are being studied by palaeontologists.

were discovered by scientists.

were being eroded.

have been preserved for millions of years.

had been buried in the sand.

may be lost forever.

are going to be protected.

may have been made by apemen.

Reduced passive clauses
They are a set of footprints **pressed** into volcanic ash.

They were discovered by a team of scientists **led** by the late Mary Leakey.

Grammar

1 **Look at the underlined sentences in the article on page 102. In which two sentences is the agent (or doer) of the verb mentioned? Why is it used there, and not in the other sentences?**

2 **Read the article about the prehistoric ruins at Jarlshof, on the Scottish island of Shetland. What problems are the ruins facing? What is being done?**

Storms and rising sea levels are threatening the prehistoric ruins at Jarlshof. People may have built the settlement as long as 9,000 years ago. The sea is eroding the island's coastline and has already destroyed much of it. Experts say we could lose the remains of this community for ever. This potential loss alarms experts. An organisation called SCAPE is monitoring the situation. People set up SCAPE to protect ancient shoreline sites. So far, SCAPE has surveyed 30% of Scotland's sites, including 3,500 which they judge to be at risk. They are going to publish the results of the survey shortly.

Are the verb structures in the text active or passive? Is it more natural to use the active or passive in a text like this? Why?

3 **Rewrite the article in Exercise 2 by changing the verbs into the passive form. Omit the agent if this is not known, irrelevant or obvious.**

4 **Look at the two sentences. Underline the relative clause and reduced passive clause. What is the difference between them?**
   a) Jarlshof is the site of a settlement which was inhabited from the Bronze Age until the nineteenth century.
   b) Jarlshof is the site of a settlement inhabited from the Bronze Age until the nineteenth century.

5 **Combine the sentences below to include reduced passive clauses as in the examples in Exercise 4. Where appropriate, make other verbs passive or omit the agent.**
   a) Remains of a stone wall revealed evidence of the settlement. A storm uncovered the remains.
   b) Tools and artefacts have shed light on life in prehistoric times. Archaeologists have excavated the tools and artefacts.
   c) Archaeologists are restoring some of the artefacts. The sea eroded the artefacts.
   d) They have found buildings. They think the buildings date back nearly 2,500 years.
   e) The artefacts provide insight into a unique way of life. The Jarlshof museum displays the artefacts.

6 **Work with a partner. Student A: look at the text on page 132. Student B: look at the text on page 133. Write a brief report and tell your partner about the site. Use passive structures.**

7 Grammar *Extra* 10, Part 1 page 142. Read the explanations and do Exercise 1.

Listening & Speaking

1 🌐 **3.13 Listen to an American hiker describing his experiences of barefoot hiking. Overall, was it a positive or negative experience?**

2 **Listen again and make notes under these headings.**
a) Where they were hiking
b) The reason for hiking barefoot
c) Two reasons for slowing down
d) The benefits of slowing down
e) Things the speaker saw on the forest floor
f) The physical sensations he has experienced on barefoot hikes
g) A 'rare sight' described in a later hike

3 **Work with a partner. Discuss these questions.**
a) Would you like to try barefoot hiking? Why? / Why not?
b) Imagine you are walking barefoot in the following situations:
   • along a shallow stream in the summer
   • along the seashore
   • through a snowy forest
   • in a grassy meadow

Describe what it would feel like, the dangers you might experience and the benefits and disadvantages of each situation. How many of these have you or your partner actually experienced? Where and when? What was it like?

Pronunciation

1 **Work with your partner. Discuss these questions.**
a) When do you read aloud, either in your own language, or in English? What sort of things do you read?
b) Which of these tips do you generally follow when preparing to read aloud in English?
   • Check the meaning and pronunciation of unknown words before you read.
   • Divide the sentences into chunks and decide where to pause.
   • Decide which words carry the main stress in each chunk.
   • Practise reading several times before you read to an audience.

2 **Read the transcript of part of the recording. What do you think the slashes represent?**

> Two years ago // my family camped amidst the California redwoods. // During a hike, my younger son decided to take his nap. Kicking off my shoes I got comfortable under a redwood and let my son nap in my lap while my wife and elder son went on ahead. Upon their return we had lunch and headed back to our campsite. On a whim I decided not to put my shoes back on and walked back barefoot.

3 🌐 **3.14 Listen to the recording, and mark on the recording script in Exercise 2 where the speaker pauses, as in the example. Listen again and underline the stressed words in each chunk. Practise reading the passage aloud to your partner.**

4 **Predict and mark where the pauses will occur in this passage with your partner.**

> The trail felt soft and cool; the cover of pine needles cushioned my footsteps. Normally, the return trip of a hike ends up being faster, but in this case I was slowed down for two reasons. Since my feet were not hardened to the outdoors, I had to look down and deliberate every step to avoid stepping on potentially painful objects, such as sharp rocks. In addition, every time I wanted to see a tree, a cloud, or a hill, I had to stop. Normally, with hiking boots, I can walk while looking all around, but in this case I could not do both at the same time. I had to separate the two activities of hiking and of admiring the surroundings.

🌐 **3.15 Listen and check. Practise reading the passage aloud with and without the recording.**

Speaking: anecdote

You are going to tell a partner about a walk you have been on. It could be a major hike, a long trek, a brisk walk or a short stroll; in an unusual or an everyday situation.

- Ask yourself the questions below.
- Think about *what* to say and *how* to say it.
- Tell your partner about the walk.

a) Where and when did you go on the walk?
b) Why did you go on the walk?
c) Had you been on the same walk before?
d) If it was a long walk, how did you plan it and what equipment did you take?
e) Were you alone or with companions?
f) What did you see, hear, feel or smell on the walk?
g) Did you meet anyone or stop on the way?
h) How long did the walk last?
i) How did you feel at the end of the walk?
j) What did you do after you arrived at the end?

Vocabulary

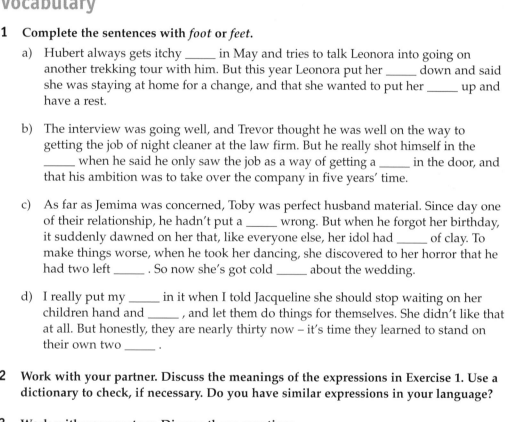

1 Complete the sentences with *foot* or *feet*.

a) Hubert always gets itchy _____ in May and tries to talk Leonora into going on another trekking tour with him. But this year Leonora put her _____ down and said she was staying at home for a change, and that she wanted to put her _____ up and have a rest.

b) The interview was going well, and Trevor thought he was well on the way to getting the job of night cleaner at the law firm. But he really shot himself in the _____ when he said he only saw the job as a way of getting a _____ in the door, and that his ambition was to take over the company in five years' time.

c) As far as Jemima was concerned, Toby was perfect husband material. Since day one of their relationship, he hadn't put a _____ wrong. But when he forgot her birthday, it suddenly dawned on her that, like everyone else, her idol had _____ of clay. To make things worse, when he took her dancing, she discovered to her horror that he had two left _____ . So now she's got cold _____ about the wedding.

d) I really put my _____ in it when I told Jacqueline she should stop waiting on her children hand and _____ , and let them do things for themselves. She didn't like that at all. But honestly, they are nearly thirty now – it's time they learned to stand on their own two _____ .

2 Work with your partner. Discuss the meanings of the expressions in Exercise 1. Use a dictionary to check, if necessary. Do you have similar expressions in your language?

3 Work with your partner. Discuss these questions.

a) When do you like **to put your feet up**?
b) Can you remember finding out that someone you knew **had feet of clay**?
c) Have you ever **shot yourself in the foot** in a work situation?
d) Can you think of a time recently when you **put your foot down**?
e) When should children **stand on their own two feet** financially, in your opinion?
f) Can you remember a time when you were **waited on hand and foot**?
g) Do you **have itchy feet** at the moment?
h) Have you ever **got cold feet** about a holiday or change in your life?
i) What is the best way of **getting a foot in the door** in a place you would like to work?
j) Have you ever **put your foot in it** in a social situation?
k) Can you remember a situation in which you tried hard **not to put a foot wrong**?

Listening

1 Do you like buying shoes? How many pairs do you own? What is your favourite pair of shoes and why? Tell a partner.

2 🌐 3.16 Listen to four people talking about their shoes on a television style programme. Match their descriptions (*1–4*) to the photos (*a–d*) on the left.

Listen again and make notes on …
a) why the shoes were bought   b) when they are worn   c) what they look like.

3 Tell your partner about the shoes you are wearing at the moment. Give as much information as possible.

Reading & Speaking

1 Read the two articles about men's and women's shoes. Which article discusses …
a) the style of a person' shoes?   b) the condition of a person's shoes?   c) both?

1 WHAT YOUR *Footwear* SAYS ABOUT YOU

THEY use them for walking, jogging and even dancing, when the mood takes them, but in the centuries since the first cavemen wrapped their feet in animal skins to protect their dainty toes from the elements, men have continued to make bizarre choices when it comes to footwear. But while it has been said that what a chap chooses to slip on his feet can say just as much about him as his carefully chosen car, beloved football team or the job he holds down, is it really fair that we hold his penchant for crocodile-hide cowboy boots against him?

Psychologist Cynthia McVey says you can indeed tell a lot about a man by what he wears on his feet, such as whether he's diligent or downright lazy, caring or couldn't-care-less. 'If they're down at heel, and in need of repair then he might not have the money to have them mended, which is okay,' she says. 'But if he hasn't given them a lick of polish and they're scruffy then he is probably not attending to detail in other areas of his life.' Sloppy footwear can be a sign of someone who's lackadaisical. But if he's too particular and fastidious, I'd be concerned he may be a little bit obsessive.' Fashion stylist Aimi Hautau agrees. 'Like ties or handbags, shoes say a lot about who a person is, about their lifestyle and what they like to do in their spare time and so on – we make a judgement about someone in about 60 seconds of meeting. So splashing out can make sense.'

2 *Shoe's* THAT GIRL?

Beware, ladies – your shoes may be giving away your secrets. No matter how coy you are with your boss, colleagues or clients, your footwear speaks volumes. And it might be saying things you'd rather not be broadcast. According to Dr Andrew Wilson, a senior lecturer in linguistics, the style of shoes or boots that you choose communicates hidden messages to the rest of the world. He said: 'Although there may be some grain of truth in the claim that shoe style preferences are linked with your actual personality, what is important in everyday life is not so much what your shoes are saying about you, but rather what other people think they are saying.'

Women who wear knee-high boots are seen as dynamic and confident. But different styles give different messages. Sharp toes and thin stiletto heels make others think you are abrasive and dominant; classic low-heeled riding boots suggest a much warmer and more approachable character. Ankle boots are viewed by others as boring and conventional. Although judged to be elegant and feminine by some, the wearers are not seen to have the same dynamic drive that a woman wearing knee-high boots has.

Glossary
a) _____ adj: seeming rude to others
b) _____ adj: behaving in a neurotic way
c) _____ adj: small and attractive
d) _____ adj: lazy or careless
e) _____ adj: messy or dirty
f) _____ adj: loose and informal
g) _____ adj: not willing to give information
h) _____ adj: very clean and neat

2 Read the articles again. Decide if these sentences are true or false.
a) Men have always had strange taste in shoes.
b) The writer of article 1 admires crocodile-hide boots.
c) According to Cynthia McVey, worn-out shoes may be a sign of laziness.
d) Aimi Hautau believes expensive shoes can help make a good impression.
e) Andrew Wilson says you cannot tell a person's personality from their footwear.
f) People who wear knee-high boots are sometimes seen as elegant and feminine.

3 Look at the highlighted adjectives in the articles. Try to guess the meaning from the context and then complete the glossary. Do you know anyone who matches these definitions?

4 Work with your partner. Discuss these questions.
a) Do you believe that you can tell someone's personality from their shoes?
b) What do you think your shoes say about you and your friends?

▲ Melanie, mother of two

▲ Saffron, student

▲ Judith, retired

▲ Poppy, TV presenter

Vocabulary & Writing

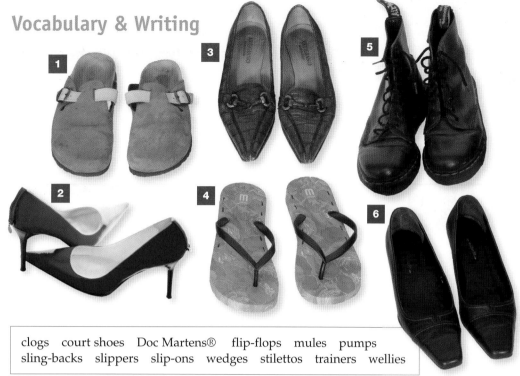

clogs   court shoes   Doc Martens®   flip-flops   mules   pumps
sling-backs   slippers   slip-ons   wedges   stilettos   trainers   wellies

1   Look at the different types of shoes in the box. Which are not normally worn by men? Which describe the shoes in the photos?

2   🌐 3.17 Work with a partner. Listen to an interview with a psychologist. Discuss which of the shoes in the photos (1–6) are being described. Which of the women on the left, Melanie, Saffron, Judith or Poppy, do you think the shoes belong to? Why?

3   Look again at the shoes in the photo. With your partner, write a description of the owner of one of these pairs of shoes. Read your description to another pair. Can they guess which shoes it refers to?

Grammar

1   Read the sentences about shoes. Which of the expressions in bold refer to a) a large difference? b) a moderate difference? c) a small difference? d) no difference?

a)   The owner of these shoes is probably **a bit** more flirtatious and feminine, and less domineering.

b)   These shoes probably belong to someone who is **somewhat** older than the other women.

c)   These shoes say 'I don't care about expensive designer fashions, there are so many other things that are **far** more interesting'.

d)   His shoes can say **just** as much about him as his carefully chosen car.

e)   These shoes are **by far** the most extravagant ones I've ever bought.

f)   The other shoes I tried on were **nowhere near** as comfortable as these.

2   Which words or phrases from the box could replace those in bold in Exercise 1?

a little   a lot   considerably   far and away   infinitely   much
nothing like   rather   slightly   way

3   Work with your partner. Write three sentences about a famous person. Use comparative structures and adjectives to compare him/her with other people.

Read your description to another pair. Can they guess who it is?

4   Grammar *Extra* 10, Part 2 page 142. Read the explanations and do Exercise 2.

Comparative structures

The other shoes are **far** more comfortable than these.

These shoes are **nowhere near** as comfortable as the others.

These shoes are **somewhat** less comfortable.

These ones are **just** as comfortable as the others.

Useful phrases

1 Work with a partner. Imagine your partner is tired. Try to persuade him/her to go out with you tonight.

2 3.18–3.21 Listen to four people trying to persuade someone to do something. For each conversation, note down what they are trying to persuade the other person to do and what the outcome is.

Listen again and note down the reasons used to persuade the other person.

3 Complete the extracts with useful phrases from the conversations in Exercise 2. Then listen again to check your answers.

Trying to persuade someone

I disagree. I think it's (1) _____ making our voice heard.

Treat (2) _____ !

Oh come on, nothing (3) _____ , nothing (4) _____ .

You might (5) _____ try.

Don't be (6) _____ !

You should cross that bridge (7) _____ . I think you should (8) _____ for it.

Expressing doubts or reservations

I can't honestly (1) _____ signing a petition.

What's (2) _____ spending so much money on shoes you're only going to wear once?

(3) _____ applying?

(4) _____ I get seasick?

Agreeing

Okay then if (1) _____ think so ...

Okay then if (2) _____ happy. But I think it's (3) _____ time, quite frankly.

Well, maybe you're right. Maybe I should give it (4) _____ .

---

4 3.22 Listen to another conversation. What is the woman trying to persuade her friend to do?

5 Listen again. Correct one of the words in these sentences so that they match the expressions used in the Recordings.

a) Come in, you know you want to, really.
b) No, absolutely not! It's out of the blue!
c) Go on, just with me!
d) Honestly, I'm not in the way.
e) You must be mad!
f) I'm still not sure I feel for it really.
g) Go on, it'll make you good.
h) Oh, alright. You've twisted my leg.

Which are used a) to persuade? b) to refuse? c) to agree?

6 Work with your partner. Write a conversation for one of these situations. A friend is trying to persuade another to ...

a) go on an expensive holiday with them.
b) take up windsurfing or mountain climbing.
c) have a new haircut.
d) go to a fancy dress party with them.

Read your conversation to another pair. Can they guess which situation it is?

Writing *Extra*

Report

1 Read a report of students' travel habits. Match the headings (*a–c*) to the paragraphs (*1–3*).

   a) Recommendations   b) Background   c) Findings

1) _____

An investigation was carried out into the means of transport currently used by students to travel into college. The purpose of the investigation was twofold: firstly, to establish how far existing public transport arrangements are meeting the needs of college students; and secondly, in line with the college's Green Transport Initiative, to consider how best to encourage students to travel to college by public transport, by bicycle or on foot, and how to minimise the use of private cars.

2) _____

It was found that just over half the students (53%), the vast majority of whom lived within a 3 km radius of the college, walked into college. However, a sizeable minority (31%) came in by car, with 6% of these obtaining lifts from fellow students. Surprisingly, only 5% of those living outside the 3 km radius used the bus, and only 11% cycled into college. The majority of students opting to use their cars cited the infrequency and unreliability of the local bus service as the main reason for this. When questioned about whether they would consider cycling, a number of respondents replied that they did not own a bicycle; further reservations centred around the perceived danger of cycling in local traffic, and the shortage of bicycle storage facilities at the college.

3) _____

In light of the findings, the following measures are proposed:

- Negotiations should be initiated with local bus companies to increase the number and frequency of bus routes serving the college.
- The City Council should be encouraged to improve existing cycle tracks, and increase the number of cycle lanes on roads into the college.
- Cycle storage facilities should be increased on college premises.
- Parking spaces should be reduced and a limited number of parking permits should be issued.
- The success of the measures should be monitored and evaluated a year after implementation.

2 Work with a partner. Discuss these questions.

   a) Why was the report written?
   b) In what way are these students' travel habits similar or different to those in your country?
   c) Do you agree with the recommendations?

3 Replace the highlighted words in the report with words in the box with a similar meaning.

> asked   conducted   determine   discovered   distributed
> focused on   mentioned   reduce   started   suggested

Underline uses of the passive in the text. Is it clear who wrote the report? Why? / Why not?

4 Match the following percentages to the quantity expressions in the box.

   0.1%   1%   10%   25%   28%   35%   47%   90%   99%

> the vast majority of   just over a third of   exactly a quarter of
> a little under half   the overwhelming majority of   one in ten
> a tiny percentage of   virtually no   a sizeable minority of

5 Work with your partner. Choose one of the topics below to ask the class about.

   a) going on regular walks
   b) walking for more than a kilometre a day
   c) walking to work or college
   d) going on walking holidays
   e) power walking or jogging
   f) doing grocery shopping on foot
   g) taking a pet or children for a walk
   h) walking in the countryside

Prepare a list of questions. Interview other pairs. Then write a report using the headings in the report in Exercise 1.

11 Words

Grammar Avoiding repetition: substitution and ellipsis
Vocabulary New words
Useful phrases Getting your point across

Speaking & Listening

When ideas fail, words come in very handy.
Johann Wolfgang von Goethe

Words are, of course, the most powerful drug used by mankind.
Rudyard Kipling

Actions speak louder than words. Proverb

1 **Work with a partner. Complete the sentences with the words in the box.**

brunch	choice	facetious	feedback	smoke	madam
peculiar	penguin	shampoo	smoke	weird	

a) _____ reads the same backwards or forwards.
b) _____ comes from combining breakfast and lunch.
c) Smog is formed by combining _____ and _____ .
d) If you write _____ in capital letters, it reads the same upside down in the mirror.
e) _____ contains all five vowels in alphabetical order.
f) _____ contains the first six letters of the alphabet.
g) _____ has been borrowed from Hindi and _____ has been borrowed from Welsh.
h) Both _____ and _____ mean 'strange'. _____ originates from Old English and _____ from Latin.

2 **Work in small groups. Discuss these questions.**

a) Can you remember the last new word you learnt in English (excluding the words from Exercise 1)?
b) Can you remember the last new word you learnt in your own language? Is it a newly-coined word, borrowed from another language or just new to you?
c) Can you think of some English words that are used in your language?
d) Can you think of three English words that people wouldn't have known 20 years ago?

Compare your answers with another group. How many of your words were the same?

3 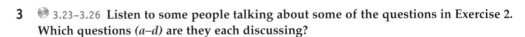 3.23–3.26 **Listen to some people talking about some of the questions in Exercise 2. Which questions (*a–d*) are they each discussing?**

Make a note of the words they talk about. Are any of them new to you? Did they mention any of the words you came up with in Exercise 2?

4 **Look at these sentences. Which do you agree with most? How many people in the class feel the same as you?**

a) Our language is being weakened by the introduction of English words and expressions. I'd like to see all of them banned.
b) I love what the internet is doing to our language. It's a global phenomenon making communication easier, as more and more words are the same in all languages.

Vocabulary

1 Look at the three titles for three different lifestyle articles. What do you think the articles will be about?

a) **Life online**   b) **Money matters**   c) **Time out**

2 Match the titles (*a–c*) in Exercise 1 to the opening paragraphs (*1–3*). Then match the paragraphs to the photos (*a–c*). Which article would you like to know more about? Why?

1 Life in the **credit crunch** is no joke. With money hard to find and businesses going bust, a lot of people are finding themselves the victims of **rightsizing**. More and more people are entering the job market and finding that they have to **upskill** to keep up. **Conspicuous consumerism** is no longer the vogue, even the super-rich are tightening their belts and in the new **lipstick economy**, the **recessionistas** are the new fashion role models.

2 Everyone, it seems, is at it: **life-casting** on blog sites, **microblogging** on social networks, uploading their **phoneography** on video and photo-sharing sites. Gone are the days when you had to wait for a postcard or a letter to keep up with family news, or for your film to be developed before you actually saw your photos. Now we're all members of the **twitterverse**, constantly updating each other on our **status**, sharing photos as we take them, and writing intimately in **netspeak** to people we've never met in **RL**.

3 Are you getting tired of the **always on, always connected** lifestyle? Craving a bit of **digital down time**? Then you need to try **unplugging**. It's the art of relaxing without the aid of your computer, mobile phone, MP3 player, etc. It entails quality **face time** with the people you love, chatting without needing an **IM** service and redressing the **joy-to-stuff ratio** in your life.

3 Look at the words and phrases in bold in the paragraphs in Exercise 2. They are all relatively new to the English language. Divide them into three groups:

a) I know what it means.
b) I've seen or heard it, but I'm not sure what it means.
c) I've never seen or heard it before.

Compare your answers with a partner. Look at the words you put in groups *b)* and *c)*. Look again at the way they are used in the paragraphs. Can you guess their meaning from the context? Use the definitions on the left to help you.

4 Check your answers with your teacher or online. Which words or phrases are most relevant to your life and lifestyle? Why? Is there an equivalent in your language?

New words

blog noun [C]: an online diary which is updated regularly

broadcast verb [T]: to send out messages or programmes on the radio or TV

consumerism noun [U]: buying and using a lot of goods and services

downsize verb [T]: to reduce the number of workers in a company

down time noun [U]: time when you relax and don't work

fashionista noun [C]: someone who is very interested in fashion or works in the fashion industry

quality time noun [U]: time you spend with someone you love, doing things you enjoy

ratio noun [U]: a relationship between the sizes of two numbers or amounts

Twitter™ noun [U]: a free social messaging service

Speaking

1   Work in small groups. Discuss which of these you write…
a) all the time.   b) at least once a week.   c) once in a while.   d) never.

> blog entries   comments on websites   emails   instant messages (IM)   letters
> status updates   text messages

What else do you write on a regular basis?

2   Look at the quotation. Do you agree that writing is more important in the 'digital age' than it used to be? Why? / Why not?

> 'As the world becomes increasingly digital, writing becomes more important. This is especially true for non-writers. If you work in an office, the majority of your communications are made with text by email or IM. Whether you like it or not, your ability to exchange ideas, collaborate with others, and ultimately succeed, hinges on the ability to write effectively.'

Reading & Vocabulary

1   Work with a partner. Think of five tips you could give a person who wants to improve their writing.

2   Compare your tips in Exercise 1 to the list (*a–g*). Are any of them the same?
a)   Keep it short and to the point.
b)   If in doubt, sleep on it.
c)   Use a clear layout for easy reading.
d)   Think before you write.
e)   Avoid repetition.
f)   Choose your style carefully.
g)   Always pause before you hit send.

The tips are taken from a website that offers 'Seven simple steps to successful writing'. What do you think the writer says about each tip?

3   Read the blog on page 113. Match the tips (*a–g*) in Exercise 2 to the paragraphs (*1–7*). Compare your answers with your partner. Were your predictions in Exercise 2 correct?

4   Work with your partner. Discuss these questions.
a)   Do you think the writer has left out any particularly important tips?
b)   Do you think you'll put any of these tips into practice in your writing?
c)   If yes, which? And how?

5   Look at the words and phrases highlighted in the article. Discuss their possible meaning with your partner. Then complete the glossary at the bottom of the article.

6   Complete the sentences with some of the words and phrases from the glossary. Make any changes necessary to the words and phrases.
a)   I find long, _____ sentences so annoying!
b)   I must admit that I'm sometimes prone to _____ and tangents when I'm speaking.
c)   It really annoys me when people _____ instead of getting to the point!
d)   I sometimes find it really difficult to make myself understood – you know, to _____ .
e)   I usually find it quite easy to _____ information from technical texts.
f)   I sometimes have to read something three or four times before it actually _____ .
g)   I really admire people who always know exactly what to say and how to say it, people who always manage to _____ .

Look at the sentences again. Are they true for you? Why? / Why not?

The writer's block

Whatever it is you have to write, the idea of a blank page – or screen – can be very daunting. Here are a few easy tips to help you overcome your writer's block.

1 _____

Before you actually start, think about what you want to say, why you want to say it and who you're going to say it to. The most important question to ask is: what response do I want to get? The answer to that obviously depends on what you're writing. It may be a memo at work. In that case, your main aim is that your reader be able to glean the most important information quickly and get back to you with a response as soon as possible. It may be an entry in your weekly blog. If so, you're probably more interested in stimulating your reader's interest and curiosity. But whatever you're writing, the next six tips are sure to help.

2 _____

Don't waste time and ink on unnecessary preambles or tangents. Make sure that everything you say is relevant to your main aim or message. Favour shorter, simpler sentences, written for maximum effect. Avoid long, rambling sentences where possible. If you're going around the houses, it's probably because you're not really sure yourself of exactly what you want to say. And if you don't know, your readers definitely won't!

3 _____

You may feel that a point needs stressing, and that you therefore want to repeat it just to make sure it sinks in. Don't. It's much better to make sure you expressed yourself clearly and succinctly the first time round. If something really needs saying again – at least find a different way to do so.

4 _____

This takes us back to the first point. Remember your reader! If you know them personally, then you'll also know how best to write to them. Make sure your style reflects both your relationship with your reader and your attitude to what you're writing. If you're writing to an anonymous audience, keep your style neutral. Remember that first impressions are vital. The right choice of words and tone can help you get off to a great start. And of course, the wrong choice can do quite the opposite! It's much easier to offend when your words aren't accompanied by facial expressions and positive body language. Don't start with a friendly 'hi' if you're writing an email to a prospective employer! Start off formally, using the usual letter conventions – there'll be plenty of time to adopt a friendly tone once you've got the job!

5 _____

Punctuation and paragraphs can be powerful tools. The lack, or misuse, of either can make a text very difficult to read. Their correct and careful use, on the other hand, can really help put your point across. Try reading your text aloud to yourself. Notice the places where you stop or pause. Does your punctuation reflect these pauses? Do the paragraphs show where you take a breath and start out on a new idea? If not, add them in. It'll make your text much, much easier to process. With longer texts you may also want to use headings or bullet points.

6 _____

No matter how brief or informal your message, always read through it again before you send it. If you're sending an email, always make sure you've included the right attachments, and are sending it to the right recipients. Don't just hit Reply All. It can save you a lot of embarrassment! And watch out for typos and spelling mistakes – each careless mistake will make you look just that little bit less professional, that little bit less capable.

7 _____

If you're writing something really important, and you're not sure you've hit the right note, then press 'save', go away and come back to it later. Do something completely different, even if it's just for five minutes. If you can leave it till the next day, all the better. It often takes no more than a few minutes to transform a draft into a polished final product.

Glossary
a) _____ verb [T]: choose sth because you think it's the best option
b) _____ verb [T]: learn or pick up pieces of information
c) _____ phrase: saying something in a very indirect way
d) _____ phrase: create the right mood or impression
e) _____ noun [C]: an introduction to a document
f) _____ phrasal verb: explain what you want to say
g) _____ adj: long and confusing
h) _____ phrasal vb: is completely understood
i) _____ noun [C]: new, and often completely different and irrelevant topics

Grammar

Avoiding repetition

Substitution

Read through **it** again.

The answer to **that** is obvious.

Do you want to improve your writing? If **so**, read these tips.

Do so at your peril.

Ellipsis
Don't.

If **not**, put them in.

If you **don't**, they definitely **won't**!

1 Work with a partner. Look at these extracts from further writing tips. What do the words in bold refer to?

> The most important question to ask is: what response do I want to get? The answer to **that** obviously depends on what you're writing. **It** may be a memo at work. In **that case**, your main aim is that your reader should quickly glean the most important information. **It** may be an entry in your weekly blog. If so, you're probably more interested in stimulating your readers' curiosity and keeping **them** interested in what you're saying.

> Punctuation and paragraphs can be powerful tools. The lack, or misuse, of **either**, can make a text very difficult to read. **Their** correct and careful use, on the other hand, can really help put your point across.

2 Look at the tip below. Substitute the sections in bold with a word or phrase from the box. You will not need to use all the words.

> either way   it   its   to do so   that   they   them   their overuse   those

The use of short, staccato sentences can make you seem rude. (1) **Short staccato sentences** can also make your arguments seem too simplistic – or impossible to follow! (2) **Whether they make your writing too simplistic or impossible to follow**, it's important to show the links between your ideas. (3) **In order to show the links between your ideas**, use discourse markers such as *as a result, on the other hand, in conclusion*. (4) **Using these discourse markers** can really help make your writing much clearer and easier to read. But beware of (5) **the overuse of discourse markers** too! Too many discourse markers can make your writing heavy and clumsy. And (6) **discourse markers** can sometimes cloud the issue. So, remember, use (7) **discourse markers** carefully and sparingly.

Compare your answers with your partner. Write a heading for the tip.

3 Work with your partner. Look at the tips (*a–d*). Which words can you cut from the section in bold without losing the meaning? Use full forms instead of contractions where necessary.

a) If you're going around the houses, it's probably because you're not really sure yourself of exactly what you want to say. **And if you don't know what you want to say, your readers definitely won't know what you're saying**!

b) You may feel that a point needs stressing, and that you therefore want to repeat it just to make sure it sinks in. **Don't repeat it**.

c) Do the paragraphs show where you take a breath and when you start out on a new idea? **If they don't show this, put them in**.

d) Also, make sure you've included the right attachments, **and that you are sending it to the right recipients**.

🔊 3.27 **Listen and check. Which words were cut? Why were they cut?**

4 Work with your partner. Make the conversation as short as possible, using substitution and ellipsis.

A: Do you do a lot of writing?

B: I used to do a lot of writing at school, but now I don't write at all.

A: What about writing text messages? Don't you ever write text messages?

B: Yes, of course, I write text messages every day! But I don't really think of writing text messages as writing. Do you think of it as writing?

A: No, I suppose I don't think of it as writing. But I do write a lot of emails at work. I think emails count as writing.

B: Yes, I suppose that what you say is true. But I was thinking more about essays and reports … now essays and reports are what I call real writing.

🔊 3.28 **Listen and check. Do you agree with the speakers? Why? / Why not?**

5 **Grammar *Extra* 11** page 144. Read the explanations and do Exercises 1 and 2.

The American author, Mark Twain, was born in 1835 and is most famous for *The Adventures of Tom Sawyer* and *The Adventures of Huckleberry Finn*, both based on his own childhood.

Speaking

1 **Work with a partner. Discuss these questions.**

a) Do you think English spelling is difficult?

b) Which words do you occasionally misspell?

c) What changes do you think could be made to English to make spelling easier?

2 **Look at this article which was written by Mark Twain. Read it aloud with your partner.**

A Plan for the Improvement of English Spelling by Mark Twain

In Year 1, that useless letter 'c' would be dropped to be replased either by 'k' or 's', and, likewise, 'x' would no longer be part of the alphabet. The only kase in which 'c' would be retained would be the 'ch' formation, which will be dealt with later. Year 2 might reform 'w' spelling, so that 'which' and 'one' would take the same konsonant, wile Year 3 might well abolish 'y' replasing it with 'i' and Iear 4 might fiks the 'g/j' anomali wonse and for all.

Jenerally, then, the improvement would kontinue iear bai iear with Iear 5 doing awai with useless double konsonants, and Iears 6–12 or so modifaiing vowlz and the rimeining voist and unvoist konsonants. Bai Iear 15 or sou, it wud fainali bi posibl tu meik ius ov thi ridandant letez 'c', 'y' and 'x' – bai now jast a memori in the maindz ov ould doderez – tu riplais 'ch', 'sh', and 'th' rispektivli. Fainali, xen, aafte sam 20 iers ov orxografekl riform, wi wud hev a lojikl, kohirnt speling in ius xrewawt xe Ingliy-spiking werld.

Which of his suggestions do you approve of?

Pronunciation

1 **Mark Twain recognised that English spelling and pronunciation are often very different. Read these sentences and cross out the silent letters.**

a) Knowing how to pronounce English words correctly is important but there's no doubt that it is one of the hardest things to learn.

b) Keep your receipt if you want to return a purchase, otherwise there's no guarantee you'll get your money back.

c) I had a really bad case of pneumonia earlier this year. Even watching the TV was tiring, so I spent most days just listening to the radio.

d) Psychiatrists can be very vague. They'll rarely give you a direct answer to a question.

e) During the flight the plane will climb to 10,000 metres above sea level.

2 **The pronunciation of British place names can be difficult too. Look at these place names and cross out the silent letters.**

a) Gloucester

b) Leicester

c) Grosvenor Square

d) Brighton

e) Greenwich

f) Guildford

🌐 3.29 **Listen and check your answers.**

3 **Work with your partner. Try reading this limerick.**

There was a young lady from Gloucester,
Whose parents thought they had loucester.
From the fridge came a sigh,
'Let me out or I'll digh!'
But the problem was how to defroucester.

4 🌐 3.30 **Listen and check. Correct the misspelled words with your partner.**

Useful phrases

1 🌐 3.31 **Listen to two people, Sue and Matt, talking about socialising online. Do they think it's a good thing to do? Why? / Why not?**

2 **Read the extract from the conversation. What exactly is Sue's point? Do you agree with her?**

Matt: So, are you saying that people who socialise online are all freaks and weirdos?

Sue: No, you know (1) that's not what I meant! (2) You're twisting my words. (3) All I said was that it can be a problem, you know, you don't know who you're talking to ... and they could be ... yes, I suppose, they could be weirdos or something ... I mean, you never know, do you?

Matt: (4) So, what are you saying then? That we should all stop using chatrooms and networking sites and whatever?

Sue: No, (5) that's not what I'm saying ... and you know it ... (6) my point is that we need to be careful, that's all ... you know, don't give away too many personal details ... don't make yourself vulnerable ...

Matt: But surely it's much safer to talk to someone at a distance than to talk to a stranger in a club or a bar ...

Sue: (7) You're missing the point ... I'm not saying that it's dangerous to chat with people online ... (8) I'm just saying that you have to be really careful when it comes to arranging to meet them in real life ... you just don't know who they are, or what they want ...

Listen again and replace the highlighted phrases (1–8) with the actual useful phrases used in the conversation.

3 🌐 3.32 **Listen to these useful phrases again. Mark the main stress. Then practise saying them with the recording.**

a) I didn't say that!
b) You're deliberately misconstruing my words!
c) That's not what I meant!
d) You're twisting my words!
e) So, what are you implying?
f) That's not what I'm saying!
g) You're missing the point!

4 **Work with a partner. Write a short exchange between Sue and Matt discussing the topic of computer games. Use the ideas in the flow chart.**

Sue thinks that Matt spends too long playing computer games

Matt asks if she's accusing him of wasting his time

Sue explains that she's worried about his eyesight

Matt says the games help him relax after a long day's work

Sue explains that she doesn't want him to stop completely and reminds him that playing often gives him a headache

Read your conversation to the class.

5 **Work in small groups. Respond to one of the statements below. Make sure you're putting your point across clearly and that your partners understand exactly what you're saying.**

- Social networks are great – they're the best way to keep in touch with friends and family.
- Face time with friends is really important.
- I'm getting tired of this always-on, always-connected lifestyle.

Vocabulary *Extra*

Origins of new words

1 Work with a partner. Look at the highlighted words. Can you explain exactly what they mean?

a) The invention of the biro revolutionised writing.
b) There was an anti-terrorism demo in the centre of town.
c) How good are you at guesstimating the calories on your plate?
d) If you don't know a word, google it!
e) More and more people are having laser eye surgery.
f) Paparazzi blamed for Madonna's riding injuries.
g) Experts say tsunamis can travel at up to 500km/h.
h) Hollywood's restaurants are full of wannabe actors waiting to be discovered.

2 Look at the words in Exercise 1 again. Match each word from the sentences (*a–h*) to its origin (*1–7*).

1 a word borrowed from another language
2 a brand name that has become a common noun
3 a noun or brand name that is used as a verb
4 a verb phrase which has been made into an adjective
5 a combination of two words
6 the initial letters of a group of words
7 a shortened word

Check your answers in the dictionary entry on the right.

3 Look at the words in the box. Do you know what they mean? Can you match them to the categories in the dictionary entry?

> decaf   facebook™ (v)   fuggedaboutit   kosher   Kleenex™
> lol   scuba   stalkerazzi

🌐 3.33 Listen to seven people talking about the words. Check your answers.

4 Work with your partner. Discuss these questions.
- Do you ever skype, facebook or youtube? If yes, how often?
- Do you think it's okay for an English language student to use slang like *lol* and *fuggedaboutit*?
- Do you think there are too many borrowed English words in your language?

5 Check your own dictionary. How does it show information about sources of new vocabulary?

Sources of new vocabulary

- **Borrowing**
Many English words are 'loanwords' from other languages, such as *paparazzi* (Italian), and *tsunami* (Japanese). Many are so familiar that we no longer think of them as borrowings, for example, *bungalow* (Hindi), *ombudsman* (Swedish).

- **Eponyms**
Eponyms are names of people, places or companies that are associated with a particular product or thing, and that become used as general vocabulary items. Examples include *Biro, Hoover, sandwich, sherry, watt*.

- **Conversion**
Conversion is the processs of changing the grammatical class of a word without changing its form. Conversion of nouns to verbs is particularly common in English – for example, *to word a message carefully*. More recently, nouns and brand names such as *Google*™, *email*, *text*, and *Skype*™ are also used as verbs.

- **Respelling**
Respellings often represent the way we pronounce certain words in informal situations – for example, *gonna* (*going to*), *pix* (*pics, pictures*), *sleb* (*celebrity*). Sometimes they develop different meanings from the original versions: for example, the word *wannabe* is a respelling of the phrase *want to be*, but it is used as a noun meaning someone who wants to be famous or successful.

- **Blending**
A blend is a combination of parts of two words, usually the beginning of one word and the end of another – for example, **glocalization** (*global + localization*), **guesstimate** (*guess + estimate*), **netiquette** (*net + etiquette*).

- **Acronyms**
An acronym is an abbreviation in which a sequence of letters is pronounced as a word – for example, **AIDS** (*acquired immune deficiency syndrome*), **laser** (*light amplification by stimulated emission of radiation*).

- **Clipping**
In clipping, the beginning or ending of a word is cut off – for example, **demo** (*demonstration*), **goss** (*gossip*).

12

Conscience

Grammar Special uses of the past simple
Vocabulary Describing street people. Verb/Noun collocations.
Expressions with *conscience*
Useful phrases Apologising

Speaking & Listening

1 Look at the photos and answer these questions.

a) Which person is the odd one out? Why?
b) Which of the people would you be more likely to give money to? Why?
c) Have you given money to anybody on the street recently? If not, do you ever give money? Who to and when?

2 🔊 3.34–3.39 Listen to six people talking about giving money to people in the street. Match the speakers (*1–6*) to the people they're talking about in column A and their attitude to beggars and giving in column B.

A	B
☐ beggars in general	☐ the government should take action
☐ people who clean car windows	☐ *1* it's better to give something other than money
☐ street performers	☐ you should only give to charity collectors
☐ *1* homeless people	☐ it's important to know where the money is going
☐ charity collectors	☐ it's okay if they do something to earn it
☐ charities in general	☐ beggars are all work-shy

3 Listen again. Which speaker do you sympathise with most? Who do you sympathise with least? Why? Compare your answers with a partner.

Vocabulary

1 Look at the words and phrases in the box. What's the difference between them? Which are a) neutral? b) potentially offensive? Which are a) more formal? b) more spoken or informal?

> bag lady   beggar   busker   down-and-out   homeless person   squeegee merchant
> street performer   street person   street vendor   tramp   vagrant   wino

2 Work in small groups. Discuss these questions.

a) Do you often see people asking for money on the streets in your town?
b) Are they tolerated or do the police tend to move them on?
c) What do you think is the best way to help people who ask for money on the streets?

Grammar

Special uses of the past simple

It's time we did something.

I'd rather they did something.

Suppose you were in that position.

Imagine you had no money.

1 Complete these sentences from the recording in Speaking & Listening, Exercise 2 on page 118, using an appropriate form of the verb in brackets.

a) I'd rather they actually _____ (do) something to earn the money.

b) I think it's high time that the government _____ (do) something about it because it really is annoying.

🌐 3.40 **Listen and check. Which tense is used? Why?**

2 Look at the expressions and sentences in bold below. Do they all refer to an action in the past? Would you use a past form in these sentences in your language?

a) **Suppose I gave him a few pounds**, what then? Would he use it to buy food, do you think?

b) **Imagine you had no home and no friends or family**. What would you do?

c) **It's about time we started thinking about other people** and not only about ourselves.

d) **It's time you asked someone for help**.

e) **I'd rather you didn't tell anybody**. I don't want my family to know I'm begging.

f) **I didn't tell anybody I'd seen her**. I didn't want to make things worse for her.

3 Complete these sentences with a verb in the appropriate form.

a) It's about time people _____ expecting others to look after them.

b) It's high time we _____ giving more generously to charity.

c) Imagine what we could do if we all _____ a little every day.

d) I'd rather people _____ something concrete to help, instead of paying out money to ease their consciences.

e) Suppose I _____ one of them a bed for the night. Would that solve the problem?

f) I'd rather local authorities _____ money on helping local youth clubs or improving leisure facilities for young people than redeveloping old buildings.

Which of the sentences above do you agree with? Compare your answer with a partner.

4 Complete the punch lines for the cartoons using *It's about time* and *I'd rather*.

_____ a shave.

_____ speak with your mouth full.

5 Grammar *Extra* 12 page 144. Read the explanations and do Exercises 1 and 2.

Reading

1   Look at the blurb of this DVD. What is the connection between international football and homelessness?

In the summer of 2006, while the football world's attention was focused on Germany, thousands of players around the globe were training hard and competing to be part of another world cup ... The Homeless World Cup.

It began in 2001 as a wild idea to give homeless people a chance to change their lives through an international street soccer competition. Five years later, the annual Homeless World Cup was an internationally recognised sports competition.

500 homeless players from 48 nations would ultimately be selected to represent their country in Cape Town, South Africa – coming from such disparate parts of the world as war-torn Afghanistan, the slums of Kenya, the drug rehab clinics of Dublin, Ireland, and the streets of Charlotte, North Carolina.

Win or lose, it would be the journey of a lifetime.

"Rarely has the HEALING POWER OF SPORTS been as genui depicted. A HEARTFELT tribute!"

Narrated by Colin Far

KICKING IT

a ball can change your life   DVD

2   Work with a partner. You are going to find out more about the Homeless World Cup. Student A: look at Article A on page 121, Student B: look at Article B on page 133. Answer these questions.

a)   How does the Homeless World Cup help people?
b)   Who founded the Homeless World Cup?

Tell your partner about your article and compare your answers.

3   Work with your partner. Decide which of the sentence endings (1–4) is correct. Underline the passages in the articles that support your answer.

a)   More or less the same number of people ...
    1   watch the Homeless World Cup as watch the official World Cup.
    2   play football as watch the official World Cup.
    3   are homeless as play football.
    4   watch the official World Cup as are homeless.

b)   The rules for the Homeless World Cup ...
    1   are the same as the official World Cup.
    2   are slightly different.
    3   are significantly different.
    4   exclude the participation of women.

c)   Most of the players at the Homeless World Cup ...
    1   found somewhere to live after the competition.
    2   got a job within six months of taking part.
    3   felt more motivated to change their lives.
    4   didn't feel there had been a change in their lives.

4   Think of two ways to complete the sentence according to one or both of the texts. One sentence must be true, the other must be false. Show your sentences to your partner. Can they choose the correct option?

The Homeless World Cup is ...
1
2

tag line

a short phrase used for advertising something, often used alongside a slogan to the main feature of a product or service

5   Work with your partner. The organisers of the Homeless World Cup are trying to raise the profile of the event. Write a 15-word tag line for their new campaign, explain what the competition is and what it aims to do. Compare your tag line with the rest of the class. Vote on the best one.

Article A

The Homeless World Cup

There are an estimated one billion homeless people in the world. That's roughly the same as the number of football fans who watched the 2006 World Cup.

What happens when football and homelessness come together? Lives change. And the annual Homeless World Cup has the statistics to prove it.

In 2006, 48 countries competed in the 4th annual Homeless World Cup. One year later ...

92% of players have a new motivation for life.

73% have changed their lives for the better.

93 players successfully addressed a drug or alcohol dependency.

35% have secured regular employment.

44% have improved their housing situation.

39% chose to pursue an education.

72% continue to play football.

The Homeless World Cup also supports and inspires grassroots football projects around the world, working with homeless and excluded people throughout the year.

Co-founded by world-leading social entrepreneur Mel Young and Harald Schmied, editor of *Magaphon*, a street paper in Austria, it is supported by Nike, UEFA, United Nations, football clubs (e.g. Manchester United, Real Madrid, SL Benfica), ambassador Eric Cantona, and international footballers Didier Drogba and Rio Ferdinand.

73% of players changed their lives for the better after participating, by coming off drugs and alcohol, moving into jobs, education, homes, training, reuniting with families and even going on to become players and coaches for pro or semi-pro football teams.

Vocabulary

1 Match the verbs (*a–f*) to the nouns to make collocations.

a)	address	your country
b)	boost	a problem
c)	pursue	employment
d)	represent	an education
e)	reunite	families
f)	secure	your self-esteem

2 Complete the sentences with the collocations from Exercise 1. You may need to make some changes.

a) Many of the players have been _____ with their _____ following the competition.

b) Some have succeeded in _____ _____ and have started working regularly for the first time in their lives.

c) Others have decided to _____ an _____ by going to night school or even university.

d) The majority have managed to _____ major _____ , such as drug addiction.

e) They are all proud to _____ their _____ at football.

f) The Homeless World Cup helps _____ the players' _____ .

3 Rewrite the sentences in Exercise 2 with a similar meaning, using the verbs given below. Make any other changes that are necessary.

a) get back *Many players have got back together with their families after the competition.*

b) get   c) do   d) deal with   e) play   f) feel better

Which version is more formal? Which verbs were used in the articles?

4 Work in small groups. Order the following according to their importance for living a happy and fulfilled life, in your opinion.

- a good education
- a good job
- getting on with your family
- good self-esteem

Do you think any of the four can exist without the other three?

1   Work with a partner. Do the quiz. Keep a note of your answers.

Ever had that guilty feeling?

Are you a worrier or do you sail through life without a care? Do our quick quiz and find out!

1   A friend is having his head shaved for charity. He asks you to join in too.

a)   You say yes straight away. Why not? It's for a good cause.

b)   You're torn – you don't really want to do it, you like your hair as it is, but you know you'll feel guilty if you let your friend down.

c)   You say no – you don't think you'd look good with a bald head – but you make a generous contribution to your friend's good cause.

2   Your elderly grandmother has asked you to go and stay with her for the weekend. She's feeling lonely and needs the company.

a)   Of course you'll go! You love staying with your grandmother – it's a great excuse for an early night and a quiet, relaxing weekend.

b)   You had planned to go out with your friends and you really don't want to go, but you know you'll feel really guilty if you don't.

c)   You explain you've got a special party arranged for this weekend, but that you'll come and visit her during the week.

3   You see a really expensive pair of trainers in a shop window. You know they're overpriced, but you really want them. What do you do?

a)   Wait for the sales. You may even be able to get them for half price.

b)   Dither for a couple of days, but then go back and buy them. When people ask you how much they cost, you lie and say they were half the price.

c)   Buy them. They'll look great with your new jeans!

4   It's Christmas, your great aunt is staying with you. She's bought you a jumper as a present. It isn't really your style. Do you …

a)   wear it all the time she's there – after all it's made of lamb's wool and it's very warm and cosy?

b)   try it on, wear it for about half an hour, but worry that someone you know might see you in it?

c)   ask her where she got it and if she's got the receipt, so you can change it for a jumper in a different style?

2   Turn to page 133 and compare your answers with the quiz results. Discuss with your partner what kind of person you think would always give the a), b) and c) answers. What does the quiz say about you?

Listening

▲ Jay

▲ Kiera

1 🌐 3.41 **Listen to a short conversation between Jay and Kiera. What is the link between the four pictures (a–d)?**

2 **Work with a partner. Answer these questions.**

a) What does Jay feel guilty about?
b) What is she going to do to ease her conscience?
c) What would you do in her position?

3 **Look at the extracts (a–e) from the conversation in Exercise 1. When the speakers say them in the recording, they drop one or two of the words. Which words do they drop?**

a) How are you doing?
b) Not too bad. And you?
c) Do you fancy coming?
d) Do you know my cousin, Susie?
e) I forgot to tell you …

Listen again and check.

4 **Who do you identify with most, Jay or Kiera? Why?**

Vocabulary

1 **Complete the sentences with the expressions with *conscience* in the box.**

a clear conscience	eased my conscience	an easy conscience
a guilty conscience	in all conscience	on his conscience

a) It was a tragic accident. He'll have it _____ for the rest of his life.
b) I was able to leave with _____ , happy that I'd done all I could to help.
c) He suffered with _____ for months after he left his wife and family.
d) I _____ by telling my boss about the mistake I'd made.
e) Can you, _____ , take their money when you know how much they need every penny?
f) You can go on holiday with _____ – I'll look after everything here for you.

2 **Which of these things would give you a guilty conscience? Add another three things to the list.**

- smoking in an enclosed space
- throwing litter on the floor
- spending money on luxury items
- eating too much chocolate
- forgetting someone's birthday
- not doing your homework
- losing your temper with someone
- not keeping a promise
- keeping people waiting
- forgetting to water the plants

Compare your answers with your partner. Which three things make you feel the guiltiest? What would you do to ease your conscience in each case?

3 **Can you think of a time when you felt guilty about doing any of these things? What did you do to make amends?**

Useful phrases

1 🌐 3.42–3.47 **Listen to six short conversations (1–6). What are the people apologising for? Who sounds most apologetic?**

2 **Listen again and complete the useful phrases.**

a) Oh, I'm _____ , it totally _____ !
b) ... I think I _____ .
c) _____ ! I had _____ you were so touchy today!
d) I'm _____ sorry.
e) I really, really _____ . ... But it _____ again.
f) We _____ that tonight's concert has been cancelled.

3 **Listen again. Notice the use of intonation and voice range. Practise repeating the useful phrases in Exercise 2 with the same feeling.**

4 **Match the apologies (a–e) in Exercise 1 to the responses (1–5). Which person feels most upset about what's happened?**

1 Yeah, well, it better hadn't!
2 Yeah, well, don't leave it too late!
3 Yes – this time!
4 That's alright. Don't worry about it. Easily done.
5 Can we just drop it, please?

What do you think the relationship is between the two people in each of the conversations (1–5)? Who do you think is making the apology in the last recording?

5 **Work with a partner. Look at the situations and decide what you would say in each. How angry do you think the other person would be?**

a) you borrowed someone's bike and damaged it
b) you lost your friend's memory stick
c) you spilt a drink over a stranger
d) you drove into the back of someone's car

Choose one of the situations and act it out between you.

6 🌐 3.48 **Listen to people saying *sorry*. Match each *sorry* (1–6) to its use (a–f).**

a) apologising for doing something wrong
b) breaking bad news
c) offering commiserations
d) asking someone to move
e) asking someone to repeat what they said
f) drawing someone's attention

What do you say *sorry* for in your language? Would you use the same expression for all six uses in (a–f)?

7 **Work in small groups. Discuss these questions.**

a) When was the last time someone apologised to you?
b) What were they apologising for?
c) How did they apologise?
d) Did you accept their apology? Why? / Why not?

Writing *Extra*

Responding to a complaint

1 🔊 3.49 **Listen to a conversation between two friends. What is Kelly upset about? What advice does Laura give her?**

2 **Read the letter Kelly received from the store manager in reply to her letter of complaint. How do you think she reacted when she got it?**

> Dear Ms Johnson,
>
> I have received your complaint about the service in one of our shops. If anyone was rude to you, it was not me, but the check-out assistant, Mrs B. Smith. I was not even present in the store when the incident occurred. The policy of our company is that staff should be polite at all times. Accordingly, the company is not at fault in any way. Nor am I, and I have been completely exonerated by an inquiry conducted by my assistant, Mr A. Toady. I regard your approach to me as a personal insult, and any future correspondence should be addressed to someone else.

Read the reply again. What were the three main mistakes the store manager made in his reply?

3 **Look at this alternative reply. How would Kelly feel if she received this letter? Why?**

> Thank you for informing me of your experience in one of our stores. I regret the incident, and the distress you understandably feel. Please accept my personal apologies, and those of the company. The policy of our company is that staff should be polite at all times. Our organisation failed to provide you with the service you are entitled to expect. The matter has been investigated, and steps have been taken to prevent a recurrence. I hope that you will have a better experience of our services in future, and will not hesitate to contact me personally with any suggestions as to how they might be improved.

Read the letter again. Underline the passages where the manager says:

a) We accept and welcome criticism.
b) We apologise for any perceived failures.
c) I, as manager, accept ultimate responsibility for what happens in the store.
d) Action has been taken following the complaint.

4 **Look at another letter of complaint. What exactly is the nature of the complaint?**

> Last week I booked a taxi from your online taxi service to take me to the airport. The taxi was booked for 7.30 a.m. and I was due to arrive at the airport at 8 a.m. to check in. The taxi did not appear so I called the help line. They promised that the taxi would be there in five minutes. When the taxi still didn't appear I tried calling other taxi services, but they were all busy. Eventually a taxi turned up, 15 minutes late. By the time I arrived at the airport the flight had closed. I had to pay for a ticket for the next flight. I enclose the receipt for the second flight and expect to receive full reimbursement at your earliest convenience.

5 **Work with a partner. Read the notes from the taxi company on the right and respond to the letter.**

6 **Read through your letter and make sure you have addressed the following points.**

- Acknowledged the original letter of complaint.
- Shown that you accept responsibility for what happened.
- Apologised and offered a way to make amends.
- Closed the letter on a positive note.

Notes:
- company policy – taxi on time or taxi fare fully refunded
- flight cannot be refunded
- offer vouchers for 3 free taxi rides as a goodwill gesture

Review D

▶ **Grammar _Extra_** pages 142–145

Grammar

1 Underline the correct alternative.

The first shoes worn by man were a type of sandal. Sandals (1) **wore / were worn** in most early civilizations. The oldest sandals (2) **found / were found** in the American south-west. These sandals (3) **date / are dated** back approximately 8,000 years. A few early cultures also (4) **had / were had** shoes. In Mesopotamia, more than 3,000 years ago, a type of soft shoe (5) **used / was used** by the mountain people who (6) **lived / were lived** on the border of Iran. The soft shoe (7) **made / was made** of wraparound leather, similar to a moccasin. Until relatively recently no difference (8) **made / was made** between left and right shoes.

2 Write the reduced passive clauses in bold as full relative clauses.

a) These highly practical and resistant shoes, **designed originally for use on boats**, are now the number one preferred beachwear for all ages.

b) They used to be strictly for beachwear, but now they can be seen everywhere, **even teamed up with a smart skirt and blouse for the office**.

c) This sturdy footwear, **previously seen mainly on muddy lanes or farmyards**, has now become the height of fashion.

Match the sentences above to the photos (_1–3_).

3 Work with a partner. Write sentences comparing the shoes in the photos in Exercise 2 with the ones you are wearing now. Use all the comparative structures in the box at least once.

> a bit more   by far   far and away   infinitely
> nothing like   nowhere near as   somewhat
> slightly

4 Look at the short conversation below. What are the two people talking about?

A: I did **it**!
B: Congratulations! Was **it** difficult?
A: No, not as difficult as I thought. I'm really pleased I've got **it**! **It**'s going to make such a huge difference!
B: I bet Beth **is** too. Now she won't have to do all the driving!

What exactly do the words in bold refer to? Check with your teacher.

5 Make the article as short as possible by replacing or dropping any unnecessary words and phrases.

Crowdsourcing: what is crowdsourcing? Who takes part in crowdsourcing? Well, everyone and anyone can take part. Everyone and anyone taking part in crowdsourcing is part of the basic concept. The term 'crowdsourcing' was first used in 2006. The term describes a process by which a company broadcasts a business problem online and issues an open call for solutions. These solutions come from any person and every person who is online. The crowd offers solutions to the problem which was broadcast by the company and they also sort through the solutions and find the best solutions. And the company doesn't have to pay a penny for the service!

6 Work with your partner. Write the verbs in brackets in the appropriate form.

a) I'd _____ (prefer) that you didn't tell anyone.
b) It's about time we _____ (make) a move.
c) It's high time you _____ (face) your responsibilities.
d) I'd rather _____ (tell) him myself.
e) If I _____ (not/know) you so well, I'd think you were hiding something from me.
f) If only he _____ (know) how she felt about him.

Look at the sentences again. Who do you think is talking, and who are they talking to? What do you imagine the situation is?

Vocabulary

1 Work with a partner. Complete the sentences with a word from the box. More than one answer is possible at times.

> energy-efficient   locally-grown   organic
> recycled   renewable   solar-powered   sustainable

a) All official forms are printed on _____ paper where possible.
b) The local restaurants often offer _____ meat on their menus.
c) There's a lot of _____ produce available in the shops.
d) Our building has _____ hot water.
e) The local government has started a scheme to help householders buy _____ kitchen appliances.
f) Our local MP is a strong believer in _____ farming.
g) The government is investing money in creating reliable _____ energy sources.

Are any of these statements true for your country?

2 Match the expressions in the box to the definitions.

> be waited on hand and foot   get a foot in the door
> get cold feet   get itchy feet   put your foot down
> put your foot in it   put your feet up
> shoot yourself in the foot

a) accidentally annoy or embarrass someone
b) sit down and relax
c) firmly refuse to do something
d) say or do something stupid that gets you into trouble
e) get a chance to start working somewhere
f) have everything done for you
g) want to travel or make a change in your life
h) suddenly feel uncertain about a plan

Have any of these things happened to you recently? Tell your partner about it.

3 Complete the expressions in the article.

Not everyone suffers during a credit 1) c_____.
In fact, some companies have found their profits soaring in the so-called lipstick 2) e_____ where people are spending money on affordable treats instead of indulging in conspicuous 3) c_____.

The art of writing seems to have made a comeback, albeit in the shape of 4) l_____casting and 5) m_____blogging. Everyone can be a writer now, publishing their thoughts and deeds in 6) s_____ updates on any number of social networks.

I'm well and truly fed up of this 7) a_____ on, 8) a_____ connected lifestyle. I'm sorely tempted to switch it all off, indulge in a bit of 9) d_____ down time and try to readjust my 10) joy-to-s_____ ratio!

4 Re-order the letters to find ten words to describe people who ask for money on the street.

a) gab dlay
b) gerbag
c) subrek
d) pamrt
e) gvanart
f) noiw
g) wndo-dna-tuo
h) lhemosse srenop
i) restet denvro
j) geueqees cahtmenr

Did you see any of these people on your way to your English class today? Tell your partner.

5 Match the two halves of the sentences.

a) He was proud to have had the opportunity to represent
b) He travelled abroad to pursue
c) After many long years she was finally reunited
d) She worked hard to address
e) Winning such a prestigious prize certainly helped boost
f) He worked for years in badly-paid jobs before he secured

1 a career in acting.
2 her confidence and self-esteem.
3 her drug problem and eventually overcame it.
4 his country at the Olympics.
5 his first professional cinema role.
6 with her family.

Look at the sentences again. Can you think of celebrities from your country, or in the news, to match each sentence?

Pronunciation

1 Look at some words from Units 10–12. Say the words and add them to the table.

> ~~conspicuous~~   development   emissions   energy
> facetious   feminine   flirtatious   honestly
> information   misconstruing   punctuation
> renewable   repetition   settlement   stilettos
> sustainable

A: ▢□□	B: □▢□	C: □▢□□	D: □□▢□
		conspicuous	

2 Underline the stressed syllables.

🔊 3.50 **Listen, check and repeat.**

Additional material

Unit 1 Speaking & Listening (page 8)

Read the information and act out a telephone conversation.

Group A
Suzi
Last night you and your boyfriend decided to go to the cinema tonight to see a film you both really want to see. Tonight is the last night it's showing. He's already cancelled once because of work. You're not too sure about your relationship at the moment. You think there must be something worrying him, but he refuses to talk about it. You're going to phone your boyfriend to make arrangements to meet. Think about what you're going to say to him and the language you're going to use.

Group B
Brian
You and your girlfriend had talked about going to see a film tonight but you've been having a hard time at work lately and you just want to have a quiet night in at home, alone. You and your girlfriend can go out another time when you're not so tired. It's not that you don't want to see her, it's just that you know you wouldn't be good company tonight. Your girlfriend will be phoning you soon. Think about what you're going to say to her and the language you're going to use.

Unit 2 Speaking (page 14)

Answers
a) baked beans: Max   c) a bar of chocolate: Janet
b) cauliflower: Julia   d) nuts: Colin

Unit 2 Listening (page 20)

Anne: Thailand
Kim: Southern India
Bill: Hungary
Steve: Spain

Unit 2 Reading (page 16)

Group B
Read the text and make notes about the changes that had taken place ...

a) in the seating area and the kitchen.   b) to the menu.   c) to the vegetable gardens.

TEXT B

Arriving on the island that second time was a totally different experience. There was now a mass of tables on a huge concrete terrace exposed to the sun. Between the tables ran waiters, carrying trays of drinks and food. Our waiter spoke to us in English and thrust menus into our hands as soon as we sat down.

I looked through the windows into what had been a small and homely kitchen, and saw four chefs sweating over huge stoves. There was no sign of Marianne or Didier and I didn't recognise their son amongst the army of waiters. On the paper tablecloth was a basket, but the bread in it was not home-made. It was what you could buy in any supermarket on the mainland.

Looking at the menu I realised that the motor boat was picking up more than just passengers: the greatly expanded menu offered dishes which could not have been created using ingredients just from the island. Worst of all, the squid was now served in batter and accompanied by chips.

I asked the waiter what had become of Didier and Marianne. They had retired about five years earlier and sold the business to an entrepreneur from the capital. Only Dominique remained. She had married a local boy and was managing the bar on the jetty. The restaurant was obviously profitable. As we sat and ate an unremarkable meal the boat came and went two or three times, bringing new customers and taking away those who had already eaten. After dinner we wandered unnoticed around the back of the main building and looked out over what had been the gardens. There were now a number of small concrete buildings, some with lights shining from the windows. The new owner had obviously decided that there was money to be made from offering tourists more than just dinner. They could now come and spend the night, have breakfast in the morning and then return to the mainland.

As we climbed aboard the boat, considerably poorer, I found myself thinking about Marianne. What she would think of her restaurant now, I could only guess. My reverie was broken as we chugged to a halt at the end of the jetty. I looked over to the car and wondered whether the satnav was still there.

Unit 2 Vocabulary (page 17)

Group B
Students from Group B: prepare to teach four of these words from your part of the review to a student who read the other part.

batter chugged concrete entrepreneur homely reverie satnav thrust

a) Read the text again and find the words.
b) Discuss their meanings with your partner. Think about the best way to explain them.

Unit 3 Grammar (page 25)

Most prefer to live in cities if given choice

According to a survey published in the press today, it would appear that most people under the age of thirty would much prefer to live in a large city if given the choice. By far the most important factor given in their answers would seem to be the fact that it is far easier to find work in larger cities. However, the results show that there is no doubt that the range of free-time facilities on offer is also an important factor in the decision to leave families and homes in rural areas.

Unit 3 Reading (page 27)

Clue
The texts describe four cities from the list below:
Bangkok, Budapest, London, Madrid, Moscow, New York, Paris, Prague, Rome, Tokyo

Unit 3 Reading & Vocabulary (page 30)

Student A
1 Below are four words from the text. Check their meanings in a dictionary if necessary, and prepare to explain the words to your partner. Your partner must listen and identify the word from the text.

a) buskers   b) check out   c) eyeball   d) gorge

2 When you have finished, listen to your partner's description of four more words from the text and identify the words being described.

Unit 4 Vocabulary (page 39)

The Urban Myth

The flat tyre
Two university friends decided to go skiing for the weekend but planned to be back on campus in time to revise for an important exam on Monday morning. However, they were having such a good time on the slopes that they knew that they would have to come up with a good excuse for not being prepared for the exam. Therefore, they decided to tell their lecturer that they had set off with plenty of time to get back and do some studying, but that they had got a flat tyre on the way back and therefore deserved to take the exam at a rescheduled time. When he heard the story, the lecturer agreed that it really was just bad luck, and suggested that they took a few days to study and do the exam at the end of the week. The students, of course, were delighted. At the appointed time, the lecturer greeted them and placed them in two separate rooms to take the exam.
The few questions on the first page were worth a minor 10% of the overall mark and were quite easy. Each student grew progressively more confident as they worked their way through the questions, sure that they had got away with fooling their lecturer. However, when they turned to the second page they discovered that really they hadn't.
The only question on the page, worth 90% of the exam, read: 'Which tyre?'

Unit 3 Reading (page 30)

Student B

1 Below are four words from the text. Check their meanings in a dictionary if necessary, and prepare to explain the words to your partner.

> a) rant b) gawp at c) handily d) eateries

2 Your partner will explain four more words from the text. You must listen and identify the words being described. When your partner has finished, explain your four words for your partner to identify.

Unit 4 Listening & Speaking (page 43)

Student A

> ### Joke 1
> A man's walking down the street and he sees this other bloke with a big dog, and he says to him, 'Does your dog bite?' The man with the dog says, 'No, my dog doesn't bite.' So the man pats the dog and gets his hand bitten off.
> 'I thought you said your dog didn't bite,' says the first man.
> 'That's not my dog,' says the other one.

Unit 5 Reading & Vocabulary (page 46)

Mostly As
You like to live life to the full regardless of the cost, and your money often burns a hole in your pocket. You are generous with your money and enjoy life's luxuries. However, your laid-back attitude to spending and credit can land you in trouble and you may need to take a careful look at your finances if you want to avoid always being overdrawn and in debt.

Mostly Bs
You take a careful approach to budgeting and like to keep track of your income and outgoings. You tend to live within your means, planning ahead and clearing your debts as soon as you can. You avoid paying over the odds for your purchases and are not waylaid by special offers – but equally you do allow yourself to indulge in the occasional treat or extravagance.

Mostly Cs
Your approach to spending is frugal in the extreme, and you economise and cut corners where you can – your friends might even accuse you of being tight-fisted. You have an eye for a bargain, and prefer window-shopping to the real thing. But does your thrifty attitude mean you could be missing out on friendships and the fun side of life?

Unit 5 Useful phrases (page 54)

Student A

1 You are a customer in a street market. You see a jacket that you would like to buy. There is a small mark on the sleeve and one of the buttons is missing. Try to negotiate a discount – ideally 20%.
2 You would like to borrow a friend's car to take your elderly aunt, who has difficulty walking, to the airport. There are no buses or trains as it is an early flight. Try to persuade your friend to lend it.

Unit 6 Speaking (page 56)

Answers

a) False: the average male brain weighs 1.4kg and the average female brain weighs 1.3kg.
b) True
c) False: 80% of the average human brain is water.
d) False: the brain is pinkish grey on the surface and white inside.
e) True
f) False: we use 100% of our brains in everyday life.
g) True
h) False: the brain is very active during sleep, but the activity is of a different type to waking activity.
i) False: we yawn more when the brain is being stimulated to allow more oxygen to the brain.
j) True

Unit 4 Listening & Speaking (page 43)

Student B

> **Joke 2**
> A woman gets on a bus with her baby and she goes up to the driver and tries to buy a ticket and the driver says, 'Oh, luv, that's the ugliest baby I've ever seen.'
> The woman is obviously absolutely furious, so she sits down and starts chatting to the man next to her and says, 'Can you believe that driver just insulted me?'
> And the man says, 'Oh, don't worry, you go and tell him off and I'll hold your monkey.'

Unit 5 Useful phrases (page 54)

Student B

1   You are a market stall holder. You are prepared to offer a very small discount for goods but only if you have to – ideally no more than 20%.
2   You have a car. The last time a friend borrowed it, it got scratched, so you would really prefer not to lend it again.

Unit 6 Reading & Speaking (page 57)

1   one point for each piece of information
2   one point for each grammar focus (there are two: The future as seen from the past. Discourse markers.)
3   1 point – clothes   2 points – clothes and colours   3 points – clothes, colours, shoes and accessories
4   10
5
6

5	0	2	2
3	3	2	1
1	3	0	5
0	3	5	1

7   fewer than five words = 0, 5–10 words = 1, 11–14 = 2, 15 = 5

Unit 6 Reading (page 58)

The Lost Mariner

The Lost Mariner is a man who could remember his childhood and the first years of his working life (he worked for the American navy) in great detail; but nothing else. His world had stopped in 1945; he believed he was a young man in his twenties, that America had won the war and Truman was the President of the USA. He was unable to remember anything that had happened to him since.

The Phantom Finger

A sailor accidentally cut off his right index finger. For forty years afterwards he was plagued by the phantom of the finger rigidly extended: whenever he scratched his nose or tried to eat he was afraid that the phantom finger would poke his eye out. He knew that it was impossible but the feeling was so strong he couldn't ignore it.

The Dog Beneath The Skin

A young man dreamt he was a dog and could smell like a dog. He woke up and found he was indeed able to smell like a dog. He could distinguish all his friends by smell; he could smell their emotions – fear, contentment, worry – like a dog. It was a whole new world but then suddenly, after three weeks, this strange transformation ceased.

Unit 7 Useful phrases (page 76)

Student A

You boss has offered you promotion. The job will mean longer hours and lots of travelling, but it will also mean a generous pay rise. You have a young family and you need the extra money, but you don't want to spend so much time away from home.

Unit 8 Listening & Grammar (page 79)

During a recent court case held in Wales, an English judge learnt a lesson about using Welsh in the courtroom. A Welshman stood in the witness box, accused of shoplifting. Defending him was a Welsh lawyer.

The lawyer asked the judge towards the end of the trial whether he could speak to the jury in Welsh. Not wishing to appear biased towards English, the judge agreed. Shortly afterwards, a verdict of not guilty was returned. What puzzled the judge was the verdict, as the defendant was obviously guilty.

Not being able to speak Welsh, the judge hadn't understood what the lawyer had said, which was: 'The prosecutor is English, the prosecution counsel is English, the judge is English. But the prisoner is Welsh, I'm Welsh and you're Welsh. Do your duty.'

Unit 8 Speaking & Listening (page 80)

Case 1
The driver was driving within the established speed limit and was not guilty of violating any driving offences. As such, he could not be made liable for the injuries to the pedestrian. However, his car was insured against accidental injuries to third parties and the driver's insurance company paid the pedestrian £5,000 in damages for the injuries incurred (a broken wrist and resultant loss of earnings). As the car was covered under a fully comprehensive insurance policy, the insurance company also paid for the damages to the car. The insurance company sought to take the children's parents to court to sue them for the damages to both car and pedestrian, but the court ruled that the parents could not be held liable for their child's having crossed the road as they had done everything in their power to try to stop her.

Case 2
The court found the footballer not guilty of deliberately seeking to injure his opponent, and although he had committed a foul, he had not premeditated an assault on his opponent. However, the club's insurance company were forced to pay damages for loss of earnings whilst the player was recovering from his injuries.

Unit 9 Reading & Speaking (page 88)

Mostly As
You are definitely a lark, or a morning person. You are alert and at your peak first thing in the morning, and go steadily downhill after that. You accomplish your best work in the morning, so try to do important tasks then and leave the afternoon and evening for winding down and relaxing.

Mostly Bs
Like most people, you are neither an owl or a lark, but somewhere in between. This means you can fit in with most schedules and can accommodate the occasional early morning or late night with little disruption to your body clock.

Mostly Cs
You are definitely an owl, or an evening person. You tend to spend the first part of the day waking up and really come to life in the evening. Getting up and fitting in with most work schedules can be a challenge, but you are able to enjoy and make the most of all the nightlife that is on offer.

Unit 10 Grammar (page 103)

Student A
Read the information about an historic site under threat. Write a brief report using passive structures, answering these questions: a) What is the problem? b) What is being done? c) What has been done? d) What should be done in future?

Lascaux caves, Dordogne, France
Bacterial and fungal infection threaten prehistoric paintings. Caves now closed to tourists. Authorities monitoring the situation. Preserving the paintings is necessary.

Unit 7 Useful phrases (page 76)

Student B

Your neighbour has invited you to go on holiday with his family to the Caribbean for a month. He will pay all your expenses but he has five small children and you will be expected to help look after them. You'd love to go to the Caribbean but you're worried you may end up being stuck with the kids all day.

Unit 10 Grammar (page 103)

Student B

Read the information about an historic site under threat. Write a brief report using passive structures, answering these questions: a) What is the problem? b) What is being done? c) What has been done? d) What should be done in future?

Wadi Mathendous rock art, Libya

Tourism and vibrations from oil-drilling threaten ancient cliff carvings. Prehistoric people drew animals and other symbols on the dry river bed. Tourists climb on the rocks, defacing the pictures. The oil-drilling must stop.

Unit 12 Reading (page 120)

Article B

Too often people associate sport with professional players behaving like spoilt children, says the social entrepreneur Mel Young. 'Sport is so much more, and we're showing governments and other agencies that this is something that works.'

This is the Homeless World Cup, which Young co-founded; an annual five-a-side football tournament contested by 48 countries from around the world, each of them represented by men and women living in temporary accommodation or on the streets.

The tournament aims to bring together homeless people from around the world to share their experiences, learn valuable life skills and boost their self-esteem.

And it does work. In a survey of participants in last year's event in Cape Town, South Africa, 73% reported that their lives had changed for the better six months later. Many had improved their housing situation, secured regular employment, were pursuing an education and/or had tackled a drug problem.

Part of the event's success is that it reaches people that other parts of the system can't reach. Young men in particular can be reluctant to accept help, but football and the idea of representing one's country is a powerful attraction.

'It's not the answer for everybody,' says Young, 'but it works for a lot of people.'

Young hopes the event can grow in the future and has dreams of getting 100,000 people involved by the end of the decade.

'We're very ambitious, because it works,' he says. 'What we're proving is that sport, and football in particular, can be used as a tool in the world of development.'

Unit 12 Reading & Speaking (page 122)

Mostly As

You always find the positive in a situation and hate putting yourself first. But watch out, people might start taking advantage of you and you could end up feeling just a little bit resentful.

Mostly Bs

My, you are a ditherer! Even the smallest decision turns into a massive dilemma. Cut yourself a bit of slack, lighten up a bit. Life isn't really that serious, you know. And even though you think people are judging you for every little thing you do, they're not! They've got better things to do with their lives!!

Mostly Cs

Wow! Pragmatic must be your middle name. You certainly know how to get the best of both worlds, and still keeping everyone happy at the same time. No regrets, no guilt and definitely no sleepless nights for you!

Grammar *Extra*

Unit 1 **Position of adverbials. Aspect**

Part 1: Position of adverbials

An adverbial can be a word (*sometimes*, *actually*) or a phrase (*in due course*, *on the TV*). Adverbials are generally used to provide additional information about a verb, an adjective or the sentence as a whole.

Adverbs of frequency are usually used between the auxiliary verb (when there is one) and the main verb: *We don't **always** make up after an argument.*

Adverbs which express possibility and probability are normally used between the auxiliary and the main verb in the affirmative: *We'll **probably** see you tomorrow.* But they are often positioned before the auxiliary in the negative: *We **probably** won't see you tomorrow.*

Adverbs of manner and **indefinite time** can also be used

between the auxiliary and main verbs. *We **quickly** finished our lunch. / We've **finally** met the deadline!*

Adverbs such as *apparently*, *presumably*, *frankly*, which comment on the sentence as a whole, usually go at the beginning of the sentence: ***Frankly**, I've had enough of the situation.* But they can also be used at the end: *I've had enough of the situation, **frankly**.*

Changes in position and meaning: most adverbials are very flexible and can be used in any of the three positions. However, sometimes a change in position can change the meaning of a sentence: *Jane **only** speaks German.* (she doesn't speak any other languages) as opposed to ***Only** Jane speaks German.* (no-one else speaks German)

▶ **Now do Exercise 1.**

Part 2: Aspect

The perfect aspect
Perfect verb forms are used to look back at an action, or series of actions that took place (or will take place) before a given point in time. *He hasn't spoken to her for three days.*

The continuous aspect
Continuous forms are used to describe an action, or series of actions, in progress at (or around) a given point in time. *She was attending an important meeting when I phoned so I couldn't*

speak to her.

Perfect continuous verb forms
The two aspects can be combined to form perfect continuous forms. Perfect continuous forms generally emphasise the length of time an action has been in progress, or the fact that it has only recently stopped. ***He'd been waiting** a long time and he was getting very frustrated. Was no-one going to help him?*

▶ **Now do Exercise 2.**

Unit 2 **Noun phrases. Describing nouns and order of adjectives. Fronting**

Part 1: Noun phrases. Describing nouns and order of adjectives

In addition to the noun, a noun phrase may contain a determiner and extra details describing the noun:

Determiner	Pre-modification	Head	Post-modification
articles possessive adjectives quantifiers, etc	adjectives nouns compound nouns	main noun	prepositional phrases relative clauses reduced relative clauses
a cup of *the*	*black espresso* *Lebanese*	*coffee* *restaurant*	*with two or three sugars* *your cousin recommended*

When there are two or more adjectives before the noun they usually follow a certain pattern. Opinion adjectives always come before adjectives that describe facts. Other adjectives follow the order below.

size	other qualities	age	shape, pattern, colour	origin	material	type

For example, *delicious fresh black Italian espresso coffee*

▶ **Now do Exercise 1.**

Part 2: Fronting

Fronting = to start a sentence with something other than the subject and the verb. Fronting is often used in journalism and literature for dramatic effect or emphasis:
Here comes John ...

Inversion: when you bring an object, complement or adverb to the beginning of the sentence you often reverse the order of the subject and the verb: ***Damien was** his name.*

Fronting questions: when you front a reported question there is no inversion: *What they were doing there, we did not know.* The fronted question follows the normal word order pattern for indirect questions, i.e question word, subject, verb: *Why he had come, I could only guess.* Notice the use of the comma after the fronted question.

▶ **Now do Exercise 2.**

Unit 1 **Exercises**

1 Put the phrases in the correct order to form sentences. More than one order is possible. Choose the one you think sounds most natural.

  a) I / watch TV / always / before going to bed / for half an hour
  b) I / worked late / last week / every night / at the office
  c) I / love reading a good book / more than anything else / quite honestly
  d) I / won't do anything special / probably / tonight
  e) I / wish I had more time / at the weekend / sometimes / to do sport
  f) I / dislike loud music / particularly / in public places
  g) I'll / have time / to do more sport / probably / once I finish my exams
  h) I / know I / I'm / eat / in a hurry / always / too quickly / but

  Are the sentences true for you? If not, change them so that they are. Then compare your sentences with a partner.

2 Complete the short conversations with the correct form of the verb in brackets.

  a)
  A: Where _____ (1 you/be)? I_____ (2 wait) here for hours!
  B   Don't exaggerate! I bet you _____ (3 just/arrive). Jack said he spoke to you half an hour ago and that you _____ (4 just/get) off the bus!
  b)
  A: How long _____ (5 you/live) in this flat? It _____ (6 must/be) a long time.
  B: Yes, this time next week, we _____ (7 be) here for five years.
  A: And when _____ (8 you/move) out?
  B   At the end of the month. We _____ (9 move) into the new flat on the July 1st. We'll be sad to go.

  Practise reading the exchanges with your partner.

Unit 2 **Exercises**

1 Write the sentences in the correct order.

  a) rust / bike / A / old / covered / in / battered
  b) great / soundtrack / thriller / An / with / a / action-packed
  c) a / man / story / no / home / with / about / A / moving
  d) high-heeled / wear / black / to / work / I / A / shoes / pair / of
  e) world / sandwich / bar / coffee / best / Italian / An / the / that / espresso / makes / in / the
  f) Asian / dishes / new / serving / a / restaurant / range / seafood / of / A / wide

  Now write three complex noun phrases describing a) one of your favourite possessions, b) a book or film you've enjoyed, or c) a place where you've eaten recently.

  Compare your sentences with your partner. Do you have similar tastes?

2 Rewrite the sentences starting with the words in bold.

  a) The curtains came **down** on her last act.
  _____

  b) Her long blonde locks had **gone**.
  _____

  c) There was a special light **in** her eyes.
  _____

  d) Her youthful beauty was **still** intact.
  _____

  e) Applause rang **loudly** through the theatre.
  _____

  f) There was **no-one else** on the stage with her as she took her last bow.
  _____

  g) No-one knew **what** would become of her now.
  _____

  Look at the sentences again. They all come from the same text. What kind of text is it? What is the event being described in the text?

Unit 3 Hedging. Inversion after negative and limiting adverbials

Part 1: Hedging

Hedging = to avoid answering a question, or making a statement, in a direct way. You can use a range of expressions to do this:

- **Verbs**
  Use verbs such as *seem, appear, suggest*.
  It **appears** that people are happier in the city.

- To further distance yourself from the answer or statement, use *would*.
  It **would** appear that people are happier in the city.

- **Passive**
  Use the passive with verbs such as *think, recognise, believe, report* and *know* to show that an opinion is not necessarily your own. *It is widely* **recognised** *that … It has been* **reported** *that …*

- **Noun phrases**
  Use noun phrases to explain your attitude to the reliability of a statement.
  Strong evidence: *there is little / no doubt, there is little / no discussion*
  Fairly strong evidence: *there is some evidence / there is some discussion / there is some doubt*
  Unreliable statement: *there is little / no evidence*

▶ **Now do Exercise 1.**

Part 2: Inversion after negative and limiting adverbials

Sometimes a negative or limiting adverbial is placed at the beginning of a sentence to create emphasis. This effect is most frequently found in writing and is considered both formal and literary.

Negative adverbials
Adverbial phrases which contain words such as *no, not, never, no sooner, not until, never before*

Limiting adverbials
Adverbials such as *seldom, rarely, hardly, barely, little* or adverbial phrases that contain the word *only*:
only after I had taken the test, **only** by bribing the officer …

Inversion
When these adverbials are used at the beginning of a sentence the subject and auxiliary verb are inverted:
Never **have** *I seen anything quite so breathtaking.* The same happens with the verb *be*: *Not only* **is** *it one of the oldest cities, it is also one of the most beautiful.* In the present simple and past simple, use *do/does* or *did. Rarely* **do** *we visit that part of town.*

▶ **Now do Exercise 2.**

Unit 4 The future as seen from the past. Discourse markers in writing

Part 1: The future as seen from the past

You can use a range of structures and expressions to talk about the future as seen from the past. You can talk about:

- **events that took place** using *would*, or *was / were to*:
  Who could have guessed that he'd become President one day? / Those **were to** *become the happiest years of his life.*

- **events that did not take place** using *was / were* + perfect infinitive: *They* **were to** *have gone to Mexico, but they had to change their plans at the last minute.*

- **future plans in the past** using *was / were going to, was / were planning to, had been hoping to, had been thinking of*:
  He **had been hoping to** *go to university, but he failed all his exams.*

- **imminent events in the past** using *was / were due to / (just) about to, on the point / on the verge of*: *I* **was about** *to leave. / He* **was on the point / verge of** *giving up.*

▶ **Now do Exercise 1.**

Part 2: Discourse markers in writing

You use discourse markers to show how ideas relate to each other and to show our attitude to those ideas.
I love silly jokes, particularly those involving slapstick, **such as** *pies in faces.*

Here are some common uses with examples of common discourse markers:

- giving examples: *for example, for instance, e.g., say, such as, including*
- emphasising one example: *in particular, particularly*
- specifying who or what exactly you're talking about: *namely, viz, i.e.*
- clarifying what you want to say: *that is to say, in other words, strictly speaking, to put it another way*
- adding information: *too, in addition, not to say, as well as, moreover*
- qualifying a statement: *or at any rate, or even, or at least*
- contrasting two things or ideas: *on the other hand, by contrast, however, nevertheless*
- emphasising a similarity: *likewise, similarly*
- introducing a question: *so, then* (when word position changes).

Notes
Too, when used as a discourse marker, is never used at the beginning of a sentence.

▶ **Now do Exercise 2.**

Unit 3 Exercises

1 Underline the most appropriate alternative, in your opinion.

   a) **It is widely agreed / There is little evidence to show** that younger people prefer to live in cities.

   b) **There is no doubt / It would seem** that there are better job opportunities in large cities.

   c) **It is generally recognised that / There is some discussion about whether** small communities offer better services to the elderly.

   d) **Research suggests that / There is some doubt about whether** most people would prefer to work from home rather than travel to an office every day.

   e) **It has been reported that / It is not believed that** most young graduates would be happy to move abroad to find work.

   f) **There is no doubt / Some experts suggest** that the future of work lies in the internet.

   Compare your answers with a partner. Do you agree? Why? / Why not?

2 There is one mistake in each sentence. Find and correct the mistakes.

   a) Never before I had felt so happy.

   b) Not until had we reached the top did we realise how far we had come.

   c) Only once the show was over we could relax and enjoy ourselves.

   d) Only after some years I understood how important that experience had been for me.

   e) Not only did I want to do it again, did I want to do it as soon as possible!

   f) Barely had I arrived when happened the strangest thing.

   Look at the sentences again. Choose two of them that relate to an experience you have had in your life. Tell your partner about the experience.

Unit 4 Exercises

1 Match the sentence endings (1–6) to the sentence beginnings (a–f).

a) I was about to go out	1 would go on to be one of the best musical groups of all time.
b) We all knew that	2 then we managed to persuade them.
c) He had planned to	3 she decided to extend her stay.
d) She was to have left today but	4 retire to the country.
e) They weren't going to go but	5 he wouldn't be coming back.
f) They started out as a small town band but	6 when the phone rang.

   Underline all the verb forms that refer to future as seen from the past. Rewrite the sentences using an alternative form.

2 Complete the sentences using the discourse markers in the box. You do not need to use all the discourse markers.

> in addition   including   in particular   not to say   or at least   so   that is to say

   a) The course provides an introduction to Spanish culture, and _____ to flamenco and Spanish guitar music.

   b) The show was based on old-fashioned slapstick humour, _____, people falling over and throwing pies in each other's faces.

   c) The show went on for far too long, _____ that seemed to be the general feeling among the audience.

   d) I thought his jokes were very macho, _____ sexist, and generally in very bad taste.

   e) The story was weak and the animation was dated. _____ why was it such a success?

   f) There were a number of guest stars, _____ footballers and TV celebrities, who all drew a loud cheer from the audience.

   Think of a show, live or on TV, that you have seen recently. Write a very brief review describing the show and your general opinion of it. Use some of the discourse markers in the grammar reference section.

Unit 5 Prepositions in relative clauses. Articles

Part 1: Prepositions in relative clauses

Prepositions in defining relative clauses

Prepositions normally come at the end of a defining relative clause in informal written and spoken styles:
The woman that / who you were talking to.

In more formal styles they come before the relative pronoun. *Who* is replaced by *whom*. Do not use *that* after a preposition.
⚠ *The woman to whom you were talking.* (NOT ~~The woman to that you were talking.~~)

Of in non-defining relative clauses

You can modify the relative pronoun in non-defining relative clauses using quantifiers and determiners such as *many, all,*

most + of. When talking about people, the relative pronoun *who* changes to *whom*:
*The audience, **many of whom** had seen the film before, all stood up and applauded.*

The relative pronoun *which* stays the same:
*He offered me a pile of books, many of **which** were battered and torn.*

Remember that you cannot use the relative pronoun *that* in non-defining relative clauses:
⚠ NOT ~~He offered me a pile of books, many of that were battered and torn.~~

▶ **Now do Exercise 1.**

Part 2: Articles

A / an, some, the: general rules of use

If something is unknown to the speaker, the listener or both, use *a / an, some* or no article. Use *a / an* with singular countable nouns.
Use *some* or no article with uncountable nouns and plural countable nouns: *I need (**some**) accommodation, for example a room in an apartment with (**some**) students.*
If something is known to both speaker and listener, use *the*:
The flat I saw yesterday was really nice.
If you are talking about something in general terms, use *a / an, some* or no article: *I love spaghetti.* If you are talking about a specific person or thing, use *the*: *I loved **the** spaghetti we had last night.*
When there is only one, use *the*: *the world, the North, the economy*

Definite article *the*: some special cases:
* use with an adjective to talk about a group of people: *the rich, the English*
* use with household chores: *the cooking, the cleaning, the shopping*

No article: some special cases:
* do not use *the* to talk about meals as part of a routine: *What do you have for breakfast?*
* use to talk about transport with *by*: *I usually go by car.*
* use with *last* or *next* in time expressions referring to the immediate past or future: *I slept well last night.*
* use with points of the compass used as adverbs: *He travelled north.*

▶ **Now do Exercise 2.**

Unit 6 Verbs of the senses. Participle clauses

Part 1: Verbs of the senses

You can talk about your senses in two ways:
* to refer to abilities or sensations (stative)
* to refer to voluntary actions (dynamic)
These verbs can be used with both a stative and a dynamic meaning: *see, hear, feel, sense, smell, taste, look*
These verbs are always dynamic: *listen, touch*

can, could and be able to

Stative verbs of the senses are often used with *can, could* or *be able to*: **I would love to be able to hear** *as well as* **I could when I was younger.**

Continuous forms

⚠ Verbs of the senses with stative meanings are not usually used in continuous forms.

I can see the car over there. (NOT ~~I'm seeing the car over there.~~)

Meaning changes

When you use *see, hear, feel, sense, smell* or *taste* in continuous forms, the meaning often changes:
I can't see that sign very well. What does it say? (*see* referring to the sight)
I'm seeing the doctor tomorrow about my back. (*see* = meet)
I think I can taste salt in this. (*taste* referring to sense of taste)
They're tasting the dessert to see if they like it. (*taste* = testing)

Continuous forms can also be used to talk about temporary states: *I'm feeling good. / I'm hearing the music.*

▶ **Now do Exercise 1.**

Part 2: Participle clauses

Participle clauses do not include a subject. They are used to avoid repetition and shorten complex sentences. They are commonly found in written texts such as reports and essays.

Present participle clauses

The present participle substitutes for the subject and a different form of the verb:
Because he was a bit shy ... → Being a bit shy ...

Past participle clauses

The past participle is substituted for the subject and the verb *be*:
James was woken by a noise, so he ... → Woken by a noise, James ...

Perfect participle clauses

The perfect participle substitutes for the subject and a verb in a perfect form:
Because she hadn't understood the question, ... → Not having understood the question, ...

Position of not

Not always comes at the beginning of the participle clause:
Not knowing what else to do, I called the police.

▶ **Now do Exercise 2.**

Unit 5 Exercises

1 Add the prepositions in brackets to the sentences and answer the question below.

a) Is that the book you were telling me yesterday? (about)
b) Who was that strange person that you were talking on the bus? (to)
c) What's the name of that restaurant that we went with Rob? (to)
d) Whom were you referring when you said some people have no idea how to behave? (to)
e) Excuse me, whom do I have the pleasure of speaking? (with)
f) I spoke to a number of different people, many whom I had never met before. (of)

Which three sentences or questions are more formal in style? Rewrite these sentences in a more informal style.

2 Complete the sentences with *a, some, the* or – (no article).

a) I usually do _____ shopping on my way home from _____ work.
b) I go to _____ small supermarket round _____ corner from my flat.
c) I buy _____ fresh fruit and vegetables and _____ bread.
d) On Saturdays, in _____ morning, I go to _____ market in _____ town centre.
e) There's _____ great fish stall there and I usually buy _____ fish and _____ shellfish. Not too much. I'm usually only cooking for one!
f) If I have _____ guests coming for _____ dinner, I'll buy _____ wine and spend _____ money on something special at _____ butcher's.
g) I love _____ shopping for _____ food. It's much more fun than _____ shopping for _____ clothes.
h) Mind you, I still love going to _____ mall with _____ friend to do _____ window-shopping.

Do you feel the same about food shopping? Compare your ideas with your partner.

Unit 6 Exercises

1 Underline the correct alternative. In one sentence both options are possible.

a) I think my eyesight is failing. **I can't see / I'm not seeing** as well as I used to.
b) A: **Can I hear / Am I hearing** things, or is there a pig in your bath?
   B: No! It's the fan. It makes a strange noise.
c) Hey, Greg, **can you taste / are you tasting** this for me? I'm not sure if I need to add more salt.
d) I sat in the garden **hearing / listening to** the birds singing in the trees.
e) Are you on YouTube™? What are you **seeing / watching**? Anything interesting?
f) We used to live above a café. We **could always smell / were always smelling** fresh bread and coffee in the morning. Delicious!
g) I **could hear / 've heard** some strange things about the new boss. Are they true?
h) I don't know what it is between those two, but I **can sense / 'm sensing** a lot of tension.

Work with your partner. Compare your answers. Explain why you chose each option.

2 Look at the transformations. There's a mistake in each one. Find the mistake and correct it.

a) Because I'm so shy, I hate going to parties where I don't know anyone.
   Because being shy, I hate going to parties where I don't know anyone.
b) Now that I've finished university, I'm looking for a job.
   Finishing university, I'm now looking for a job.
c) I was impressed by the publicity, so I signed up for this course.
   Impressing by the publicity, I signed up for this course.
d) I was brought up to be independent, so I hate having to follow orders!
   Having brought up to be independent, I hate having to follow orders.
e) I find it difficult to understand the grammar, so I make lots of mistakes!
   Finding difficult to understand the grammar, I make lots of mistakes.

Are any of these sentences true for you? Compare your answers with your partner.

Unit 7 Complex sentences. Speculating about the future

Part 1: Complex sentences

Simple sentences only contain one clause: *I called Tom.* A complex sentence contains two or more clauses:
(1) *I called Tom* (2) *because I was bored.*
(1) *Feeling bored* (2) *I called Tom* (3) *who was still at work.*

Complex sentences are used to show the link between ideas and events and to avoid unnecessary repetition. The main clause describes the main or central event: *I called Tom.* A main clause is similar to a sentence: it typically contains a subject and a verb. The other clauses are subordinate clauses and add information about the main event: *Because I was bored, I called Tom, who was still at work.*

Linkers are often used to introduce subordinate clauses.

I called you because I wanted to talk about the project. Relative pronouns are also used: *… the project that starts next week.*

Subject pronouns, auxiliaries and main verbs can often be dropped in subordinate clauses: *I called you to talk about the new project.*

Participle clauses are often used to combine sentences and avoid repetition. They are particularly common in more formal written styles: *Needing to talk to someone, I picked up the phone.*

▶ See page 138 Unit 6 for more information about participle clauses.

▶ **Now do Exercise 1.**

Part 2: Speculating about the future

Modal verbs

will = you are confident that something will happen: *Time travel will one day be possible.*

may / might = there is a possibility, but you're not 100% sure: *Time travel may / might one day be possible.*

could = it's logically or physically possible, but you are not saying that it will definitely happen: *It could happen one day.*

should / ought to = you think it is logical / reasonable to expect that something will happen, although there may be unforeseen setbacks: *It should happen fairly soon if our projections are correct.*

Adverbs with *will* and *won't*:

You can use adverbs such as *certainly, almost certainly, definitely, easily, probably* with *will* and *won't* to clarify or modify your speculations: *We will probably have colonised the moon before the end of the century.*
The adverbs usually come between *will* and the main verb but before *won't*: *We certainly won't have developed a way to*

travel through time.

Adverbs with *may, might* and *could*.

You can use the adverbs *possibly / (very) well easily* with *may, might* and *could*: *Our grandchildren may / might / could well travel to the moon.*

Phrases: the following phrases can also be used to speculate about the future:
be sure to / bound to = you're confident that something will happen: *They're bound to find a clean alternative to oil.*

be (highly) likely to / that = you're fairly confident but not 100% sure: *It's likely to happen in the next twenty years.*

be (highly) unlikely to / that = you're fairly confident something will not happen: *It's highly unlikely that people will ever live on the moon.*

Note: use *to* + infinitive after *likely / unlikely* when the subject of the verb is the same: *We're likely to be late.* Use *that* when the subject is different: *It's likely that we'll be late.*

▶ **Now do Exercise 2.**

Unit 8 Paraphrasing. Using modals to talk about the past

Part 1: Paraphrasing

The normal word order in a sentence in English is: subject verb object adverb: *They called the police at once.*
However, this order is often varied to add emphasis or avoid repetition. You can change the order in a number of ways:

- Using the passive: *The police were called at once.*
  You use the passive to bring the object of an action to the beginning of the sentence.
  ▶ See page 142 Unit 10 for more information about the passive.

- Using participle clauses: *They called the police as soon as they heard the bang.* → *Hearing a bang, they called the police.*
  You often use participle clauses to highlight relationships

of cause and effect, or the sequence of events.
▶ See page 138 Unit 6 for more information about participle clauses.

- Varying the position of adverbials: *As soon as they heard the bang, they called the police.*
  ▶ See page 134 Unit 1 for more information about the position of adverbials.

- Using cleft sentences: we use clauses with *it* or *what* plus *be* to focus attention on the information that follows: *it was the bang that made them call the police; what made them call the police was the bang*
  ▶ See page 32 for more information about cleft sentences.
  ▶ **Now do Exercise 2.**

Part 2: Using modals to talk about the past

Modal + infinitive: Use *would* to talk about (1) past habitual actions: *We would drive to town every Sunday.* (2) to explain that someone refused to do something: *They just wouldn't accept no as an answer.*
Use *could* as the past form of *can* to talk about abilities, possibilities and permission: *I couldn't believe my eyes. / We could do whatever we liked.*

Modal + have + past participle: use *should / ought to have* to suggest that a past action was not good or advisable. *You shouldn't have signed it* → I don't think it was a good idea to sign it.
Use *may / might / could have* to speculate about possible past

actions: *They might have made a mistake* = I don't know, I'm just suggesting a possible explanation.
Use *would have* to give an opinion about past events: *They wouldn't have said something that rude, surely.* = I don't believe they could say something like that.
Use *can't have* to say that you think a past event was impossible: *He can't have forgotten. He never forgets appointments.*
Use *must have* to say that it is sure to have happened: *He must have got caught in traffic.* = It's the only explanation.

⚠ Note that you can't use *can have* or *mustn't have*. *He may / might / could / must have forgotten.* ✔ (NOT *He can have forgotten*). *She can't have liked it.* (NOT *She mustn't have liked it.*)

▶ **Now do Exercise 2.**

Unit 7 **Exercises**

1 **Combine the three simple sentences to make one complex sentence. Use the words in brackets. Do not re-use the words that are crossed out.**

a) I needed a new phone. Someone had stolen mine. I went to the shop to buy a new one.
(needing, because, I) _____

b) There was a new PDA. It had some great new features. One of the features was a built-in satnav system.
(that, such as, it) _____

c) I thought about it for some time. I decided it was too expensive. I bought a simpler model.
(having, so) _____

d) I thought about it again. I realised I just needed a straightforward phone. I use my phone to make calls and send text messages.
(thinking, I use) _____

e) I'm happy with my purchase. It's smaller and lighter. It looks really good!
(because, being, it's) _____

Write two complex sentences describing the last time you bought a phone or other electronic gadget.

2 **Underline the correct alternatives.**

a) I **may / won't** well have to do some work over the weekend.
b) I probably **won't / might not** be taking another holiday until next year.
c) I think I **could / should** be able to get this exercise done fairly quickly.
d) It's highly unlikely **to be / that I'll be** going out tonight.
e) **I'm bound to / It's unlikely to** get a new job before the year's out.
f) I **certainly won't / won't certainly** be studying English this time next year.

Are the sentences true for you? If not, change them and then compare your new sentences with a partner.

Unit 8 **Exercises**

1 **Complete each sentence so that it means the same as the one above it.**

a) Grammar is the most difficult aspect of learning a language.
It's _____ .
b) Grammarians often make grammar rules appear more difficult than they really are.
Grammar rules are _____ .
c) Grammar is best learnt by using and being exposed to the language.
The best way _____ .
d) I learnt my first language through exposure, so I think it's the best way to learn a language.
Having _____ .
e) Studying grammar rules and doing grammar exercises is a waste of time.
It's a _____ .
f) I think it's important to study the rules of the language because it helps me learn more efficiently.
What helps me _____ .

Do you agree with the statements? Discuss them with your partner.

2 **Put the words in the correct order to make sentences.**

a) must / He / have / forgotten / keys / his / or / something
b) window / The / may / purpose / have / left / on / open / been
c) climbing / out / actually / front / The / have / stuck / got / he's / door / could / and
d) can't / wanted / He / do / it / have / to
e) into / my / lost / keys / I / my / get / flat / once / couldn't / and / back
f) the / doormat / under / kid / When / I / we / used / leave / key / young / was / to / a / the

Which sentences refer to the picture? Which of these sentences do you think are most probable? Can you think of any other explanations? Look at the sentences that don't refer to the picture. Are they true for you? Compare your answers with your partner.

Unit 9 Concessive clauses and adverbials. Regrets and past conditionals

Part 1: Concessive clauses and adverbials

You use concessive clauses and adverbials to contrast two situations or to show that an action or event is unexpected or surprising: *Although I slept for ten hours, I was still tired the next day.*

You can use linkers such as *even though, although, though* to introduce a concessive clause. Use a comma after the concessive clause: **Even though** *I had slept well, … /* **Although** *I'm usually a good sleeper, …*

You can use *even so, yet, however* and *that said* at the beginning of a sentence. Always use a comma after the linker. *I usually sleep very well. However, last night was an exception.*

However and *though* can both be used at the end of a sentence: *I slept well. I was still tired in the morning,* **though / however**.

Use *despite* and *in spite of* with a gerund or noun: **Despite having** *slept for ten hours, I was still tired. /* **In spite of the comfortable bed**, *I still couldn't sleep.*

You can also use adverbial phrases such as *try as I might, strange as it may seem, hard as I tried* to highlight the contrast with the main clause. Use a comma to separate the phrases from the main clause: **Try as I might**, *I just couldn't get to sleep.*

▶ **Now do Exercise 1.**

Part 2: Regrets and past conditionals

You can use sentences with *I wish, if* and *if only* to talk about regrets: **I wish / If only** *I'd said goodbye. /* **If I'd gone to the party**, *I'd have been able to say goodbye.*

Use the past perfect or *could have* + past participle with *wish* and *if only*:
(1) **I wish I'd gone** to the party. (2) **I wish I could have gone** to the party.
(1) *I'd gone* tells us you didn't go: (2) *I could have gone* tells us that for some reason you were unable to go.

If and conditional sentences: use *if* + past perfect simple or continuous to talk about a past situation: **If I hadn't been** *working late … /* **If the car hadn't broken down** *…* Use a modal (*would, could, might, should, ought to*) + *have* + past participle to describe the desired past action: **I would / could have gone** to the party. Use a modal + infinitive to talk about

a desired (but impossible) present result: **I wouldn't / might not feel** *so bad.*

Substituting for *if*: (1) drop *if* and invert the subject and the auxiliary verb: **Had I gone to the party** *…* (2) Use *but for* with a noun (noun + gerund): **But for the car** *breaking down … /* **But for** *that last-minute job …*

Regret: use *regret* + verb + *ing* or *having* + past participle, the meaning is the same: **I regret not going** to the party. / **I regret not having gone** to the party. You can use similar structures with *I'd have liked*: **I'd have liked** *to go /* **I'd have liked** *to have gone.* The two structures mean the same.

Other phrases: *it's a pity, it's a shame*. With these phrases you use the past simple: *It's a pity / shame* **I didn't / couldn't / wasn't able to** *go to the party.*

▶ **Now do Exercise 2.**

Unit 10 Passive structures. Comparative structures

Part 1: Passive structures

You use the passive when you want to a) focus attention on the object of an action and establish the topic of a sentence b) when the agent of the verb is not known, generic, or obvious c) to refer back to the previous sentence in a text. Passives structures are more common in formal written styles, such as news reports. Active sentences are more common in informal speech.

Focusing attention: the subject of the passive sentence is the topic of the sentence; this is what we are talking about: **The prehistoric ruins of Jarlshof** *are being threatened by storms and rising seas.*

Unknown agent: when you do not know who performed an action, or when the agent of the action is generic and/or obvious (for example, *people, the police*) a passive structure is usually used: *The settlement was built 9,000 years ago.* is preferred to *People built the settlement 9,000 years ago.*

Referring back: the passive structure is often used in order to refer back to the topic at the end of the previous sentence in a text: *Experts* **are alarmed** *by this loss. The situation* **is being monitored** *by an organization called Scape. Scape* **was set up** *to protect ancient shoreline sites.*

▶ **Now do Exercise 1.**

Part 2: Comparative structures

Modifying comparative structures
Use these modifiers with comparative structures to show …

*   a large difference: *far, a lot, considerably, infinitely, much, way*: *He's* **way** *more intelligent than me.*
*   a moderate difference: *somewhat*, rather**:
    A **rather** *bigger house than ours.*
    *both of these modifiers are fairly formal in style
*   a small difference: *a bit, a little, slightly*:
    It's just **slightly** *smaller than the last one.*
*   no difference: *no*: *It's* **no** *faster than going by bus.*

Use these modifiers with structures with *as … as …* to show:

*   a large difference: *nowhere near, nothing like, not nearly*:
    He's **nowhere near** *as tall as his father.*
*   a small difference: *almost, nearly*:
    She's **almost** *as good as her sister.*
*   no difference: *just*: *He's* **just** *as bad as ever.*

You can also use modifiers to intensify superlative structures: *She is* **by far / far and away** *the best teacher.*

▶ **Now do Exercise 2.**

Unit 9 Exercises

1 **Link the two sentences using the words and phrases given. Make any necessary changes.**

1 I'm usually a really heavy sleeper. That night every single noise and movement seemed to wake me up.
   a) although   b) even so   c) despite

2 They reassured me and offered me kind advice. But I was still worried about the situation and couldn't sleep a wink.
   a) in spite of   b) try as I might   c) even so

3 I went to bed tired and depressed. I woke refreshed and ready to face the day.
   a) even though   b) however

2 **Complete the sentences with an appropriate form of the verb in brackets.**

a) If only _____ (I/stay) a little longer that night, I _____ (find out) what happened to Jon and his friends.

b) If things _____ (go) a little bit differently that day, I _____ (not be) in the mess I'm in now!

c) I wish _____ (pay) more attention to my parents' advice when I _____ (be) younger.

d) He wished he _____ (take part) in the competition, but his parents wouldn't let him.

e) If they _____ (not/talk) to each other at the time, they _____ (hear) what the policeman said.

f) _____ (I/tell) him about it sooner, he could have done something about it.

g) I really regret _____ (stay) at home now. It sounds like I missed a great party!

h) I'd really have liked _____ (see) the film last night. Was it good?

i) It's a shame you _____ (not/meet) Laura. I think you would have liked her.

Unit 10 Exercises

1 **Read the article and rewrite the phrases in bold as passive structures. Add by + agent where necessary.**

First meeting imminent

(1) **Government officials were still finalising plans** last night for the first face-to-face meeting with intelligent life from outer space. (2) **They first established contact** over three years ago but (3) **they only made the information public** once (4) **a team of international experts had confirmed** without a shadow of a doubt that Gaters are indeed friendly.

(5) **The ETF (Earth Task Force) are issuing daily bulletins** on the state of communication with Gat, the Gaters' home planet. (6) **They have reported** that Gaters have been trying to make contact with us for over 25 years but their messages of peace and goodwill had fallen on deaf ears.

(7) **Government officials are still to confirm the exact location and date of the meeting**. But (8) **we are expecting a visit** could take place anytime from June 27th onwards. There has been much speculation concerning the Gaters' physical appearance, however (9) **the authorities have not released any information on this point**.

1 Plans _____ .	6 It _____ .
2 Contact _____ .	7 The exact location _____ .
3 The information _____ .	8 A visit _____ .
4 It _____ .	9 No information _____ .
5 Daily bulletins _____ .	

2 **Add the words and phrases in the box to the sentences.**

> as   by far   considerably   just   less   more   no   slightly

a) He's more patient than I ever gave him credit for.

b) There really isn't much difference between the two of them, I suppose this one is just more attractive.

c) She's better than the last one as far as I can make out. Just as pompous, just as full of herself.

d) I'd say that this year's holiday was as good as last year's, wouldn't you?

e) This is the worst film I've ever seen!

f) I don't know, it's no different from his other films, just as outrageous, just violent.

g) I think your job is far stressful compared to Randy's. You don't know how lucky you are!

h) This novel is far challenging in terms of plot and characterisation.

Unit 11 Avoiding repetition: substitution and ellipsis

Substitution

You can often substitute nouns and verbs with pronouns and possessive adjectives in order to avoid unnecessary repetition. This is equally common in writing and in speech.

Pronouns and possessive adjectives

Use pronouns such as *it, they, them, that, this* to substitute for nouns, noun phrases and clauses:

*The castle was beautiful set against the sunset. **It** stood out clearly against the darkening sky.*

It here refers to *the castle*.

Think about what you want to say and why you want to say it.

It in this instance refers to the clause 'What you want to say'.

You can also use possessive adjectives to refer back to nouns and noun phrases used earlier in a text:

*Discourse markers can really help you make your writing much clearer and easier to read. But beware of **their** overuse.*

Their refers back to the discourse markers in the previous sentence.

So: you can use *so* to substitute for a verb or verb phrase:

*Do you want to improve your writing? If **so**, read these tips.*

So refers to the verb phrase 'want to improve your writing'.

*Many writers include anecdotes to make their writing more memorable. If you do **so** too, make sure they are short and amusing.*

So refers back to the act of including anecdotes.

Omission of words (ellipsis)

You can often drop or omit certain words in a sentence without losing the meaning of the sentence. What and how much you choose to omit depends on the context and the people you are talking or writing to. When you use ellipsis it is important that the words you drop have either been used previously or can be understood from the context.

Main verbs

You can often avoid repeating a main verb after an auxiliary:

*If you don't know what you want to say, your readers definitely won't (**know**).*

The second *know* can be dropped without losing the meaning of the sentence.

Pronouns and auxiliaries

You can drop repeated pronouns after *and* or *but*:

*Make sure you've included the right attachments and (**that you**) are sending them to the right recipients.*

When the auxiliary is repeated, it too can be omitted:

*Make sure you've added a relevant subject line and (**that you have**) signed off appropriately.*

Negative verb phrases

At times it is possible to omit all the verb phrase, apart from *not*:

*I should be able to join you later. If **not**, I'll call.*

not = I can't join you later. This is understood from the context.

To + infinitive

You can drop the infinitive after *to*.

*Do you do a lot of writing? I used to (**do a lot of writing**).*

*Tom asked me to go out with him tonight, but I don't want to (**go out with him tonight**).*

▶ **Now do Exercises 1 and 2.**

Unit 12 Special uses of the past simple

The simple past can sometimes be used with reference to the present or future.

- **In conditional sentences**

  You use the past simple with *if, I wish* and in other conditional clauses to say that we think a present or future event is unlikely or impossible:

  *If I **were** rich / If I **had** more time / I **wish** I **could** speak Russian / If I **won** the lottery* – none of these things are true or likely to come true, therefore you use the past simple and not a present or future verb form.

- **In reported speech**

  The past simple is often used to refer to the present in reported speech.

  *He said he **was** the greatest footballer on earth. He said he **did** it every day.*

  The actions he is talking about are still true in the present, but his words are being reported in the past. In this case the present is also possible.

- **With it's (about / high) time**

  Use *It's (about / high) time* to say that you think something should happen now or very soon. You always use the past simple after *It's (high / about time)*:

  *It's **time** these kids were in bed / went to bed. / It's **about time** the politicians did something about it.*

  The action is in the future, although the idea is that the action should really have happened already.

- **With would rather**

  Use *I'd rather* + subject + verb to explain that you don't want someone to do something, or that you're not happy with a present situation. You always use the past simple, and not a present tense, to talk about the action you don't like:

  *I'd **rather you didn't smoke** when I'm eating. / He'd **rather we didn't use** his car.*

  When *would rather* is not followed by a subject you do not use the past simple. Instead you use an infinitive: *The government **would rather spend** money on health care than helping the elderly. / I'd **rather not work** in the evenings.*

▶ **Now do Exercises 1 and 2.**

GRAMMAR EXTRA: EXPLANATIONS

Unit 11 Exercises

1 Look at the words in bold. Which refer to ...

a) texting?
b) texting while crossing a road?

> Love (1) **it** or hate (2) **it**, texting is here to stay. Some people do (3) **it** occasionally, only when (4) **it**'s completely necessary; others are totally obsessed. They (5) **do it** on the bus, as they walk down the road, even as they cross the street. (6) **This latter use** has become a hazard on the busy streets and sidewalks of some American cities where authorities are making moves to have (7) **it** banned.

2 Rewrite the text below avoiding the repetition of the words in bold. Use substitution and ellipsis.

My daughter never calls her friends anymore. She prefers to text (1) **her friends**. She says that (2) **sending text messages** is quicker and easier. Not only (3) **is it quicker and easier**, she also claims that sending a text message is more efficient. She claims that there are fewer misunderstandings and arguments when she texts her friends than when she speaks to (4) **her friends** on the phone. Asked why (5) **texting her friends was less problematic**, she explained that texting gave her more time to think, (6) **it gave her more time** to choose her words and (7) **it gave her time** to change and perfect her message before she sent it. When you speak, she explained, once the words are out, you can't change (8) **the words**. You have said (9) **the words that** you have said. And you have to deal with the consequences (10) **of what you have said**.

Unit 12 Exercises

1 Read the sentences. Change the verbs to the past simple where necessary.

a) If I have more time, I would definitely want to do voluntary work with a local charity.
b) If I have enough money at the end of the month, I always give some to charity.
c) The government representative explained that they have done everything in their power to ensure early release of funds.
d) A national children's charity warned that homelessness is not a problem that affects only adults.
e) I think it's about time we all stop thinking about shopping as if it is some sort of sport or national pastime.
f) I'd rather give money to charities than to the government; I think they'd make wiser choices about how to spend it.
g) It's high time somebody does something about the growing number of homeless people on our streets.
h) I'd rather the government spends money on providing homes and education than on short-term job creation schemes.

2 Write five sentences explaining how you would like to see the world change in the future.

I wish _____ .
If only _____ .
It's high time _____ .
It's about time _____ .
I'd rather _____ .

Work in small groups and exchange your ideas. Which are the most common, interesting or unusual ideas?

Recordings

Unit 1

 1.01

Joanna

Well, I like to be able to take an active part, so it helps if there aren't some people who hog the conversation all the time, and also people need to have a sense of humour about things, I think, not to take things too seriously and you need a conversation that flows, so that you can … well, you don't get stuck on one point.

1.02

Mike

Um, a good conversationalist. I'd say it's someone who's, who's got a point that they want to put across during the conversation. Someone with something to say as opposed to someone who just talks endlessly about various subjects and doesn't engage in one particular subject, and I'd say it was someone who listens to other people as well, um, that's what I'd say.

1.03

Phil

When people aren't really interested in what you're saying, that's very annoying indeed. Also, people who interrupt you continually with grunts or opinions of their own or whatever, and also some people don't care about whose turn it is to talk, so they just, you know, butt in when you're in the middle of a thought and obviously, you know, when the topic's boring, that's very irritating. And sometimes, you know, the conversation goes nowhere, it's going nowhere, and that's, that is also extremely irritating.

1.04

Jessica

I really hate it when I'm with someone who just drones on and on in a conversation, and who doesn't give you a chance to speak at all. Oh, and I also really hate it when they just carry on and they don't care whether or not you are interested at all in what they're saying. They seem oblivious to how you're reacting to them. I hate that.

1.05

Bryony

Um, it's good when you're talking about things which you've got in common with the person you are talking to, like you're on the same wavelength and you can share the same tastes or experiences so you know where the other person's coming from. It's also nice if you can share a joke or a personal story or an anecdote or something like that.

1.06

Rafe

I can't stand it when you have to do all the talking yourself, when the other person's not responding. Or when they are responding, but it's with monosyllabic answers, you know, they're just going 'yeah', 'uh', 'hmm', and that's all you're getting back. And when you have to work to keep the conversation going. That's, that's really bad, when you're having to hunt around for things to say because you're just not getting anything back.

1.07

(B = Brian; S = Suzi)

B: Hello?
S: Hi, it's me!
B: Hiya! How are you doing?
S: Fine, a bit stressed out, had a hard day at work, you know, the usual.
B: Yeah, me too.
S: So, what about the film then? I just phoned the cinema to check the times and it's on at 7 o'clock and 9.30. Which do you reckon?
B: Listen, love, do you mind if we go another night? I'm tired, I just fancy a quiet night in, you know, bit of a veg on the sofa, watch some footie on TV.
S: But it's the last night. You said you really wanted to go!
B: Why don't you go with your sister? You said she wanted to see the film …
S: This is the third time you've pulled out. What's going on?
B: Nothing. I just don't fancy it tonight, that's all.
S: Come on, if there's something wrong you can tell me. I'm not going to fly off the handle.
B: There's nothing wrong …
S: Yes, there is. You've been off for days. You don't talk to me, you don't want to see me.
B: That's not true.
S: Are you bored with me? Is there someone else? Have I done something wrong?
B: No, no, of course not.
S: You never used to shut yourself away like this, you used to want to spend time with me. What's changed?
B: Nothing's changed. Of course I want to see you.
S: But not tonight, eh? The football's more interesting, I suppose.
B: Oh, you know that's not true. It's just that I'm tired, that's all. It's been a hard day. I just need a quiet night in …
S: Alone!
B: Look, if it's that important to you, I'll come. What time did you say?
S: No, forget it! I wouldn't want you to go out of your way or anything!
B: Don't be like that. Come on, shall I come and pick you up?
S: No, forget it. I've gone off the idea. Let's just drop it.
B: Look, I'd love to do something tomorrow, yeah?
S: Whatever. Just please yourself. You always do!
B: Suzi, don't … Suzi. Suzi?

1.09

1

(W1 = Woman 1; W2 = Woman 2)

W1: I'd been waiting and waiting and waiting and, you know, I was beginning to think, like, you know, like, he wasn't coming or something …
W2: Why didn't you phone him … or text, text him … or whatever …
W1: Yeah, well, you know, I thought he might have got caught up at work or something and I didn't really want to … I didn't want him to feel … to think … you know, that I was like hassling him, you know?
W2: So, what did you do?
W1: Well, actually he phoned me! He'd been waiting for me … but in another restaurant … in another restaurant on the other side of town!
W2: What … ?
W1: Turns out there are two Italian restaurants called Casa Mia, and neither of us had realised! I had no idea.
W2: Me neither!
W1: Yeah, and so, like, you know, neither of us had realised and we'd both, you know, thought of the other one and …
W2: So, what happened? Did you go to him? Did he come to you?
W1: He came to me. He was driving … he had his car … it was easier for him. He was really sweet about it actually, really, really apologetic and we …

1.10

2

(W = Woman)

W: Mmm. Yes, well … I'm just on the train actually. It's just coming into the station now.
W: What? Ah, yes, well … We've been working on it all week.
W: Yes, yes, it's almost done.
W: Yes, of course, we all understand how important it is and we've already completed the initial plans, we're just waiting for the final details to come through …
W: Yes, yes, of course, I'm sure we'll have finished by then …
W: What? Sorry? I can't hear you very well …
W: Yes, yes, don't worry. We're working on the final details now. We'll be sending it to the printer's this evening …
W: Yes, yes, this evening … or tomorrow morning at the latest …
W: Sorry, what's that? You said you'd been promised it by the end of last week?
W: I really don't think that's possible … You must have been talking to the wrong person … I mean, there must have been some kind of misunderstanding.
W: Yes, of course. I understand your concerns, and I'll make sure it gets done this evening.
W: Of course, absolutely. I'll be taking care of it personally. You can be sure of that.
W: Yes, yes, I'll bring it round later this evening. You can count on that.
W: Goodbye.

1.11

1

(S = Sue; J = John)

S: Hey, John! Fancy meeting you here! How are things?
J: Sue? What a surprise. I wasn't expecting to see you here. You look great!
S: Thank you! You too. So, what are you doing here? On holiday? On business?

J: Yeah, on business. I'm at the conference. I forgot you lived here now. I should have got in touch …

2
(M = Man; W = Woman)
M: Sorry, have you got the time?
F: Yeah, just a sec … it's ten past three.
M: Shouldn't the number three be here by now?
F: Yeah, but it's often a bit late …
M: Especially when there's so much traffic.
F: Yeah, it's really busy today, there must be something going on in town …
M: It's that new exhibition, probably, you know, the travel fair or something …

3
(J = Jay; R = Ruben)
J: Hi, you must be Ruben. I've heard a lot about you.
R: All good, I hope!
J: Of course. I'm Jay, by the way. I work in accounts.
R: Hi Jay, pleased to meet you. So, how long have you been here?
J: Feels like forever, no, only joking, about three years actually. Before that I was …

4
(A = Alison; C = Claire)
A: Great party, isn't it?
C: Yeah.
A: So, how do you know Kim?
C: We work together.
A: Oh really? At the school? Are you a teacher too?
C: No, I'm the receptionist.
A: Okay. Um, Sarah, right?
C: Yes, how did you know?
A: Ah, well …

Unit 2

 1.12

1
Erm, bitter coffee in a plastic cup and milk in plastic containers. Yeah, either that or a greasy burger on a plastic tray. Looks great in the picture but tastes disgusting and is definitely over-priced.

2
Erm … watermelon maybe, or strawberries … no, I know, big bowls of fresh salad with home-made dressing, served with cheese, bread and a glass of chilled white wine.

3
Roast dinners, you know, huge plates of roast lamb served with mashed potatoes and tiny, sweet green peas, and on top of it all, swimming in it, the best gravy you have ever tasted.

4
Crunchy milk chocolate biscuits dipped in coffee, curled up on the sofa watching your favourite film.

5
No food really, I mean, I associate it more with not being able to eat anything, well, at first at least … and later … maybe chocolate or fruit for some reason … I don't know, something like strawberries, yes, succulent, sweet strawberries with fresh cream.

6
I don't know, hot chocolate? Er, no, fish 'n' chips or a Chinese takeaway – or some kind of microwaveable convenience food that doesn't need any cooking.

 1.13
Anne
The food? Mmm, it's superb, really hot and spicy, but quite delicate too. Kind of like a cross between Indian and Chinese food but with its own special flavours too. They use a lot of lemon grass and coconut and a lot of fish. I really liked the soups. You can buy them from stalls on the corner of the street. You choose the meat you want in your soup and the kind of noodles – long thin white rice noodles, or big fat, thick yellowish ones, and there are these tubs of spices too and you choose as much or as little of whatever you want. Then you sit there on the street, or in the market or wherever you are, and eat it. I had some for breakfast one day – it was great! Really great!

1.14
Kim
The food? Well, it took a bit of getting used to actually. I like hot, spicy food, but this was too much for me at the beginning. I reckon I built up a kind of immunity to it as time went by though and I got to like it by the end. It's nothing like the kind of food we get in restaurants back home. I loved the ritual of it, going to the small street cafés where they serve your food on a banana leaf. They wash the leaf and then serve a huge helping of rice right in the middle and give you generous helpings of all the various different sauces on offer that day. You don't get a knife and a fork. You eat with your right hand, making little balls of rice and then soaking up the sauce with these little balls – it takes quite a long time to get good at it. When you've finished they bundle the banana leaf up with any leftovers and throw it out on the street where the goats and cows eat them. I love that side of it too – nothing goes to waste!

1.15
Bill
The food? Well, to tell you the truth I didn't really like it that much. It isn't the healthiest of diets. Everything is either fried or cooked in pig's fat and, hmm, I don't really like cabbage that much and that's a staple part of their diet, like a lot of places in Central Europe. It's usually pickled and served with sour cream – so, no, it isn't really my favourite. Having said that, there were some things I loved – the bread, for example, it's really soft and tasty, and so many different kinds, and the scones, and pastries too, are really good. And some of the soups, the various kinds of goulash – that's their national dish – and the bean soups are really delicious and the paprika makes them quite spicy – great on a cold day.

1.16
Steve
The food? It isn't particularly elaborate, but it's good. The seafood is especially good, and there's just such a variety, so many different kinds of shellfish, I wouldn't know the names for half of them in English. Another favourite of mine is the grilled green chilli peppers. They serve them up by the plateful to be shared between friends over a beer or two. There's always one that's so spicy it almost blows your head off. More than anything else I love the eating out culture. It's quite informal, you go to a bar and order huge platefuls of various different

specialities and share them, everybody eating off the same plates. It's very sociable – a really nice social eating ritual.

1.18
Conversation 1
(J = John; M = Mrs Dersty)
M: Hello?
J: Hello. This is accounts. Could I speak to Mrs Dersty?
M: Speaking.
J: I have your expense claim form here, but I'm afraid we won't be able to reimburse your dining expenses.
M: Oh, and why is that?
J: Because you could have used the company's dining facilities.
M: Yes, but it was a breakfast meeting with a client.
J: That may be, but it's company policy.
M: I think you'll find that it's only company policy if we're entertaining in-house guests.
J: I see. Well, we'll need to double-check that and get back to you.

1.19
Conversation 2
(G = Girl; M = Mother)
G: You bought strawberries?
M: Yes, what's wrong with that?
G: But they're out of season!
M: So what if they're out of season?
G: Well, apart from the fact that it doesn't help the environment, imported fruit doesn't taste as good.
M: That's a load of rubbish. These strawberries are absolutely delicious!
G: Yeah, but how much did they cost?
M: They were on offer.
G: Yeah, but they must have cost a fortune. Imported from Spain! What about the environment?
M: Okay, okay, I suppose you're right, it's not brilliant for the environment, but I couldn't resist them.

1.20
Conversation 3
(A = Anna; B = Ben)
A: I can't believe he got her a Hoover for her birthday.
B: Oh, I don't know. It's the thought that counts.
A: No! Come on! He couldn't have given it much thought, if that's all he came up with.
B: You gave me a drill on my last birthday!
A: So?
B: I rest my case.

1.22
a) The best way to eat fish is raw.
b) French cuisine is the best in the world.
c) People who smoke in restaurants are inconsiderate.
d) If you want to get to the top, you have to start at the bottom.
e) Life is too short to waste time worrying about what other people think.
f) Travel is the best way of broadening the mind.

Unit 3

1.23
(M = Mike; S = Sue)
M: Thank you, John, and now it's back to

the studio for the answers to last week's quiz. Sue?

S: Thanks, Mike. Hello, yes, and there are a few surprises in the answers this week. So, let's start with the first question, which I think held the biggest surprise for our contestants.

According to data collected by the UN, 53% of the world's population live in cities, whilst 47% live in rural areas. In the EU the percentage of people living in urban centres rises to a staggering 74% and an even higher 87% in the USA. It would appear that there is a steady movement towards urban areas and that the proportion of city dwellers will continue to rise.

Although it may seem a fairly straightforward question to answer, there is still some discussion as to which is the world's largest capital. This is mainly due to the difficulty in deciding where the world's largest cities actually end as they all tend to be surrounded by a mass of satellite towns which all merge into one large agglomeration. If we take 'city' to mean a metropolitan area, then Tokyo, with a population of more than 32 million, is easily the world's largest capital city. Mexico City and Seoul both vie for second position with populations of just over 20 million.

Likewise, it is very difficult to tell which is Europe's noisiest capital, mainly as there don't seem to be any standardised noise pollution measurements across the countries of the EU, and very few exhaustive studies have been carried out. However, it is widely recognised that Athens is the European capital which suffers from the worst noise pollution levels. It's not known whether this information is based on popular opinion or on statistical data from the Greek authorities, although a recent government report seems to suggest that it's true. Judging from the entries we've received, this will come as quite a surprise to some of our listeners.

On to the fourth question. There is still some debate over this one. The Syrians claim that their capital city, Damascus, is the world's oldest city, though other Middle Eastern inhabitants would claim that their capitals are just as old. Sources seem to suggest that the Syrians are right and that their capital is indeed the oldest in the world, having been continuously inhabited since 5000 BC.

Question five was pretty straightforward. There is no doubt whatsoever about which of the world's capital cities is the highest. La Paz, in the Bolivian Andes, stands four kilometres above sea level.

And finally, the last question, again a fairly straightforward question. The first city to have reached a population of 1,000,000 was Rome, which had a population of over a million during the heyday of the Roman Empire in 133 BC. London reached the mark in 1810 and New York in 1875. Today there are over 300 cities in the world that boast a population in excess of one million.

So, the winners this week are, Jane Turbot from Whitstable in Kent, Carol Jackson from St Andrews …

1.24

(S = Sharon; D = Derek)

S: Have you seen this? The article about that new survey …

D: Yes, I was reading it earlier. No surprises there, I don't think … seems pretty obvious to me. You don't need a survey to tell you that, do you?

S: Yeah, well, I don't know, I mean it's not that simple is it? I mean, some people like living in the country …

D: Yeah, and you can see why; less stress, less traffic, less smog … but I don't think it's just a simple question of what you like, you know …

S: No, it's more like … well, it seems like it's a question of work and money more than anything else, I mean …

D: Yeah, it said that, didn't it? The main reason was that they couldn't find a job in the country …

S: Well, it doesn't say that exactly, but yes, it says it's, er, it's, you know, easier to find work in large cities and I reckon that's true. Don't you?

D: Yeah, but I don't think that's the main reason. I mean, it might be the main reason for older people … you know, no jobs, rural unemployment, whatever …

S: Yeah, there's a lot of that …

D: But it seems to be talking more about young people … I mean, the statistics here are referring to people under thirty and you know, I reckon that even if, even if there were plenty of jobs in the rural areas, well, they'd still go to the cities, wouldn't they?

S: Do you think so? Maybe you're right. Maybe it's more a kind of lure of the bright lights thing …

D: Yeah, you know, nightlife, music, youth culture in general …

S: Yeah, it says something about that, doesn't it? That bit where it talks about, what is it … 'leisure time activities' or something like that?

D: 'Free time facilities'.

S: Yeah, that was it.

D: … pubs and clubs more like!

S: Yeah, and cinemas and exhibitions and stuff as well …

D: No, discos and the chance to meet other young people more like …

S: Yeah, okay, the social side of things, but it's important, isn't it?

D: Yeah, this survey seems to reckon it's the second most important factor, in fact, after getting a job. You know, if young people decide to leave their homes in the country, then they reckon the social side of things is the second most important thing they consider. What other things do you think they mentioned?

S: Oh, I don't know. Maybe they said there were more opportunities for continuing their education, like going to colleges and stuff. They might be thinking about facilities for their families in the future, like being near good schools and stuff. Um, what about better living conditions … more modern houses which need less work doing to them and stuff?

D: Yeah, I suppose they're all things you'd have to think about, aren't they?

S: Yeah, the survey makes quite a lot of sense.

D: Hmm.

1.25

[H = Helen; R = Robert]

H: Well, I don't really think it's particularly dangerous. Not any more than any other large city. You have to be sensible, take the normal precautions. I mean, I wouldn't walk down a street and stare at somebody and I certainly wouldn't walk home alone, and I wouldn't go down unlit alleys, you know, dark alleys at night, and obviously there are certain areas that you just know you wouldn't go into, but I think on the whole it's not a particularly dangerous city.

R: Yeah, I think I agree, but, um, actually there have been a couple of stories in the papers recently about this spate of muggings that's been going on.

H: Oh yeah, I read about that. Yeah, because they say things are changing and things are getting worse in the city. I did have a friend, actually, she was on the underground, and her wallet was snatched from her bag just as the train was coming into the station, and of course they got off straight away and there was absolutely nothing she could do about it.

R: Well, I sympathise with her. I mean I've seen that happen too, and, er, you've just got to watch it in a place like that, or like the street market. You've got to be really careful there because there is a big crowd and a lot of pickpockets and they can steal something and run away.

H: But I don't think it's really dangerous. They're not violent people, you just have to be sensible and keep your eyes open, and …

R: Well, I don't know. This article I read they said that a lot of the thieves were carrying knives, which means if you resist then, er, you could get badly hurt, so that really makes you think, doesn't it?

H: Hmm, I said it wasn't violent, maybe it is. I heard about a group of tourists the other day who were mugged. What do you do if you see something like that? You don't really know what's going on and you don't really want to get involved in case you get hurt.

R: Yes. I think it's stupid to try and be a hero. I mean you could get very badly hurt and all they want is just money. I mean I know that is a terrible thing to say, but it's just money. It's not worth losing your life for.

H: I suppose so. Apparently these guys had a knife and they cut one of the women's handbags from her shoulder. I think she thought they were going to stab her husband actually.

R: Did you hear if anybody was hurt at all?

H: No, no-one was hurt. Apparently the woman had had her passport stolen, and her travellers cheques taken, but the sad thing was that they had only just arrived and they didn't want to leave all their stuff in the hotel. They thought it was safer with them.

R: Yeah, well, that's a problem with tourists though, isn't it? They're easy targets. They stand out in a crowd, thieves know they're probably carrying money and documents around and they don't speak the language, and they're vulnerable, aren't they?

H: Well …

R: I mean it happens to locals as well. There is a friend of mine who was jumped from behind, you know, and they got her bag and they ran away, and she tried to run after them but the thieves were too quick, obviously.

H: Was she hurt at all?

R: No, no, but she was really angry.

H: Of course.

R: She didn't lose anything really valuable so, um, she didn't report it to the police in the end, actually.

H: I think she should have done that actually. I think it's quite important when something like that happens because it might be mild at the moment but they could get worse. I think they need to know if a crime's happened, actually.

R: Yeah. Well, I mean, there should be more police around anyway, shouldn't there? There should be more police on the streets at night.

H: I think you're right.

R: You could be on main streets and there's nobody, just a police car driving up and down every now and again, would …

H: You'd feel better protected I think.

R: Yeah, and it would put the muggers and thieves off, wouldn't it?

Unit 4

1.29

Simon

Actually, this was my favourite book when I was a child. It's called the *Lord of the Rings*. It's a real epic, it's a classic really – it was written for kids but actually lots of adults read it as well. It's massive, three books in fact, but such a brilliant read! It's set in a fantasy world called Middle Earth and it has fantasy characters like, erm, elves, and dwarves, and monsters and dragons and all sorts of mythical creatures like that. And it tells the story of these creatures called hobbits who are a bit like a humans but not really humans. Er, the main character is called Frodo and he's the one who's got to get rid of the ring. Well, it's a very special ring that was crafted a long, long time ago by the Dark Lord, who is the villain of the story. And it's an extremely powerful ring, the ring of power you might want to call it, because everyone who puts it on becomes invisible. And, basically, this book is about their quest, the quest of the hobbits and their companions, to destroy the ring, because, um, if the Dark Lord gets hold of it he can rule the world. Oh, and there's this other character called Gandalf who is a wizard, and he's on the side of good, and he helps Frodo and his companions to vanquish the Dark Lord. And, well, anyway, they have all sorts of, kind of, adventures and there are lots of battles and stuff and well, in the end Frodo throws the ring into a volcano and that's the end of the ring. Basically, it's about the battle between the forces of good and evil and in the end, the good triumphs over evil. It's, um, a really powerful story, a real page-turner. You get totally engrossed in the story, it's so well-written, it's really magical. I couldn't put it down. It's been made into a film now, quite an epic actually, and very popular.

1.30

1

(F = Fiona; J = Jeremy)

F: So, have you ever been conned?

J: I'm ashamed to say I have actually, yes. Um, it was years ago. I was a student and I had a car, um, and it had a particularly distinctive sound about it, cos it was like a diesel engine and I wanted to get a different car so I took it to a second-hand car salesman and he conned me into believing that the sound that the engine makes was in fact a fault and it was on its way out, and he said he would do me a favour by offering me a very small amount of money just to take it off my hands. And I remember at the time thinking, 'Is this really right?' and then I was kind of almost frightened to challenge him on it, and so I said, 'Okay, fine, yeah', and he gave me a very small amount of money for something that was in fact in perfect condition, and I could have got a lot more money for it at another time.

1.31

2

(M = Martin; J = Jennifer)

M: Do you have any experiences of being conned?

J: I do, actually, um, and this was at home. Someone knocked on my door.

M: Right.

J: A really nice lady. You know, very sort of young and bright and she said, um, 'Can you lend me £5 because I'm here to see my mum? She's not very well. I've run out of change.' Really, honestly I thought, gut feeling, yeah, she seems plausible. She said, 'I'll come back, I'll come back in twenty minutes and I'll pay you.' And so, yeah, I gave her the money. And I'm usually quite sort of, you know, you can see when someone's lying but this, this lady was really lovely. Very well dressed and …

M: How old was she?

J: Oh, she must have been about her early twenties and she ran off with my fiver and never came back. Absolutely unbelievable. I mean I guess I was quite silly to have done that but she just completely conned me.

1.32

3

(M = Martin; A = Anne)

M: Do you have any experiences of being conned?

A: Yeah. Well, it's quite embarrassing actually. You know those phone calls you get and they say oh, you've won a holiday and all you need to do is answer a few questions.

M: Yeah.

A: So I answered a few questions about, you know, my ideal place to go and how much pocket money I'd need and how much … you know, all that kind of stuff and maybe have some extra money for … to buy some clothes and things like that and they kept me on the phone for ages and I was really excited and I put the phone down thinking I'd actually won a holiday and then I didn't hear anything and then I got the phone bill and it cost me £15 that phone call, so I didn't get the holiday.

M: How did you feel?

A: And I was gutted and felt quite stupid.

1.33

4

(G = Georgina)

G: Yeah, this is something that happened to me when I was living abroad and I was living in a flat and something went wrong with my loo, and so I got my boyfriend to get a plumber, to send round a plumber, and so the next day there was a knock on the door. This guy arrives and said, 'I'm a plumber.' So I said, 'right, come in, have a look, there it is', and he had a look at it and said, 'oh yes, you'll need a new something' – I don't know what it was – 'but it'll cost you £20, um, so I can go off and get it now if you like' and so I gave him the £20 and, of course, never saw him again. And then that evening I said to my boyfriend, 'I don't think much of the plumber you sent,' and he said, 'What plumber? I never sent a plumber.' So what had happened, obviously, was that this guy was just coming round, knocking on doors and hoping to find someone gullible like me who'd hand over the money.

1.36

So there was this pensioner, right, and he was driving along the motorway, right, and he gets a call from his wife. Now of course he shouldn't pick up the phone, but he does. 'Take care,' she says, 'I've just heard on the radio that some idiot is driving down the motorway the wrong way.' So he says, 'One idiot? I can see hundreds of them.'

1.37

So there's this businessman riding on the train after a hard day at the office, and this young guy sits next to him and says, 'Call me a doctor, call me a doctor,' and the businessman says, 'Well, what's the matter, are you ill?' And the guy, the young guy says, 'No, no, I've just graduated from medical school.'

1.38

A sandwich walks into a pub and orders a pint of Guinness, and the barman says, 'Sorry, don't serve food.'

1.39

A: I've got one. A mouse goes into a pub and goes up to the barman and says, 'Got any cheese?' and the barman says 'No, it's a pub, we don't sell cheese.' So the mouse goes 'Oh!' and scampers out. The next day the same mouse comes in the same bar. Goes up to the barman. 'Got any cheese?' And the barman says 'Look, I told you yesterday this is a pub, we sell beer, we sell spirits, we don't sell cheese, okay?' The mouse goes 'Oh!' and scampers out. Next day same mouse, same pub, comes in again, goes up to the barman and says, 'Got any cheese?' and the barman says, 'Look, I told you yesterday. If you come in here again I'm going to nail you to the bar and the mouse goes, 'Oh!' and scampers out. Next day, same mouse comes into the pub again, goes up to the barman, 'Got any nails?' The barman says no. 'Got any cheese?'

B: I didn't get that at all.

1.40

(W1 = Woman 1, W2 = Woman 2)

W1: I had a really scary experience when I went camping with my friend by the seaside. Actually, it was the first time either of us had been camping.

W2: Really?

W1: We pitched our tent right near the edge of a cliff so we had a beautiful view over the bay.

W2: Oh, lovely!

W1: But then during the night a wind got up, and started blowing harder and harder.

W2: Oh no!

W1: At first I thought we could just sleep through it but eventually I realised that the tent was going to blow away if we didn't act fast.

W2: Oh, how scary! You must have been terrified!

W1: So, anyway, we got up and started to pack our things up.

W2: Right.

W1: … and we were just about to start taking the tent down to pack it away in the car when I realised I couldn't find my car keys.

W2: Oh, what a nightmare! That must have been awful!

W1: So, I hunted high and low, and anyway, to cut a long story short, eventually found them lying on the grass outside the tent.

W2: What a relief! I bet you were pleased!

W1: Yeah, and fortunately we managed to get everything in the car before the rain started.

W2: Oh, good!

W1: But, all in all, it was a pretty horrendous night, and I don't think either my friend or I are in a hurry to go camping again!

W2: I'm not surprised!

1.42

1

So, anyway, I finished the meal and I called the waiter to pay the bill. And I opened my bag and, guess what? My purse wasn't there.

…

But you'll never guess what happened. This man at the next table leaned over and offered to lend me the money.

…

Obviously I said no. I mean, I didn't know him and it would just have been too embarrassing.

1.43

2

We'd actually been travelling for two days but we'd run out of money. So I hadn't eaten for two days! I was absolutely starving!

…

It was the last bus home and there was a long, long queue. I was thinking, what if we don't get on? We'll have to spend the night in the bus station.

…

But, anyway, in the event, we managed to get the last two seats on the bus.

1.44

3

I'd known about the concert for ages, it was one of my favourite groups playing. But for some reason I hadn't got round to phoning up for tickets. And when I did eventually phone, all the tickets had sold out.

…

But then, the next time they were playing, I phoned up well in advance of the concert date. And so this time we managed to get seats right in the front row.

1.45

4

I was at a party with my girlfriend, and I saw this guy I'd known ages ago at school. And I was just about to introduce him to my girlfriend when I realised I'd completely forgotten his name.

…

Luckily I didn't have to introduce him though, because he immediately introduced himself.

…

Or perhaps it wasn't so lucky as it turned out… He spent the rest of the evening talking to my girlfriend!

1.46

5

I was sitting at the table, having breakfast, and suddenly there was this knock on the door.

…

It was the postman. He handed me an envelope which I had to sign for, because it was special delivery. And so I opened it and you'll never guess what was inside - a cheque for £5,000!

Unit 5

2.01

1

Ah, well bizarrely enough it's a department store. I just love the ease of being able to go in, do your food shopping, buy electronic goods, maybe buy some clothes and then I normally end up in the book section and I'll buy some books that I probably don't need, but it's all under one roof, so it's absolutely perfect.

2

Oh, actually that's my responsibility. I don't like other people doing that for me, to be honest. I like to, you know, go and have a good look around and pick the produce that I really, really like the look of and the smell and all the rest of it, so er, yeah, I quite enjoy that. That's not one of my most painful chores.

3

It's going to be a house, which is a bit of a necessity. It will be lovely to unpack and spread my stuff around a few rooms. I know that it's going to cost a lot and organising finance is tricky, but a house is something I've always dreamed of having.

4

I have to say I'm really not. I like to consider everything I buy. Um, what I tend to do is I visit all the shops and I'll assess all the different prices and perhaps some shops you might get additional things thrown in, for example. Inevitably, I end up going back to the first shop probably because that's where I've asked all the questions and I feel a certain sense of customer loyalty perhaps, but I might check prices online, for example, and certainly do the rounds, but I like to put a lot of work in before I actually purchase anything.

5

Well, when I was much younger I was shopping just before Christmas with my parents and I got separated from them which was really scary at the time and, fortunately, I guess I knew to ask somebody at the counter and they put an announcement over the tannoy and, um, I waited there and eventually was reunited with my parents, but I remember it being quite traumatic and really, really scary.

6

Oh, my God – I love it. I mean anything and everything to do with shopping – I'm there. I mean, they call me the plastic bag lady because I'm constantly with bags, you know – down the high street. I mean retail therapy, it's got to be the best thing for anyone.

2.02

(P = Presenter)

P: Good evening and welcome to *The Money Show*, the programme that helps you navigate the world of spending and saving, and manage your personal finances. Today we've asked you the listeners to write, email or call with your top tips for saving money or making it go further. The lines are open now on 0359-67678888, that's 0359-67678888, if you'd like to share your ideas.
First off, we've had an email from Tony Price, who says: I've made huge savings by cancelling my gym membership. I found I was only going once or twice a week which was not only making me feel guilty for not going more often, but was also costing me a fortune in monthly subscription fees. With all the money I've saved, I've bought a bicycle and now I get my exercise for free. And on top of that, now that I'm cycling to work, I'm saving on train fares as well! Thank you very much, Tony, for that idea. How to save money and get fit at the same time – can't be bad! And here's another idea from Gemma Banks. Gemma writes: It really makes sense to buy things in the sales whenever you can. Why pay over the odds when, if you wait for the sales, you can get it for half the price? And if you buy in bulk, you can also stock up on presents so you're never at a loss if you need a birthday gift for someone.
I agree, Gemma, in fact I can't honestly understand why anyone buys things at any other time. And talking of purchases, here's a tip from Penny Nowell, who writes: My top tip for saving money is to stop buying designer label clothes. My wardrobe used to be stuffed with top-of-the range clothes and accessories I hardly ever wore. Then a friend said to me, 'Face it, Pen – celebrities are given expensive clothes to wear – they don't actually go out and buy them. You're not a celebrity and never will be. How can you justify paying over the odds because a top designer has had his or her name sewn into the label? And can you honestly tell the difference between an exorbitantly-priced designer bag and one bought at a fraction of the price down the market? Get your clothes at a market or in discount shops and you'll save a fortune.' Thank you, Penny. So, those of you with a penchant for upmarket clothes,

take note – not sure I come into that category myself, though. And here's another money-saving idea from Paul Moore who's emailed us with the following suggestion: if you're an impulse buyer like me, my suggestion when you're waiting at the till with your new purchase is to count to ten and ask yourself: 'Do I really need this?' The chances are the answer is no. Even if it's half price, if you don't need it, you're not saving money. So, put it down, walk away and believe me, you'll feel a lot happier, and a lot richer, when you get home. Plus the fact that your house won't be cluttered with stuff you're only going to give away or get rid of in a few months' time.
I like that suggestion, Paul. I'm sure we'd all be a lot happier if we could just be content with the bare necessities of life. And talking of bare necessities, here's a tip from Sally Richards …

🔘 **2.03**

(B = Bill; M = Marina)
B: So, have you got any experience of bargaining?
M: Yeah, yeah, I have actually. I was in Turkey and I've got a bit of a passion for rugs, and I saw this kilim and I really liked it but it was way over-priced and er … but I got into this whole bargaining thing with this guy and because I, in a way, I kind of liked it – I mean it was lovely, but I also didn't really want it and so because I didn't really want it, I just made up a price, you know, and really low. I started really low.
B: Well, don't they say, go like a fifth of the price or something? (Yeah, that's right.) I mean, I know it's probably different in different countries but I know in Egypt they kind of literally go a fifth of the price, you know, and you think what, you're kind of insulting them but …
M: But anyway, and so, because I didn't really care about it that much, there wasn't a huge emotional investment. I just, you know, I just made up a figure (Brilliant!) and, basically, we got it just above the figure that I had quoted.
B: It's good fun though, isn't it?
M: Yes and no. What about you?
B: No, I really enjoy it. I think because they are so used to doing it, you know, in Turkey and Egypt and, you know, a lot of places other than England probably, and maybe America, I think they enjoy it. You know, they get a kick out of it and they know that they've got a margin that they can sell it at and they try and get the most out of you and I think it is a challenge for them, you know, and I've never left a bargain or a haggling situation not feeling happy and the seller not feeling happy. And that's always a good thing. You know, you go into a shop in this country and you know you've been ripped off but you still buy it because you want it or you need it.
M: But, you know, I think at the moment you can actually bargain here as well.
B: Do you think?
M: Yeah, yeah, definitely.

🔘 **2.05**

(M = Market stall holder; C = Customer)
C: Excuse me, how much is this vase?

M: This one? It's 50 euros. Solid marble.
C: Hmm. Yes, it's beautiful, but it's a bit more than I was prepared to pay. Could you give me a discount, do you think?
M: Well, I suppose I could give you ten percent off. So, that would make it 45.
C: Hmm. The thing is, it's a little bit chipped, here at the top, and I wanted to give it to someone, as a present.
M: Well, I suppose I could knock off another 5 euros. But that's as low as I'm prepared to go. It's solid marble. Hand carved. You won't get another one like it.
C: Yes, yes, I can see that, but I'm afraid it's still a bit above my price range. I think I'll leave it, thanks.
M: Tell you what, you can have it for 35, and I'll throw in this little box as well.
C: Oh, right. Is that your best price?
M: Yes, I can't go any lower than that or I'll be giving it away.
C: Okay, I'll take it. Thanks very much.
M: Thank you. That's 35 euros please. You've got yourself a bargain.

Unit 6

🔘 **2.09**

1
Hmm, that's a difficult one. I think a crossword. Um, I don't think I've ever completed one, to be honest. And I've got a degree! Yeah, I mean, I've spent hours and hours … especially the cryptic ones – I always need help. But, um, you know, we get there in the end!

2
Oh, I've got absolutely wonderful and clear memories of playing chess with my dad. I mean we used to spend hours actually and, er, he taught me everything I know virtually and, and you know, I've gone on to play throughout my life and I find it a wonderful thing to pass on to my kids.

3
I'm absolutely obsessed with Sudoku. I play it all the time, if I'm on a train or a bus or I can actually spend hours sitting at home doing it, it's quite sad!

4
Well, I think those hand held game things are just pointless. I mean, I don't see, I really don't see the point in them. People say, you know, it improves eye/hand co-ordination and all that kind of stuff but I don't get it, I don't like them and I don't see how people can spend hours and hours playing them.

🔘 **2.10**

Mike
Mmm … sight I suppose. Yes, the most important one is sight I suppose … I mean, if you're blind, if you can't see, then although you can lead a full life and all that, I think it does make you more vulnerable, more dependent on other people, I don't know, for silly little things like, for example, like shopping in a supermarket or whatever and I would really hate it if I couldn't see what things or people looked like … or the expression on a person's face when they're talking to you. I mean, you wouldn't even know if they were looking at you or whether they looked interested in what you were saying.

🔘 **2.11**

Maria
No, I haven't, but I read this article about a man who'd gone deaf and then his hearing was restored to him, and he spoke about how isolating it can be if you can't hear. He said that you miss out on a lot of things, that although you can communicate fine when you need to, you miss out on the subtleties of a conversation, and the thing he missed most was humour … the humour in spontaneous conversation … because it all gets slowed down when you're signing. And he really missed listening to music, that was the worst part he said. That, and not being able to hear his wife's voice. And he said that it was really strange to start with when he regained his hearing. Everything sounded much louder. He said he actually misses total silence sometimes, just not hearing anything, and that it can be really relaxing.

🔘 **2.12**

Helen
Um, I don't know … but maybe smell I suppose … like someone can just walk past you on the street and you can catch the smell of their perfume and it reminds you really strongly of someone … or food … I can't remember where I was the other day, but I suddenly smelt the most wonderful cooking smells: coconut oil and eastern spices and it reminded me so strongly of my holidays in Thailand … I could see the palm trees, taste the food, feel the sun on my skin … yes, I think smell triggers the strongest, most vivid memories.

🔘 **2.13**

Nick
This may seem like a strange answer, but maybe touch … you know, the sense of touch … I think it's probably the one we take most for granted, being able to feel things and it's not, it's not, you know, a sense that's limited to one part of your body either – it's everything, every single pore, every single bit of your skin. I remember seeing a documentary about a man who'd been born deaf and mute and had later lost his sight in an accident – he lived a full life – he was eighty-something and he still worked and even travelled. He just lived his life totally through his sense of touch. In this programme, they showed him visiting other people like him in Japan. It was amazing – they used an international signing language which was based on touch – they would touch each other and sign on each other's palms, and they could feel each other talking – and it showed them going to a drum concert too – like a traditional Japanese drum concert – and they could feel the music, I mean they could feel the vibrations of the drums, even though they couldn't hear them. It was just totally amazing.

🔘 **2.14**

Petra
Well, usually I'm renowned for my sense of smell! Sometimes I can smell things that no-one else notices. That can be good because I'm really sensitive to things like gas leaks and anything that smells bad … things like food that's gone off. My mum often asks me to smell meat or fish or milk or whatever to see if it's okay … but recently I've had quite a heavy cold and it's really affected

my sense of smell. I mean, I can smell really strong things, like coffee or if something's burning in the kitchen, but I can't smell other things like perfume so I don't know how much to put on. And I really miss the subtler smells in the kitchen. It affects my taste too. Everything tastes so bland.

🔵 2.16

(A = Adam; B = Brad; D = Dylan)

A: Do you mind budging up a bit?
B: No, of course not.
A: Thanks. Dylan, would you mind not sitting there?
D: Why?
A: You're leaning on my jacket.
D: Sorry!
A: So, Brad, have you decided?
D: Decided what?
A: Mind your own business!
D: Oh, come on!
B: Dylan, would you mind getting us some drinks?
D: Yes, I would.
B: Oh, come on! It's just boring work stuff.
D: Oh, okay. I don't believe it for a second.
B: You know I'll cover for you while you're away.
A: Would you?
B: Yeah, really, no problem.
A: Hmm, but what about Peter? Do you think he'll mind?
B: No, of course not. Mind you, Nicholas will.
A: Really, why?

Unit 7

🔵 2.20

This exciting new mobile phone prototype looks more like a piece of space-age jewellery than a phone. It's made up of two pieces: the wristband is the phone itself whilst the silver hoop, which looks like it should be part of a pendant, is actually the earpiece. When used in this mode the phone offers safe and easy hands-free voice calls, but it's also a great way of carrying your phone. You can't forget your phone when it's attached to your wrist! And the earpiece can be worn as a clip on your shirt or T-shirt.

When you're not wearing it around your wrist it can open out into a fairly traditional phone size and shape with all the familiar features: keypad, camera, music player. The earpiece can be worn separately or clipped onto the phone and the phone brought up to your ear.

But possibly the most innovative feature is the fact that it also folds out even further and the transparent touchscreen converts into a full size qwerty keyboard, or an interactive map.

🔵 2.22

(J = John, S = Sue)

J: So, what trendy new gadget are you going to wow us with today, Sue?
S: Here it is, John, it's an e-reader – or an electronic reading device to give its full name.
J: Doesn't look very exciting to me. Give me a good old-fashioned paperback any day.
S: Ah, but this is so much more than a book. It's a thousand books, all stored in one small device. The e-reader is

going to do for books what the iPod did for music. No more hunting around in bookstores, no more dusty bookshelves … books have gone digital. No more torn pages or newsprint stains on your fingers. All you need now is this – one small, slim gadget that you can fit in your pocket or bag and take with you wherever you go with all the books, newspapers, magazines and comics you could possibly ever need.

J: You've been reading too much hype! I bet you can't use it in the bath! And anyway, I love the smell of dusty old bookshelves – my house would look very bare without them …
S: Yes, but think of this, you're going on holiday, you're packing your bags, you've got to that point when you have to decide which books to take with you. How many can you fit in your luggage? Which one are you going to take on board with you? What if you don't like it? What if you finish it halfway through the journey and have nothing left to read except the in-flight magazine …
J: Horror of horrors …
S: Well, this is the answer. No more difficult decisions about which to take and which to leave behind. You can take them all with you … and if you need a map or a local guidebook when you're away, this little device connects to the internet and you can download everything you need, completely free of charge.
J: Yeah, but first you have to go hunting round to find an internet café or a wi-fi hotspot or whatever …
S: No, not at all … it uses mobile phone networks … and it automatically downloads the latest versions of newspapers, magazines and all your favourite blogs … anything you want to read really, it's there, at the push of a button.
J: Yes, but looking at a small screen like that for hours on end can't possibly be good for your eyes … I mean, it's like sitting in front of a computer for hours on end …
S: Ah, but it isn't … there's no light on the screen, so no glare and very little eyestrain, no more than reading a normal paper book … you can even read it in strong sunlight … this is the shape of books in the future.
J: Yes, but it isn't a book. I'm sorry, but I really don't think any device, no matter how slick and quick and easy to use, can possibly replace a much-loved book.
S: Yes, yes, and when the first trains were built nobody wanted to go on them because they thought the human body would be sure to explode if it travelled at over 40 miles an hour …
J: Yes, I know, I know, and no-one thought there'd be a market for personal computers back in the 1960s …
S: And think about the environmental impact – okay, so most of the paper for books is made from recycled wood pulp … but what about the costs of making the paper, printing the books and then shipping them all over the world? Not to speak of the mountains and mountains of newspapers trashed every single day … you know, it may not save the planet, but it'd definitely cut down on carbon

gas production if we all gave up paper publications and turned to e-reading instead …

J: Mmm … I can see you're definitely sold on the idea … but do you think it'll survive a windy afternoon on the beach?
S: Why not give it a go? Have this one on loan for a week and we can talk about it again in the next programme … I'm sure it'll give you plenty to write about on your blog, which, by the way, you'll be able to read on your new e-reader!

🔵 2.23

1

(C = Carla; B = Bette)

C: I don't know if I want to do it … I mean, I do, but then …
B: Oh, come on, it's not such a big deal, is it? I mean, everybody does it … even my mum's got one.
C: Yeah, but the thing is, once you've done it, there's no going back … You know, what's done is done and all that …
B: Ah, yes, sorry, I obviously hadn't thought through all the possible consequences. I mean this could have a truly life-changing effect, couldn't it?
C: Oh, stop it! It's just that, you know, once it's there, I can't get rid of it, can I? Oh, and what if I decide I don't like it anymore?
B: Ah, well, you'll just have to live with the consequences, won't you? But no, seriously, I think it'll look really good. Go for it. Go on. You know you want to.

🔵 2.24

2

(M = Mrs Taylor; A = Austin)

M: So, have you had a chance to think about it, then?
A: Yeah, but the thing is, I keep going round and round in circles … I mean, you know, it's a big decision.
M: It certainly is. I mean, you know, it's the next four years of your life … and not only that … it will effect what choices you have afterwards as well … but remember, it isn't the end of the world if you start a course and then decide it isn't for you … Lots of people change their minds, you know. I think you have to go for the choice that you feel happiest with now – what feels best for you at the moment.
A: Yes, I suppose you're right …

🔵 2.25

3

(A = Anna; R = Rachel)

A: I've been thinking about what you said … you know … how I should stop dithering all the time … how I should learn to be a bit more assertive … stand up for myself and all that …
R: … and?
A: Well, I've made up my mind … I'm going to tell them tomorrow!
R: You mean, you're actually going to hand in your resignation?
A: Yup, that's right! At long last!

🔵 2.26

4

(P = Peter; S = Stuart)

P: It's a great honour … I'm very flattered that you think I'm capable … but I need time to think about it …

S: Look, why don't you sleep on it? Talk to your wife about it. You can let us know tomorrow …

P: Okay, thanks. I will. I'll call you first thing in the morning. Once I've had a chance to think it through properly … I mean, it really is a great honour… but, as you say, I need to talk to my wife about it.

S: That's fine … we understand. It's a big decision.

P: Okay, thank you. I'll call you in the morning.

Unit 8

🔘 **2.27**

1

(D = David; M = Margaret)

D: So, have you spoken to Mike?

M: Yes.

D: And does he reckon you have a case?

M: Well, he says I certainly have a case but it'll probably cost me more than it's worth to take them to court. So, I'm not sure what to do.

D: Well, I think you should sue them, even if you only get minimal compensation. It's the principle that counts. People can't just go round spreading lies and rumours like that. What I mean is, you have to stand up for yourself, you know, show that it's important to you.

M: Yes, I agree. The only reason I'm hesitating is because I don't want any more bad publicity.

D: Well, it might not all be bad, and you know what they say, there's no such thing as bad publicity. But, if you want a second opinion, the best person to ask is Fred MacIntyre.

M: But, surely it's too late now, anyway? I mean it's been almost three weeks since they published the article …

🔘 **2.28**

2

(R = Rani; D = Daniel)

D: Well, I suppose what I should have said is, 'Yes, officer. I'm sorry, but I was in a terrible hurry.'

R: But you didn't.

D: No, I tried to deny it, you know, make out that I couldn't possibly have been doing 100 miles per hour.

R: And?

D: And, he gave me an on-the-spot fine and said that if it happened again I'd lose my licence.

R: Ooh, how much?

D: Fifty pounds.

R: Ooh!

D: That's a lesson I won't forget in a hurry!

R: What, don't lie to a policeman?

D: No, it's better to be late than fifty pounds worse off!

🔘 **2.29**

3

(F = Fiona; D = Doug)

F: Yeah, being on the jury was a really weird experience.

D: How long did it last?

F: Ooh, a couple of weeks. It was fascinating , seeing how a court works, you know, how formal it all is and everything. We had to stay in a hotel overnight because we couldn't come

to a verdict in one day. That was quite exciting.

D: Really? What was it for then? Murder?

F: No, nothing that drastic! It was your usual story of a guy setting up a company, borrowing money from banks, getting things on credit and then using the company money to buy himself and his girlfriend some nice treats, you know, a Ferrari, a Rolex …

D: A couple of diamond rings!

F: Exactly. But the main issue was that the accused used to be a local politician. Didn't you read about it in the papers? It was quite big news at the time.

D: Yeah, now you come to mention it, I do remember something … John Limes or something like that?

F: Yeah, John Limey.

D: And what did you decide?

F: Well, in the end the verdict we returned was unanimous – guilty!

🔘 **2.30**

1

Well, I suppose it's not really an offence is it, not, not a serious offence? I just think people do it without thinking. Um, they see other people do it so they do it themselves and then you end up with a really filthy street. People should think more about the environment, about their surroundings and perhaps rather than punishing them they should, they should have a deterrent fine or, or, you know, enough of a fine to make them think twice about doing it again, frankly.

🔘 **2.31**

2

Well, first of all I think the damage these things do should not be underestimated. This is in no way a nuisance crime. It is extremely, extremely serious. It can have worldwide effects. It can lose businesses and individuals millions of pounds and I think the punishment should reflect this. It's a difficult one because I think perhaps prison is too harsh, but perhaps we should consider community service. I mean, a lot of these people that commit this kind of crime are obviously extremely talented and have a lot of knowledge and maybe that could be put to better use.

🔘 **2.32**

3

A: I think it's really tricky because some people do it out of necessity. You know, a mum might do it for her children because she hasn't got a choice, but then some people just do it because others are. You know, they're copying their mates. No … no-one really gets hurt (True.) unless it's a, you know, very small company but, you know, no-one gets hurt. So, I … I think it's one of those things where if you are going to punish them – something a bit softer – you know, therapy, counselling, to try and find out why … why they did it in the first place.

B: Do you think that would work and stop it, do you?

A: I think it would help them, yes.

🔘 **2.33**

4

F: Well, I … my main concern is that, you know, it's usually the super-rich who get away with this and, er, and because they

are so wealthy they can employ, you know, excellent lawyers (Yeah) and they, they just wriggle out of it. Now I think the crime, I think it's an enormous crime and I think it needs to be punished accordingly …

M: How do you mean?

F: Well, I think a minimum of five years really, I think so you know. Erm … because they are depriving people, you know, they're, they're depriving the country actually, of huge amounts of money by siphoning all this – you know, they're siphoning off their own wealth and I just don't think it's … I think it's a really serious crime.

M: Fair enough.

🔘 **2.34**

5

M: I think these guys are quite evil really, I mean I think they're preying on innocent people and they're getting other people to do their dirty work by using the power of the word. I think they're quite low. I really think they need to be er … punished quite severely, myself.

F: And how? How would you do that?

M: Well, I mean, you know, a long prison term I … I think is the only way, really. Get them off the streets and then they … they can't continue to do it, can they?

🔘 **2.35**

6

M: Well, I actually don't think it's a crime at all. To be completely honest, I … I love seeing it, I love seeing it, I've, you know, seen it all over the world. There's this place in Portugal where it's just everywhere and it's beautiful.

F: Really?

M: Yeah, and it brings the tourists in to look at it. You know, the locals love it, they add to it all the time. I mean let's face it … it's artwork, it really is. It's street art and it's just beautiful and I mean, I don't think there should be any … any punishment. If anything, these people should be paid for decorating and making our streets look brighter and, yeah, a more interesting place.

F: Wow.

🔘 **2.36**

(T = Tim; A = Anne)

T: Have you ever had anything stolen?

A: Er, yes, I have, a brand new car! I'd had it for just under a month.

T: You're kidding!

A: No!

T: You were insured, of course?

A: Of course, but the insurance company wouldn't pay up.

T: What do you mean, wouldn't pay up? I mean, a brand new car and you didn't insure it against theft?

A: Of course I did, and I was insured against theft … but they just didn't want to pay up. It was a bit of a complicated case … Fortunately, my boyfriend at the time was a lawyer so in the end, we managed to sort it out.

T: So, what happened then?

A: Well, you see, these three teenagers stole my car … they'd broken out of this special school for young offenders and well, it seems they wanted to run away, so they decided to pinch a car – my car!

Anyway, while they were driving away they started arguing and drove the car straight into a tree.

T: Oh, no!

A: The car was a write-off, a total write-off. I couldn't believe it when I saw it!

T: What about the kids?

A: Well, they weren't seriously hurt or anything, miraculous really, considering … but they got arrested of course and sent back to the school. I was just relieved I'd taken out insurance and I was already thinking I'd get another car with the insurance money … maybe buy a second-hand one this time and make a bit of money on the deal!

T: Sounds like a good idea … but they wouldn't pay up, you said?

A: Yeah, when I explained to the insurance company what had happened, they told me they would need to see my insurance documents. So, I went down to the garage where my car had been towed, only to find that all my documents had mysteriously disappeared from the glove compartment.

T: So, what did you do?

A: Well, I went back to the insurance people and explained the situation and they said it didn't matter because they had their own copy of the original contract and that anyway, I wasn't covered.

T: But didn't you say … ?

A: Well, I thought I was covered but they said I was insured against theft, but that the car had been found, so technically it was no longer stolen. The problem was that I wasn't covered for any damage incurred in the event of theft.

T: Surely they can't include such a ridiculous clause?

A: Well, apparently they can and they did. The box with this condition had been ticked. I hadn't read all the small print in the contract.

T: But why not? You really should have read it before signing it, you know. You were almost asking for trouble.

A: Thanks! Yeah, I suppose with hindsight I ought to have done, but I couldn't be bothered at the time.

T: But couldn't you have asked your boyfriend to check it over for you? He was a lawyer, wasn't he? Or you could have asked a friend.

A: Well, I suppose I could have done, but you know how these things are, they're standard forms so I thought I'd be all right. Anyway, I have no idea if I had actually ticked the box or not. I might have done but I didn't have my copy and so they might have simply ticked the box themselves to save them having to pay out the equivalent of £8,000.

T: They wouldn't have done that, surely? That's quite a serious accusation …

A: I don't know. They certainly could have done it if they'd wanted to.

T: It would have been far too risky, I mean, you might have found your copy of the contract.

A: Not if they had it.

T: What do you mean?

A: Well, the man who ran the insurance company office was the brother of the man who owned the garage where my car was towed. I reckon they must have taken it from the car, along with all the other documents.

T: That sounds too far-fetched, they wouldn't have dared do something like that, surely? I mean, I know you must have been upset at the time, and of course, you may be right … but they can't have just stolen the documents like that!

A: I know it all sounds very improbable, but it all looked terribly suspicious at the time.

T: So, what happened in the end then?

A: Well, my boyfriend decided the best way to get the money back would be to sue the boys' school, which he did, and four years later we got the money back. Not that I saw much of it.

T: What, all swallowed up by the lawyers?

A: Yeah, my husband.

T: Oh, you married your boyfriend!

A: Yeah, to avoid the legal fees!

🌐 2.39

1
A: Have you heard? Robyn and Steve are getting married.

B: Really? No kidding? That's great news.

2
A: So, what do you think to the news?

B: What news?

A: Jeff is leaving the team.

B: What? But that can't be right! I mean, they just made him captain.

3
A: Katy says she going to pay for the damages.

B: Yeah, yeah, pull the other one!

A: No, honestly, she is. She told me so herself.

B: Yeah? Well, I'll believe that when I see it.

4
A: So, anyway, Rik reckons the boss is going to give us an extra bonus at Christmas.

B: Yeah, and pigs might fly!

A: No, honestly, that's what everyone's saying. He's really happy with the way business is going and he wants to thank everyone for their hard work.

B: Okay, I'll take your word for it, though I won't be convinced until I've got the money in my hand.

Unit 9

🌐 3.01

(A = Anne Kramer; S = Simon Holmes)

A: Well, a very good morning to you and welcome to this week's edition of *Science Matters* with me, Anne Kramer. Today we have in our studio Dr Simon Holmes, who is an expert on body clocks, circadian rhythms and all things sleep-related, and who's going to tell us a little bit more about what it all means. Simon, a very warm welcome to the programme.

S: Thank you.

A: So, first of all, tell us, what exactly are circadian rhythms?

S: Well Anne, circadian rhythms are essentially the changes that occur in our brain and in our body over the course of a day – our daily cycle of sleeping and waking if you like. In fact 'circadian' is a Latin word meaning 'around a day'. In other words, we operate in cycles of just over twenty-four hours, broadly in tune with the cycles of nature. And all animals and most plants live according to these rhythms. But in the animal kingdom, the rhythms vary according to whether an animal is a diurnal or nocturnal creature.

A: Diurnal or nocturnal? What's that exactly?

S: Well, basically that refers to whether the animal is awake during the day or during the night. As you know, we humans are diurnal, not nocturnal creatures. That means that we are active during the day and sleep during the night. Whereas some animals, such as bats or owls or foxes, are largely nocturnal – they sleep by day and hunt by night.

A: I see. And how exactly does that tie in with our body clock? And what is a body clock in fact?

S: Well, a body clock is actually just as it sounds, it's, it's a mechanism in the body that works a bit like a clock and that regulates our circadian rhythms. Nobody knows exactly how it does this, but we do know that it interacts with signals, such as variations in sunlight and environmental activity, noise and so on, and then it, if you like, fine-tunes our feelings of sleepiness and wakefulness to keep them in sync with the external cycle of dark and light.

A: I see. So, is that why we tend to wake up earlier in summer and need more sleep in winter, for example?

S: Exactly. But research has shown that the normal circadian rhythm for most people is, as I say, roughly twenty-four hours – twenty-four hours and eleven to fifteen minutes to be precise, that's according to some research, though other scientists have put it slightly higher, at more like twenty-five hours.

A: Ah, that's interesting, Simon because you say that humans are diurnal not nocturnal creatures, but that's not true of everyone, is it? Is it not the case that some people are owls and other people are larks – by nature, perhaps? What does science have to say about that?

S: Well, you're quite right, and it's important to stress that there is actually quite a lot of individual genetic variation in the pattern of circadian rhythms. It does seem that some people are genetically larkish and others genetically owlish, if you like. And these rhythms also fluctuate with age. Young children tend to be larks and then, sometime around the onset of puberty, it all changes. Adolescents start needing a lot more sleep, and shift to waking and performing better later in the day. And then, around the age of twenty or so, it all changes. And then, in later stages of life, it shifts again, and elderly people tend to become increasingly larkish.

A: So, does that explain why most teenagers seem to be physically incapable of getting out of bed at a sensible time in the morning? Like my nephew, for example, who never surfaces until it's time for lunch!

S: Well, you could be right!

A: So, I can tell my sister that my nephew will just grow out of it then, in due course?

S: Well, yes, he may do! Or he may just be one of nature's owls, I suppose.

A: And what happens, Simon, when these circadian rhythms get disrupted? Say, if we cross over to a different time zone, or have to work night shifts? How does our body clock adapt?

S: Well, obviously, if we cross over several time zones all at once, as on a long international flight for example, our body struggles to adapt to the change, and that's when we suffer from what's known as jet lag.

A: Ah, yes.

S: Now, jet lag is a condition that affects us when our body clock is out of sync with our destination time, and the body's natural rhythms are upset. And it manifests itself in all sorts of symptoms, such as fatigue, insomnia, irritability, nausea, loss of appetite and even mild depression.

A: And what about night workers?

S: Yes, night workers, people who work on a night shift, are also prone to all sorts of physical and psychological problems, especially if they aren't able to catch up with their sleep during the day.
And moving on now to sleep patterns, there are a number of interesting questions …

3.02

James
(M = Mark; J = James)

M: You've been to the Himalayas, haven't you?

J: Yeah, I had this one unforgettable night up in the mountains, in Nepal, it was actually, and it was a full moon and we were up in the mountains. So we were in the jungle, below the snow line – we could see the snow line up in the mountains up ahead, but as the moon rose – because it was a very big, low, pale moon and we watched it come up through the mountains. We just couldn't take our eyes off it and the hours just passed, you know, just conversing about the sky, basically, as you watched the moon rise and change colour (Wow!). It lit up the whole valley (Amazing!) of the Himalayas and the snow and it was just beautiful and of course then, you'd choose a little area of the sky – we had binoculars and microscope – no, not microscope, (Telescope.) telescope, thank you, and we just concentrated on a square and watched the shooting stars as they would fly past and you could be guaranteed, within about five minutes, to see a shooting star.

M: Amazing.

J: And it just took all night. We had a little fire dug in the ground keeping us warm and some food and the next minute the sun is coming up.

M: Brilliant.

3.03

Rosie
(R = Rosie; M = Matt)

R: I went to Glastonbury festival and it's great. It's just completely manic. The whole experience is crazy, but I was really lucky because I was there when it was sunny and so there was no rain (oh great!) and I think it's crucial when you're at Glastonbury, to have at least one morning when you see the sun come up, so there's clearly no point in going to

bed because everyone's up anyway and it's really noisy. So we just went out and went dancing and stuff and then sort of just mooched about some fields and sat on top of this hill and watched the sun come up and it was amazing, and it was quite hard to stay awake all that time, but it was definitely, definitely worth it.

M: And how was the next day?

R: The next day was … A lot of sleeping was involved in the next day, which is a difficult thing to achieve in Glastonbury.

3.04

Phillip
(P = Phillip; F = Flic)

P: A few years ago there was an American talk show host that come over to do one show in London and me and my friends are massive fans so we really wanted to see the show. So, we went to the South Bank where they were filming the night before and camped out to try and get tickets and, unbelievably, there were about, I think, about twenty people there in front of us but we thought, oh, that's fine, we'll camp out, that will be great and we spent the whole night on the South Bank and obviously just didn't sleep. It was an absolute nightmare. It was so cold and we felt awful the next day but the thing that kept us going was that we were going to see this show – literally our hero, and go and see this talk show host. The next day when they were about to film the show they called the people in and had a line and we didn't realise we were the standby line and they had twenty tickets and there were twenty people in front of us and so we slept out the whole night and spent the whole night there and didn't even get to see the show, unfortunately. We were really upset.

F: That's awful. Did you see it on the TV when they showed it?

P: Yeah, we did, but it wasn't the same.

3.07

(K = Kieran; F = Fiona)

K: Have I told you about my holiday in Peru?

F: No, I don't think so. Where did you go?

K: Um, I went to Machu Picchu which was somewhere I'd always wanted to go.

F: Oh wow, that must have been amazing.

K: Yes, it was fantastic in many ways – seeing the ruins is really awe-inspiring, and the setting is magical – right in the middle of the jungle – but in other ways it was a bit disappointing.

F: Oh, what do you mean?

K: Well, for a start, it was packed with tourists which meant that you couldn't really get a proper feel for the atmosphere of the place. I'd have liked to have gone there in the low season, when there are fewer visitors, but unfortunately I couldn't get time off work then.

F: Oh, right, that's a shame.

K: And another problem was the altitude. I started suffering from altitude sickness as soon as I arrived so I just went straight to bed. I think if I'd taken those altitude pills I would have been okay.

F: Yeah, I've heard about that. They say it takes a couple of days to acclimatise …

K: That's right, yeah … I'd also been

planning to get up early the next day to see the sun rise over the ruins but, unfortunately, I was just too exhausted – I slept right through the alarm. Then the next day it was pouring with rain so obviously there was no sunrise. And then it was time to leave, which was a shame. I only had two days there. It's a pity I couldn't have gone for longer.

F: Oh well, at least you got some good photos hopefully?

K: No, that was another problem. It was raining so hard that my camera got soaked and the photos didn't actually come out.

F: Oh no! Still, at least you've got your memories?

K: Yeah. I don't regret going, not in the least. But I think I'd like to go again with more time and maybe read a bit more about the history beforehand so I could understand more about what I was seeing, and it would all be more meaningful. And perhaps not go on my own next time, either. Um, maybe you'd like to come with me?

F: Ah, we'll see …

3.10

1

A: Hi, what are you up to tonight?

B: Actually I'm up to my eyes with work tonight.

A: Oh, that's a shame. I just thought we might go out for a drink to celebrate the end of term.

B: That would have been brilliant, but I'm afraid I've got to hand in a report first thing tomorrow morning. Thanks anyway.

A: Never mind. Some other time perhaps.

2

A: How about getting together sometime over the weekend to discuss the holiday?

B: Sounds good. My place or yours?

A: You could come round here if you like. Would 11 on Sunday be a good time?

B: Actually, could we make it a bit later? Say, twelve-ish?

A: That'd be fine. See you around twelve on Sunday then.

B: Cool. See you then.

3

A: We're having a party on Friday night, from about eight onwards. Do you fancy coming along?

B: That'd be fab. Thanks! Can I bring anything?

A: No, that's fine. Just yourself! And bring along a friend if you like.

B: Great, see you on Friday, then.

A: Yeah, look forward to it.

Unit 10

3.12

(C = Chloe; M = Mother)

C: Mum! You left the lights on again.

M: Sorry?

C: You left the lights on again. When I came downstairs this morning all the lights were on. And the computer and the printer were plugged in, and the television was still on standby. Just think how much energy that was consuming.

M: Oh, this isn't going to turn into another carbon footprint lecture is it? It was bad enough you coming into the bathroom this morning and turning off the tap while I was still brushing my teeth …

C: Well, someone's got to think about our carbon footprint, haven't they? You'd already been in the shower five minutes before that. You could easily have a shower in two minutes instead of five.

M: Chloe, I hardly think that one person cutting down their shower by three minutes a day is going to have a massive effect on reducing our carbon footprint.

C: Yes, Mum, but if everyone said that, nothing would change. We've all got to do our bit to combat climate change. If you spent two minutes in the shower instead of five, you'd save 7,000 litres of water a year. And you'd have three extra minutes a day as well, that's 18 more hours per year you'd gain. Just think what you could do with all that extra time!

M: Chloe, I'm all for doing my bit. I put out my paper and glass to be recycled. I get biodegradable plastic bags when I go shopping at the supermarket. And I even reuse them sometimes.

C: Yes Mum, but that's all you do. That's just a drop in the ocean. You're not going to save the planet unless you make some major changes in your lifestyle.

M: Like what, for example?

C: Like cycling to work instead of taking the car. Did you know that the average car produces three tonnes of CO_2 a year? If everyone in this country went to work by bike instead of taking the car, that's a million tonnes of CO_2 a year we'd save.

M: I hate to mention this, Chloe, but I don't seem to recall your refusing any lifts recently. And I also can't recall your being overjoyed when I turned up in the car to pick you up from Sam's the other night when it was pouring with rain …

C: Okay then … yeah … well … but when are you going to stop flying everywhere? You do know, don't you, that planes are the major contributor to climate change? If you go by train you cut back on emissions by ninety percent on every trip.

M: Ah, so planes are the bad guys, are they? I seem to remember parting with a considerable amount of money to pay for a certain round-the-world ticket for a certain person's gap year. And quite honestly, I can't see the point in giving up flying when the rest of the population are quite happily going everywhere by plane. Why be so eco-friendly that you make yourself miserable?

C: Honestly! You are so selfish. The icecaps are melting and the polar bears are dying and all you can think about is your own comfort.

M: Well, I'm afraid I'm not going to give up my holidays abroad just to make a couple of polar bears happy. Now, if the lecture's over, I'm going to make myself a cup of tea and have my breakfast. I have a busy day ahead.

C: Mum! You filled the kettle right up to the top! You only need to put in a tiny bit of water if you're only making one cup of tea. And as well as that, …

3.13

Two years ago my family camped amidst the California redwoods. During a hike, my younger son decided to take his nap.

Kicking off my shoes, I got comfortable under a redwood and let my son nap in my lap while my wife and elder son went on ahead. Upon their return, we had lunch and headed back to our campsite. On a whim, I decided not to put my shoes back on, and walked back barefoot.

The trail felt soft and cool; the cover of pine needles cushioned my footsteps. Normally, the return trip of a hike ends up being faster, but in this case I was slowed down for two reasons. Since my feet were not hardened to the outdoors, I had to look down and deliberate every step to avoid stepping on potentially painful objects, such as sharp rocks. In addition, every time I wanted to see a tree, a cloud, or a hill, I had to stop. Normally with hiking boots, I can walk while looking all around, but in this case I could not do both at the same time. I had to separate the two activities of hiking and of admiring the surroundings.

A few side-effects made me very happy with my decision. Since I was focused on looking down, I noticed many more things on the forest floor; banana slugs, beetles, caterpillars, ants, leaves and cones, among others. Since my footprint was much smaller, softer, and flexible, and I was focused on where my next step was landing, I believe I was more nonviolent. Since my son and I fell way behind, we saw different things. We saw a coyote. We noticed and took a side trail going down a rocky cliff that took me a good extra half-hour to traverse. But it was at the pace my son loved. And, of course, we saw many questioning smiles from passing hikers who doubtlessly had a good discussion later about a barefoot hiker carrying his boots.

Since then I have tried to hike barefoot as often as I can, through as many terrains as possible (and I must admit that it has not been injury-free – I have to live with cuts and bruises). I enjoy the ability to walk through water or sit with my feet dangling in cold streams. I appreciate the sensations that my feet send to me – cold, heat, pain, pleasure. I feel more grounded and allow my feet to explore the different materials that they encounter. Just as my fingers are happy playing with sand, holding a piece of bark, or touching a petal, my toes enjoy wiggling in a puddle, scraping against a textured rock, pressing on a bed of pine needles, or rolling over a cone.

Last but not least, I found that hiking slowly opens up more possibilities. Once, hiking with a large group, I fell behind. Suddenly the park rangers closed the park to cut down an ailing giant redwood. People inside could not leave until this was complete. My friends waited outside in the parking lot while I saw a rare sight, a giant redwood crashing down causing a small cascade of falling trees. An earth-shattering, deafening, beautiful, and sad event that I was lucky to experience, only because I decided to hike barefoot and slow down.

3.16

1
I wear these shoes mainly for work. I'm on my feet all day so I really need sensible low-heeled shoes that are going to be hard-wearing. They're a bit scuffed and they could do with a bit of a polish, but actually no-one looks at my feet so I reckon I can generally get away with it.

2
I've had these trainers for about three years now and to tell you the truth I wear them day in, day out. They're probably not the trendiest style out but I tried on loads of pairs in the shop, and the others were nowhere near as comfortable as these. They're a bit worn-out now but I hate buying shoes so I always make mine last longer than they probably should.

3
I saw these shoes in a sale and I couldn't resist buying them. I take a size 46 and I need a wide fitting too, so sometimes it's hard to get shoes that fit properly and look good as well. I mean, they're just classic lace-up brogues but I think they're reasonably stylish and they're good for wearing on occasions when I need to look smart.

4
I got these shoes for my sister's wedding, to go with a red outfit. There's a matching handbag too. They're designer shoes, and they're by far the most extravagant ones I've ever bought, they cost an arm and a leg. And they're not the most comfortable of shoes either – I had to take them off after the ceremony and again after all the photographs because my feet were killing me and to be honest, I've hardly worn them since. But I love the little pointy toes and I think they make me look quite elegant, even though I tend to wobble a bit on the high heels.

3.17

(P = Presenter; M = Margaret Banks)

P: Welcome back. Now, as promised, I'm joined in the studio by psychologist Margaret Banks who has written a brilliant book called *Let your shoes do the talking*, which promises to help us discover what people's shoes REALLY say about them. Margaret, welcome.

M: Hello, Poppy.

P: Now, we've asked some of our audience today to bring in their favourite pair of shoes. Margaret, would you care to take a look at them? What kind of person do you think would wear these, for example?

M: Hmm, well, I'd say that these shoes certainly suggest someone who is creative and idealistic, who perhaps has an alternative, slightly hippy lifestyle. The shoes are designed to be comfortable and good for your feet. And the vibrant colour to me indicates someone who is pretty self-assured and comfortable with herself.

P: Great! Well, we'll be finding out soon if your predictions about the wearer are correct. In the mean time, would you mind taking a look at these shoes?

M: Oh yes. These shoes tell me that their owner is fashion-conscious and glamorous. She's certainly no shrinking violet, but probably a bit more flirtatious and feminine, and less domineering than someone who might wear boots, for instance. They're really for a woman who's looking to make a red carpet entrance.

P: I see. Very interesting … And how about these ones?

M: Right, these shoes probably belong to someone who is somewhat older than the other women, and perhaps rather quiet, conservative and conventional. She is a follower rather than a leader, and perhaps not very dynamic.

P: Oh. I see. Um … okay, finally, what about these?

M: Right, well clearly the owner is young and perhaps quite trendy, and someone with a carefree and rather casual approach to life. The shoes give off a playful, fun vibe. They say, 'I don't care about expensive designer fashions, there are so many other things that are far more interesting.'

P: Fantastic! Right, thank you so much Margaret, for your assessments. Now it's time to reveal how accurate your predictions were …

🔊 3.18

1

(Y = Young woman; M = Man)

Y: Excuse me, sir. Can you sign this petition to save the rainforests?

M: Well, um, it's a good cause but I can't honestly see the point in signing a petition. No-one's ever going to take any notice of a few signatures.

Y: Oh, I disagree. I think it's well worth making our voice heard. If we get several thousand signatures, I think people will sit up and listen and then our message will start to get home.

M: Well, okay then, but I don't honestly think it'll make any difference.

🔊 3.19

2

(K = Kathy; S = Sally)

K: Oh, Sally they look gorgeous! You should get them.

S: Yes, but they're so expensive. What's the point spending so much money on shoes you're only going to wear once?

K: Oh, go on! It's your sister's wedding, it's once in a lifetime. Treat yourself! You'll regret it if you don't buy them.

S: Well, it's a lot of money, but … okay then. If you really think so.

🔊 3.20

3

(M = Matt; T = Tom)

M: Hey Tom, have you seen this advert for a fitness trainer at the Carlton Health Centre? You should apply.

T: What's the use of applying? They're bound to get loads of applications, from people far more experienced than me.

M: Oh, come on, nothing ventured, nothing gained. You might as well try. You never know, you may get shortlisted for an interview.

T: Yes, but even if I got an interview, I wouldn't get the job. I'm hopeless in interviews.

M: Oh, come on, don't be defeatist! You're a qualified trainer. Just send in an application! It's worth giving it a go.

T: Well, okay then, if it'll make you happy. But I think it's a waste of time, quite frankly.

🔊 3.21

4

(J = Jess; M = Maria)

J: Hey, guess what? Sarah and Ruth are going sailing next summer and they want me to go with them.

M: Jess, what a fantastic opportunity! You must go.

J: Hmm, I'm not sure. I've never done any sailing before. What if I get seasick? And what if I don't like sailing?

M: Well, you should cross that bridge when you come to it. I think you should go for it. You'll really enjoy it.

J: Well, maybe you're right. Maybe I should give it a try.

🔊 3.22

(S = Steph; P = Pam)

S: Come on, you know you want to, really.

P: No, absolutely not! It's out of the question! I'll freeze!

S: No, you won't. You'll love it, really. Go on, just for me! Mary went in last week, you know. She loved it.

P: Honestly, I'm not in the mood and I haven't got a costume anyway.

S: I told you, I've got an extra one. You can borrow it. Look.

P: Hah, you must be joking! That's hideous! I'm not putting that on.

S: Okay, okay, you can have this one. It's brand new!

P: Hmm, well, … I'm still not sure I feel like it, really.

S: Go on, it'll do you good. Just think how much better you'll feel when you come out!

P: Hmm … Oh, alright. You've twisted my arm. But I get to use the towel first when we get out.

S: Fair enough! Let's go.

Unit 11

🔊 3.23

(G = Gillian; K = Kevin)

1

G: Gosh, there are loads, aren't there? Like blogging.

K: Oh, yeah.

G: Anything to do with…

K: Anything internet-wise, yeah.

G: Yeah, absolutely. World Wide Web.

K: Even online. I mean, it's two words that would have existed, but put them together and suddenly it's a whole new …

G: Yeah, completely, I think, you know blogging.

K: Surfing.

G: Online surfing.

K: Surfing, which again would have existed but is different now. It's amazing.

🔊 3.24

(T = Trudy; S = Sue)

2

T: Yeah. Mellifluous. Isn't it lovely? It was used to describe an actor's voice of mellow, sweet sounding, flowing – I just thought it was beautiful. How about you?

S: Well, I heard this thing called impostor syndrome which is something that apparently we, well, a lot of us feel, which is that we don't really have the skills that we say we have or we feel inadequate about those – you know, about a certain job we are doing, which I thought was really interesting.

🔊 3.25

(C = Carolina)

3

C: Well, I think there's a lot of words in English that are currently in Spanish. A lot to do with technology – for instance,

we say download which is not a Spanish word, it's English. We also – we say lunch – it's very bad because of course it's *comida* in Spanish but now, we've inherited this word – lunch.

🔊 3.26

(C = Carolina; M = Mike)

4

C: It was, I think, sidewalk.

M: Really?

C: Yes, it's very strange for me, you know, because I thought it was pavement (right), like the thing that you walk on when you are off the road.

M: And how did you learn that?

C: I was in New York and they said to me, you have to cross onto the other sidewalk. I didn't know what he said, what are you talking about, you know, but yes so that I learnt. It was great.

🔊 3.31

(M = Matt; S = Sue)

M: So, are you saying that people who socialise online are all freaks and weirdos?

S: No, you know I didn't say that! You're deliberately misconstruing my words! My point was, that it can be a problem, you know, you don't know who you're talking to … and they could be … yes, I suppose, they could be weirdos or something … I mean, you never know, do you?

M: So, what are you implying? That we should all stop using chatrooms and networking sites and whatever?

S: No, that's not my point … and you know it … what I want to say is that we need to be careful, that's all … you know, don't give away too many personal details … don't make yourself vulnerable …

M: But surely it's much safer to talk to someone at a distance than to talk to a stranger in a club or a bar …

S: You just don't understand … I'm not saying that it's dangerous to chat with people online … my point is that you have to be really careful when it comes to arranging to meet them in real life … you just don't know who they are, or what they want …

Unit 12

🔊 3.34

1

Well, I don't think it's such a good idea to give money because, er, well, I'd be really worried that somebody would spend it on alcohol rather than something nourishing or, you know, because they always say, like, 'penny for a cup of tea' or whatever. Um, so what I think I might do is, um, buy a sandwich or hot drink or something in winter or … and give it to them there, or maybe, find some old clothes.

🔊 3.35

2

Yes, I usually put a couple of coins in a donation box, um, I mean, obviously if it's, if I'm not in a hurry and if it's easy to get at the change. Um, the thing I don't do is I don't believe in giving money to beggars.

🔊 **3.36**

3

Well, I never give any money to anybody. As far as I'm concerned, it just encourages them. You know, I pay my taxes so the state will look after these people. I mean that's what we're paying all these high taxes for and you know what, quite frankly, I just think it's sheer laziness. I mean, I think they could get up off their bums and get a job if they really wanted to. It's just that they don't want to work.

🔊 **3.37**

4

Well, I don't mind giving money to people who are doing something to earn it, I mean, you know I'd rather they actually did something to earn the money, you know like, like street artists or, or buskers. I mean, I think someone who is actually playing music, it puts people in a good mood on the way to work, so you know, I usually give those people something. A few pennies.

🔊 **3.38**

5

Yeah, I never give money on the street any more. Um, I, um, I do give money through my bank, um, to charities that, um, I'm particularly concerned about. Once a month they get money from my bank. And that way I find I know where it's going and it also means that you're giving extra money because of tax relief.

🔊 **3.39**

6

Oh, it really annoys me. These people with their squeegies. I don't see why I should give money for cleaning my windscreen. I haven't, I haven't asked them. I think it's high time that the government did something about it because it really is annoying. No, I never give them anything.

🔊 **3.41**

(K = Kiera; J = Jay)

K: Hey, Jay, how you doing?
J: Hi, not too bad, you?
K: Listen, we're planning a weekend away – we're going to Tom's grandparents' place in the country. Fancy coming?
J: Oh, I'd love to … But I can't …
K: Why?
J: I promised I'd look after my neighbour's cat. She's away on holiday. I have to go round and feed it every day – and I promised I'd water the plants and …
K: Hey, the plants'll survive for a weekend without water, won't they … ?
J: Yeah, I suppose so …
K: And you can put some food out for the cat … I mean, it's not like a dog, you don't have to take it out for walks or anything, do you?
J: No, but … well, you know, I promised … and, well …
K: I know, you hate letting people down! You and your guilty conscience. You need to lighten up a bit! Hey – I've got an idea!
J: What?
K: You know my cousin Susie?
J: Yeah …
K: Well, she doesn't live very far from you … and she'd do anything, absolutely anything for a bit of extra money … why don't you ask her to do it for you? Give

her a couple of quid, you know … you'll be doing both of you a favour …
J: Well, I don't know … I mean, she's only 15 … what if something happened? What if she lost the key? Or … or …
K: Or what? Oh, you're such a worrier! What can possibly go wrong? Look, if it makes you feel better, give her your mobile number – then, if anything does go wrong, she can call you … and if you really feel you need to, you can make an extra copy of the key and leave it with my mum or something …
J: Yeah, I suppose so …
K: And you can go away with a clear conscience …
J: Yeah, but …
K: No buts … oh, and yes, forgot to tell you … Paul's coming …

🔊 **3.42**

1

A: Did you phone the restaurant?
B: Oh, I'm sorry, it totally slipped my mind! I'll do it right now.
A: Yeah, well don't leave it too late – there might not be any tables left!

🔊 **3.43**

2

A: Oh, hi there.
B: Hello.
A: Look. I've been wanting to talk to you about the other night.
B: Oh.
A: Yeah, well, the thing is, I've been thinking about what you said and how I reacted and I think I owe you an apology. I overdid it.
B: You certainly did. You were completely out of order! All I said was that you played better before you started spending half your life in front of a computer screen.
A: Yeah, yeah, I know. I'm sorry. I completely over-reacted. Friends?
B: Yes – this time! Next round's on you though.
A: Okay, okay.

🔊 **3.44**

3

A: Listen, I'd rather not talk about it if you don't mind.
B: Sorry! I had no idea you were so touchy today!
A: Can we just drop it, please? I'm not in the mood.

🔊 **3.45**

4

A: Erm … excuse me … but I think that's my bag you've got.
B: Sorry? What did you say?
A: I think that's my bag.
B: What? Oh. Oh yes, oh dear. I'm so terribly sorry. I thought it was mine.
A: That's alright. Don't worry about it. Easily done.

🔊 **3.46**

5

A: How did the meeting go yesterday? Sorry I wasn't there, by the way.
B: Sorry! Is that all you can say? I had to deal with all those people on my own and all you can say is sorry? It's just not good enough. You think you can apologise and everything's going to be

okay? Well, it doesn't work that way.
A: Look, I really, really am very sorry. I know I left you to carry the can. But it won't happen again. I promise.
B: Yeah, well, it better hadn't!

🔊 **3.47**

6

We regret to inform you that tonight's concert has been cancelled due to circumstances beyond our control. We apologise for any inconvenience caused. All tickets will be refunded at the box office.

🔊 **3.49**

(K = Kelly; L = Laura)

K: You know, I was in the supermarket yesterday and the check-out assistant was really, really rude to me …
L: Rude to you? What do you mean?
K: Yeah, well, she was … I was in the queue, and she'd started … started ringing stuff up … and I didn't have a lot … milk, some bread, you know … and then I put my had in my pocket … And it was … it was … so embarrassing …
L: What?
K: I'd forgotten my purse, I mean, I had a … a little bit of money on me, but not enough.
L: Oh, yeah, that happened to me the other day, too …
K: … and so I told the woman on the till, you know, I said , like sorry, I think I'm going to have to put some stuff back … nicely, you know, I wasn't rude or anything …
L: Yeah?
K: Yeah … and she just flew off the handle … started going on and on at me … 'Can't you check before you come in the shop? Can't you see you're wasting me time?' … I suppose she must have been having a bad day or whatever …
L: So what did you do?
K: Well, I was really embarrassed and I didn't know what to say, so I just said, okay, forget it, and walked away… maybe I should have tried to calm her down … I … I don't know …
L: Yeah, but, I mean she was shouting at you …
K: Yeah, but the worst thing was that as I walked away I heard … I heard her say … say … 'stupid cow' … or something like that, under her breath.
L: Woah!
K: Yeah, and well, it … it got to me … I turned round and said, like, 'say that again? What did you say? Say it to my face!'
L: Good for you!
K: Yeah … but by now everyone was looking… and I was going to ask her for an apology … or … I don't know … ask for … ask to speak to the manager or something … but I lost my cool … I just turned round and walked out … and now … well, now it's too late to do anything about it …
L: No, it isn't. Write to the manager. Go on, write and complain. I would.
K: Yeah, but, you know, she was probably just having a bad day …
L: Okay, so what? She really shouldn't have treated you like that … go on, get it off your chest ….
K: I don't know …
L: Come on, I'll help you.

Phonetic symbols & Irregular verbs

Single vowels

/ɪ/	ship	/ʃɪp/
/i:/	need	/ni:d/
/ʊ/	put	/pʊt/
/u:/	pool	/pu:l/
/e/	egg	/eg/
/ə/	mother	/'mʌðə/
/ɜ:/	verb	/vɜ:b/
/ɔ:/	saw	/sɔ:/
/æ/	back	/bæk/
/ʌ/	bus	/bʌs/
/ɑ:/	arm	/ɑ:m/
/ɒ/	top	/tɒp/

Diphthongs

/ɪə/	ear	/ɪə/
/eɪ/	face	/feɪs/
/ʊə/	tour	/tʊə/
/ɔɪ/	boy	/bɔɪ/
/əʊ/	nose	/nəʊz/
/eə/	hair	/heə/
/aɪ/	white	/waɪt/
/aʊ/	mouth	/maʊθ/

Consonants

/p/	pen	/pen/
/b/	bag	/bæg/
/t/	tea	/ti:/
/d/	dog	/dɒg/
/tʃ/	chip	/tʃɪp/
/dʒ/	jazz	/dʒæz/
/k/	cake	/keɪk/
/g/	girl	/gɜ:l/
/f/	film	/fɪlm/
/v/	very	/veri/
/θ/	thin	/θɪn/
/ð/	these	/ði:z/
/s/	snake	/sneɪk/
/z/	zoo	/zu:/
/ʃ/	shop	/ʃɒp/
/ʒ/	television	/'telɪvɪʒən/
/m/	map	/mæp/
/n/	name	/neɪm/
/ŋ/	ring	/rɪŋ/
/h/	house	/haʊs/
/l/	leg	/leg/
/r/	road	/rəʊd/
/w/	wine	/waɪn/
/j/	yes	/jes/

Infinitive	Past simple	Past participle
be	was/were	been
beat	beat	beaten
become	became	become
begin	began	begun
bet	bet	bet
bite	bit	bitten
break	broke	broken
bring	brought /brɔ:t/	brought /brɔ:t/
build /bɪld/	built /bɪlt/	built /bɪlt/
burn	burnt/burned	burnt/burned
buy /baɪ/	bought /bɔ:t/	bought /bɔ:t/
can	could /kʊd/	(been able)
catch	caught /kɔ:t/	caught /kɔ:t/
choose	chose	chosen
come	came	come
cost	cost	cost
deal /di:l/	dealt /delt/	dealt /delt/
dig	dug	dug
draw	drew	drawn
dream	dreamt/dreamed	dreamt/dreamed
drink	drank	drunk
drive	drove	driven
eat	ate	eaten
fall	fell	fallen
feel	felt	felt
find	found	found
fly	flew	flown
forget	forgot	forgotten
freeze	froze	frozen
give	gave	given
go	went	gone/been
grow	grew	grown
hang	hung/hanged	hung/hanged
hear	heard /hɜ:d/	heard /hɜ:d/
hide	hid	hidden
hit	hit	hit
hold	held	held
hurt /hɜ:t/	hurt /hɜ:t/	hurt /hɜ:t/
keep	kept	kept
know	knew /nju:/	known
lay	laid	laid
lead	led	led
leave	left	left

Infinitive	Past simple	Past participle
lend	lent	lent
let	let	let
lie	lay/lied	lied/lain
light	lit/lighted	lit/lighted
mean	meant /ment/	meant /ment/
must	had to	(had to)
pay	paid	paid
put	put	put
read	read /red/	read /red/
ride	rode	ridden
ring	rang	rung
rise	rose	risen
run	ran	run
send	sent	sent
set	set	set
shake	shook	shaken
shine	shone	shone
shoot	shot	shot
shrink	shrank	shrunk
sing	sang	sung
sit	sat	sat
sleep	slept	slept
slide	slid	slid
smell	smelt/smelled	smelt/smelled
speak	spoke	spoken
spend	spent	spent
split	split	split
spoil	spoilt/spoiled	spoilt/spoiled
spread	spread	spread
stand	stood	stood
steal	stole	stolen
stick	stuck	stuck
swear	swore	sworn
swell	swelled	swollen/swelled
swim	swam	swum
take	took /tʊk/	taken
teach	taught /tɔ:t/	taught /tɔ:t/
tear	tore	torn
think	thought /θɔ:t/	thought /θɔ:t/
understand	understood	understood
wake	woke	woken
wear	wore /wɔ:/	worn
win	won /wʌn/	won /wʌn/

Macmillan Education
Between Towns Road, Oxford OX4 3PP
A division of Macmillan Publishers Limited
Companies and representatives throughout the world

ISBN 978-0-2300-0932-5

Text © Ceri Jones, Tania Bastow, Amanda Jeffries, Sue Kay & Vaughan Jones 2010
Design and illustration © Macmillan Publishers Limited 2010

First published 2010

Designed by 320 Design Limited
Photographic research and editorial by Sally Cole, Perseverance Works Limited
Illustrated by Beach pp10, 42, 43, 48, 52, 80, 84, 85, 91, 99, 114, 119, 141; Ed
McLachlan pp11, 12, 16, 17, 21, 22, 40, 44, 51, 54, 63, 64, 71, 76, 83, 86, 96, 105,
108, 115, 116, 123, 139, 145; Gary Andrews p79.
Cover design by Andrew Oliver

Authors' acknowledgements
The authors would like to thank Liz Townsend, Nicola Gardner, Madeleine Williamson,
Stephanie Parker, Katie Stephens, Andrew Hornsby-Smith, Rafael Alarcon-Gaeta, 320
Design Limited, Sally Cole (photo researcher) and James Richardson (sound producer)
for their hard work on this project.

The author and publishers are grateful for permission to reprint the following
copyright material:
Material from 'One man's rubbish…' by Ben Child, copyright © Ben Child 2006, first
appeared in The Guardian 08.03.06, reprinted by permission of the author;
Material from 'It shoe makes sense to pay out' by Sarah Howden 2008, copyright ©
Sarah Howden, first appeared in Edinburgh News 17.03.08, reprinted by permission of
the publisher;
Extracted material from 'Men Are From Mars, Women Are From Venus' by John Gray
Ph.D., copyright © John Gray Ph.D. 1992, reprinted by permission of HarperCollins
Publishers US & UK;
Material from 'The Future of Mobile Phones: A Remote Control For Your Life' by William
Webb, copyright © William Webb 2007, first appeared in The Independent 14.05.07,
reprinted by permission of the publisher;
Material from 'We can be winners' by John Ives, copyright © John Ives 2007, first
published in The Guardian 24.07.07, reprinted by permission of the author;
Material from 'How I lived on £1 per day for a year' by Kath Kelly, copyright © Kath
Kelly 2008, first published in Daily Mail 06.09.08, reprinted by permission of the
author;
Material from 'Shoe's that girl' by Elaine Singleton, copyright © Elaine Singleton 2007,
first appeared in Lancashire Evening Post 12.11.07, reprinted by permission of the
publisher;
Extracted information from 'Lonely Planet Publications' for Spain, ed.1, 1997, Central
Europe ed.2, 1997, also extracted information on London, Japan & New York City
from website www.lonelyplanet.com.au; reprinted by permission of the publisher;
Material from 'Times Online Obituary: Michael Jackson' copyright © News International
Syndication, London 26.06.09, reprinted by permission of the publisher;
Material from 'Train station spreads love', copyright © News International Syndication,
London, first appeared in The Sun 18.02.09, reprinted by permission of the
publisher;
Material from 'Man's earliest footprints may be lost forever' by Robin McKie, copyright
© Robin McKie 2008, first appeared in The Observer 13.01.08, reprinted by permission
of the publisher;
Material from 'The Man Who Mistook His Wife for a Hat' by Oliver Sacks, copyright ©
Oliver Sacks 1985, reprinted by permission of Wylie Agency LLC. US, Pan Macmillan
UK and Simon & Schuster US;
Material from '10 writing tips from the Masters' first appeared on website
www.pickthrbrain.com 06.09.07, reprinted by permission of the editor;
Material from '10,000 historic sites at risk from climate change' by Rob Edwards,
copyright © Rob Edwards 2007, first appeared in Sunday Herald, reprinted by
permission of the author;
Material from 'Teleportation and Forcefields Possible Within Decades' says Professor
Michio Kaku by Matthew Moore, copyright © Matthew Moore 2008, first appeared in
The Daily Telegraph 02.04.08, reprinted by permission of the publisher;
Material from 'Kissing banned at railway station' by Paul Stokes, copyright © Paul
Stokes 2009, first appeared in The Daily Telegraph 18.02.09, reprinted by permission
of the publisher;
Material from 'Northern Lights: Light at the end of the Tundra' by Nigel Tisdall,
copyright © Nigel Tisdall 2008, first appeared in The Daily Telegraph 10.11.08,
reprinted by permission of the publisher;
Material from 'How to apologise without taking the blame' by John Kay, copyright
© John Kay 2004, first appeared in The Daily Telegraph 07.04.04, reprinted by
permission of the publisher;
Material from 'Humour across frontiers' by Richard D Lewis, copyright © Richard D
Lewis 2005, first published by Transcreen Publishers, reprinted by permission of the
publisher;
Pop-Up article from website - http://www.snagfilms.com/films/title/kicking_it/
used with kind permission;
Article 'Barefoot Hiking: Feel more grounded without shoes' copyright © Rajesh Shah,
first appeared in Resurgence Magazine 2006, reprinted by permission of Planet
Syndication;
Adapted extracts from 'Leicester Square' by David J. Clee used from website
www.londonnet.com.
Definitions from the Macmillan English Dictionary for Advanced Learners 2nd Edition
© 2007, Macmillan Publishers Ltd www.macmillandictionaries.com

The author and publishers would like to thank the following for permission to
reproduce their photographs:
Alamy pp89(bl), 103, 106(d), 118(l), 124(r, ml, l, mr), Alamy / Adrian Buck p8(tl),
Alamy / dmac p19(tr), Alamy / John Fox p14(2), Alamy / John Henshall p33(t),
Alamy / Art Kowalsky p33(m), Alamy / Andre Matone p88(r), Alamy / Paddy
McGuiness p51, Alamy / Gary Roebuck p56(bml), Alamy / Hugh Threlfall p56(ml),
Alamy / Ulana Switucha p10(br), Alamy / Werner Dieterich p19(tl), Alamy / Carol
and Mike Werner p74; AP / Peter Byrne p87(r); Bananastock pp41, 66(br), 90(br),
123(b), 126(ml); Brand X pp19(tm) ,27, 46, 117(l); British Museum (with thanks
to the trustees of the British Museum) p126 (t); Comstock p14(tr); Corbis pp15,47,
61(tl),66(tl, bl), 81(r), 90(br), 104(t, b), 107(b), 110(tr), 111(bl), 112, 115, 118(r,
tr), 123(ml), Corbis / Timothy Bell p23(b), Corbis / Construction Photography p32
(tm), Corbis / Creasource p81(ml), Corbis / Klaus Hackenberg p56(bl), Corbis /
Frithjof Hirdes p56(br), Corbis / Gaetano p61(br), Corbis / Jphammes Kroemer p88(l),
Corbis / John and Lisa Merrill p4-5(b), Corbis / Max Rossi / Reuters p38, Corbis / Bob
Sacha p31(b), Corbis / Norbert Schaefer p45, Corbis / Jed Share and Kaoru p4(m),
Corbis / LWA-Dann Tardif p8(tm); Digital Stock p95 (b) Digital Vision pp4 (Tl), 14(l),
20(t), 39(l), 81(bl), 90(ml); Getty pp89(r),90(tl), 90(tl), 104(mt), 107(bl), 113,
123(tl), 125, Getty / Mieke Dalle p60, Getty / Jason Homa p9, Getty / Grant Faint
p89(l), Getty / Image Bank p4(t), Getty / SambaPhoto, Getty / Fredrik Skold p81(tl),
Getty / Bill Sykes Images p8(tr), Getty / Taxi p14(3), Getty / Time Life p73(t),
Getty / Steve West p82(l); Fancy p93; Fotolibra pp32 (bl), 50(t), Fotolibra / Steven
Everitt p68(r), fotolibra / Michael Webberley / MWPI p68 (l), 110(tm); Goodshoot
pp26, 90(tr); Hacker p122; Harper Collins Publishers p6(tl); Homeless world cup
p121; Image Source pp14 (tl, m, r), 25, 31(tl, tm), 53, 90(bl), 90(bl), 104(mb),
107(tm, bm), 126(r); INKCINT Cartoons / John Ditchburn p100 (m); Jupiter p101(tl);
Krywinski / Martin p29(t); MEDIO Images p100(tl); Macmillan Publishers Ltd p117(t);
Nokia Corporation p70; Pan Macmillan p39(br, bl); Photolibrary pp94, 118(m),
126(bl), Photolibrary / Atlantide SN.C p30, Photolibrary / Alex Bartel p32(r),
Photolibrary / Collection CNRI p56(tl), Photolibrary / Dizinno Tony p62, Photolibrary
/ Sylvain Grandadam p25, Photolibrary / Fraser Hall p32(bm), Photolibrary / S Lee
Studios p20(m), Photolibrary / Graham Monro p10(bl), Photolibrary / NONSTOCK
p56(bmr), Photolibrary / Lewis Real p82(l), Photolibrary / Sichtwandel p14(4),
Photolibrary / Shine Pictures p50(ml), Photolibrary / Vale and Betts p18; Pixtal p29
(br); PHOTOALTO pp59(t), pp101 (t, b), 104(m), 106(b), 106(a), 111(br), 120(l),
PHOTODISC pp101(bl), 107(t), 117(r); Rex p106(c), Rex / Aderari p37(tr), Rex / Rick
Coles p32(m), Rex / Harry Goodwin p37(b), Rex / Nils Jorgensen p78, Rex / John Alex
Maguire p23(t), Rex / Mason's News Services p75, Rex / Geoffrey Swaine p87(l); Science
Photo Library p102(b, t), Science Photo Library / Laguna Design p72; Scope Features
p49; Snag Films p120(r); Stockbyte pp20 (b), 111(bm); Superstock pp32 (t), 35

Commissioned photography by Rob Judges p.107

Printed and bound in Spain by Edelvives

2014   2013   2012   2011   2010
10 9 8 7 6 5 4 3 2 1